The Role of the Romanies

The Role of the Romanies

Images and Counter-Images of 'Gypsies'/ Romanies in European Cultures

edited by
Nicholas Saul and Susan Tebbutt

LIVERPOOL UNIVERSITY PRESS

First published 2004 by
Liverpool University Press
4 Cambridge Street
Liverpool L69 7ZU

Copyright © 2004 Liverpool University Press

The right of Nicholas Saul and Susan Tebbutt to be identified as the editors of this work
has been asserted by them in accordance with the Copyright, Designs and Patents Act,
1988.

British Library Cataloguing-in-Publication data
A British Library CIP record is available

ISBN 0–85323–679–8 hardback

Typeset by Servis Filmsetting Ltd, Manchester
Printed and bound in the European Union by Bell and Bain Ltd, Glasgow

Contents

Preface

This book emerges from a conference held in autumn 2000 on 'The Role of the Romanies: Images and Counter-Images of "Gypsies"/Romanies in European Cultures' at the University of Liverpool. The papers presented to the conference have been extensively refereed and revised for publication in dialogue with the editors. No publication of this kind is possible without assistance from many quarters, the providers of which are too numerous to mention individually. Nonetheless, the editors would especially like to thank their generous sponsors: the British Academy, the Goethe Institute (Manchester) and the Austrian Cultural Institute (London). Thanks are also due to the University of Liverpool for its support, and in particular to the librarians working with the Gypsy Collections.

Notes on Contributors

Thomas Acton, FRSA, is Professor of Romani Studies at the University of Greenwich, where he has worked since 1974. As a student he ran the first Gypsy Council caravan summer school in 1967 and he has supported the work of the Gypsy Council and the International Romani Union since then. He has written and edited numerous books and papers in Romani Studies including *Romani Culture and Gypsy Identity* (University of Hertfordshire Press, 1997), and *Scholarship and the Gypsy Struggle* (University of Hertfordshire Press, 2000).

Claudia Breger is Assistant Professor of Germanic Studies at Indiana University (Bloomington) where she teaches twentieth-century literature and culture. She received her PhD (1996) and her Habilitation (2003) at the Humboldt University, Berlin. Her publications include *Ortlosigkeit des Fremden. 'Zigeunerinnen' und 'Zigeuner' in der deutschsprachigen Literatur um 1800* (Cologne, 1998), several co-edited volumes and multiple articles on contemporary German culture with an emphasis on issues of gender, race, and sexuality. Her *Habilitationsschrift, Szenarien kopfloser Herrschaft – Performanzen gespenstischer Macht. Königsfiguren in der deutschsprachigen Literatur und Kultur des 20. Jahrhunderts*, is forthcoming with Rombach.

Colin Clark teaches Sociology in the School of Geography, Politics and Sociology at the University of Newcastle upon Tyne. His research interests are mainly located in the broad field of ethnic and racial studies, specializing in Romani Studies; he has published work on topics such as identity and stereotypes, the economics of self-employment, health promotion, access to education, social security and, more recently, immigration and asylum issues. He is the author, with Donald Kenrick, of *Moving On: The Gypsies and Travellers of Britain* (University of Hertfordshire Press, 1999).

Carmel Finnan lectures in German Studies at Mary Immaculate College, University of Limerick, Ireland. She has published on various aspects of twentieth-century German literature and culture, including Weimar culture, women's literature, contemporary Swiss literature and German–Jewish relations since 1945.

Ian Hancock is Director of the Romani Archives and Documentation Center at the University of Texas. Born in England, he received his doctorate from the School of Oriental and African Studies, London, and has taught in Texas since 1972. His work on behalf of Romanies earned him the Gamaliel Chair in Peace and Justice in 1997 and the Norwegian Rafto Foundation's international human rights prize in 1998; in the same year President Bill Clinton appointed him as the sole Romani representative on the US Holocaust Memorial Council. He has published widely in the fields of both Creole Studies and Romani Studies; his books in the latter field include *The Pariah Syndrome: An Account of Gypsy Slavery and Persecution* (Karowa Publishers, 1987), *A Handbook of Vlax Romani* (Slavica, 1995) and *We Are the Romani People* (University of Hertfordshire Press, 2002). Several of his published articles are available on the Archives website at www.radoc.net

Katharine Hooper has been Special Collections Librarian at the University of Liverpool since 1990, and curated the exhibition *Picturing Gypsies* at the University of Liverpool Art Gallery to accompany the 'Role of the Romanies' conference. An edited version of the gallery talk appeared in 'News from the Gypsy Collections, Liverpool', *Romany Routes* (June 2001). Other publications about the Gypsy Collections include 'A Record of Romani Heritage' in the *Library Association Record* (November 1999, with Julie Allinson) and the forthcoming 'Poachers of Pedigrees: Sources for Family History in the Gypsy Collections at the University of Liverpool' in *Romany Routes*.

Slawomir Kapralski is an Associate Professor of Sociology at the Centre for Social Studies in Warsaw, Poland and a Recurrent Visiting Professor at the Central European University, Budapest, Hungary. He conducts research on the relation between social memory and collective identity, on the cultural perceptions of time and space, and on nationalism and minorities in central and eastern Europe. His latest publications include a book edited with Paul V. Smith: *Democracies, Markets, Institutions: Global Tendencies in Local Contexts* (Warsaw, 2002), a report on how the Roma perceive democratic transformations in Poland (in *Lost Dynamics? The Immaturity of Polish Democracy*, Warsaw, 2002), and an essay on Auschwitz as a site of memories (in *Polin: Studies in Polish Jewry*, 15, 2002).

Donald Kenrick has recently retired from a career as an organizer of adult education, during which he pioneered basic education courses for

Gypsies. He was at one time Honorary Secretary of the Gypsy Council. He has written extensively on the history, language and social situation of the Romanies. His books include *Gypsies under the Swastika* (with Grattan Puxon, University of Hertfordshire Press, 1995), *Gypsies: From India to the Mediterranean* (University of Hertfordshire Press, 1993) and *A Historical Dictionary of the Gypsies (Romanies)* (Scarecrow Press, 1998).

Ken Lee is a post-modern Diasporic. Romani-Irish, an untrustworthy half-breed, born in a horse-drawn caravan in Ireland, raised and educated in England, he later emigrated to Australia. His first academic qualifications were in Geography, and he taught in the Department of Geography at the University of Newcastle, NSW Australia for over twenty years. Ten years ago he transferred to the Department of Sociology and Anthropology, where he recently completed a doctoral degree entitled 'Constructing Romani Strangerhood'. He does not look like a Gypsy.

Yaron Matras is the author of *Romani: A Linguistic Introduction* (Cambridge University Press, 2002) and *Untersuchungen zu Grammatik und Diskurs des Romanes* (Harrassowitz, 1994); he is the editor of the interdisciplinary journal *Romani Studies* (continuing the *Journal of the Gypsy Lore Society*), and of several collections on Romani linguistics, including *Romani in Contact* (Benjamins, 1995), *The Romani Element in Non-Standard Speech* (with Viktor Elsik, Harrassowitz, 1998), *Grammatical Relations in Romani: The Noun Phrase* (with Peter Bakker and Hrsito Kyuchukov, Benjamins, 2000), and *The Typology and Dialectology of Romani* (Benjamins, 1997). He is also the author of numerous journal articles on Romani linguistics and other aspects of linguistics.

Eve Rosenhaft is Reader in German Studies at the University of Liverpool. She is the author or editor of a number of volumes, including *Beating the Fascists? The German Communists and Political Violence 1929–1933* (Cambridge University Press, 1983), *Rationale Beziehungen? Geschlechterverhältnisse im Rationalisierungsprozeß* (Suhrkamp, 1993) and *State, Social Policy and Social Change in Germany 1880–1994* (Berg, 1997), and has recently published articles in English and German on the origins of life insurance in the eighteenth century, British council housing, and black people in Germany in the 1930s, as well as on the Nazi persecution of Sinti and Roma.

Anthony Sampson is an international author and broadcaster, based in London. He was born in 1926. After Oxford University he went to

South Africa for four years, editing the new black magazine *Drum*. Back in London he joined *The Observer* in 1955 and wrote *Anatomy of Britain* (Hodder and Stoughton) in 1962, followed by major books about multinational corporations, including *The Seven Sisters* (Bantam, 1976) about the oil companies and *The Arms Bazaar* (Bantam, 1978) about the weapons trade, which were translated into 15 languages. From 1980 to 1981 he served as editorial adviser to the Brandt Commission on North–South problems. In 1997 he published *The Scholar Gypsy* (John Murray) about his grandfather John Sampson, the Romani scholar and Librarian of Liverpool University. In 1999 he published the authorized biography of Nelson Mandela. He has been Chairman of the Society of Authors and a member of the Scott Trust, owners of *The Guardian* and *The Observer*. He lives in London and Wiltshire with his wife Sally, a magistrate. They have two children. His latest work is a new version of his *Anatomy of Britain*, called *Who Runs This Place?* (John Murray, 2004)

Nicholas Saul is Professor of German at the University of Durham. He is the author of *Poetry and History in Novalis and the German Enlightenment* (Modern Humanities Research Association, 1984) and *'Prediger aus der neuen romantischen Clique': Zur Interaktion von Romantik und Homiletik um 1800* (Königshausen & Neumann, 1999). He has edited volumes on literature and science, threshold metaphors, the body in German literature, and literature and philosophy in Germany, and has also published essays on authors from Frederick the Great of Prussia to Hugo von Hofmannsthal and Botho Strauß.

Susan Tebbutt is Head of German Studies at Mary Immaculate College, University of Limerick. Editor of *Sinti and Roma: Gypsies in the German-Speaking World* (Berghahn, 1998; German translation Peter Lang, 2001), she has published widely on the Romanies. In 2001 she held a Charles H. Revson Foundation Fellowship for Archival Research at the Center for Advanced Holocaust Studies, United States Holocaust Memorial Museum, Washington, DC, and is at present working on a monograph on Romanies and genocide.

Introduction
The Role of the Romanies: Images and Counter-Images

Susan Tebbutt and Nicholas Saul

The history of the representations and self-representations of Romany culture can be seen in terms of a dramatic analogy, as a series of negotiations between the Romany actor or role-player and the *gadzo* (non-Romany)[1] author (and vice versa). These negotiations result in the hybrid images under investigation in this volume and raise questions about the nature of roles and role-playing.

It might seem unorthodox to apply the notion of 'role' to the analysis and interpretation of the way in which Romany culture presents itself and is presented in a predominantly *gadzo* environment. For this is really an ethnic and cultural issue, whereas a 'role' tends to be a sociological rather than a cultural concept. Roles may be understood as 'socially defined expectations that a person in a given social position follows', or as sociology's fundamental tool for describing and analysing the behavioural interface between the individual and society. Yet roles in this sense are more than just repeated predictable behaviour patterns exhibited by individuals in a group or other context.

Definitions of role share a common origin in the world of drama. The role played may be viewed as the locus of conflicting energies. To play a role in society means to make a compromise between the constraints that a social system of roles imposes on the individual performer, and the ways in which self-realization is achieved. The actors, or role-players, may have varying degrees of freedom in the performance of the role, and the status of the (absent) author of the script will vary. Improvisation may dominate or be inadmissible.

In the English language the phrase 'to play a role' can be applied to two diametrically opposed activities. On the one hand it can mean 'to be a significant part of an enterprise', and on the other hand it can be used to mean 'to act out a role imposed by a third party'. These two possible interpretations are of crucial importance when it comes to examining the

---

[1] The word *gadzo* is a transliteration of the Romany word. Other spellings include *gadżo*, *gorgio*, *gadjo* and *gaujo*.

role or roles played by the Romanies in Europe over the centuries. The matter is further complicated by the fact that it is possible for a person or group of people to be 'playing a role' in both senses outlined above. Thus the Romanies may for example be instrumental in the rise to fame and fortune of Gypsiologists, but in the process are themselves acting out assigned roles which are not necessarily true reflections of their actual 'role' in society, but masks that conceal the truth.

The roles may be played out to an audience of Gypsiologists, to people in particular geographical locations, to linguists, literary and cultural historians or students of the Holocaust. The role of the Romanies may be manipulated by directors or scholars, writers and the media world. The performance, in turn, may be recorded for posterity and preserved in special collections, memorial sites, archives or works of art.

These different aspects are reflected to a greater or lesser degree in all the chapters in this book, which are grouped around four main thematic areas:

1. Romany[2] Studies and its parameters (Sampson, Hooper, Lee).
2. Constructions and concoctions of Romany culture (Matras, Kenrick, Hancock, Acton).
3. Orientalism and gender issues in literature (Saul, Breger, Finnan).
4. Memory, records and the Romany experience (Tebbutt, Rosenhaft, Kapralski, Clark).

Running across the warp of these themes, the weft threads of role-playing cross over and under and back again, engaging the reader in speculation as to whether it is ever possible to state clearly whether the Romanies are in control in historical, media or literary representations, at any given point in social history, media or literature, or whether they are being manipulated by that most visible weaver of Romany roles, the *gadzo*.

1. Romany Studies and its Parameters

The volume begins with three chapters about the genesis, development and scope of Romany Studies. Against the background of Europe's social and cultural history, Anthony Sampson begins to move the shuttle backwards and forwards with the weft threads of the beginnings of Gypsy Studies. The setting of Liverpool, a city of many contrasts, a

---

[2] The spelling 'Romani' is normally reserved for the adjective describing the language of the Romanies. Some scholars also use this spelling for everything to do with the Romanies. Within this volume the usage may thus vary from article to article.

melting pot of many nationalities, is where his grandfather John Sampson first develops his love for the Romani language, a love that later develops into an almost frenzied obsession, inspired by the work of George Borrow. For John Sampson the aim was to find the 'venerable Gypsy', a romantic goal coloured by the desire to preserve the Romanies' distance from the rest of society, lest in edging closer the Romanies might begin to act out a role that was not their 'natural' one. Sampson records his grandfather's work facilitating the portrayal of the Romanies as important players in the preservation of the Romani language. Out of this fascination there evolved the Special Collections at the University of Liverpool. Although John Sampson's attitude towards the Romanies, their language, music and folk tales might in some ways seem paternalistic, and it might be argued that the Romanies were actually playing out the role imposed by the researchers, arguably the overall picture should be seen instead as a triumph for the Romanies, the key players in the history of Romany Studies. It is John Sampson's legacy *and* that of the Romanies that are commemorated by the University of Liverpool in the 'Gypsy Collections'.

Just as John Sampson owed his academic success to the Romanies, so the Gypsy Lore Society could not have been founded at the end of the nineteenth century had there been no Gypsies. Katharine Hooper analyses the scholarship, organization, passion, fieldwork and collections of the Gypsylorists, from John Sampson and Scott Macfie to Dora Yates and, more recently, Yaron Matras. The Gypsy Collections at Liverpool[3] include photographs, old woodcuts, manuscripts, press cuttings, posters, books and edicts, and constitute a mixture of 'erudition and romanticism' – institutional recognition of the culture and history of the Romanies being considered worthy of appropriate storage, display and memorialization.[4]

The Gypsies are depicted in exotic costumes playing roles, but the majority of these manipulated, indeed marketed, roles are created by non-Romanies. Although references to the Romani language are based on oral evidence given by Gypsies from various countries, few of these informants are ever named, notable exceptions being the Wood family of Welsh Gypsies recorded by Dora Yates. On balance the Romanies are

---

[3] See the University of Liverpool website http://sca.lib.liv.ac.uk/collections/gypsy/intro.htm (accessed 14 April 2004).

[4] Greenwich University is home to the first ever British Professor of Romany Studies, Thomas Acton, and runs regular conferences about issues relating to Gypsies and Travellers. The University of Leeds is one of the few other academic institutions in Europe to have extensive collections relating to the Gypsies. See the website at www.leeds.ac.uk/library/spcoll/spprint/26600.html (accessed 14 April 2004). The University of Sheffield has the National Fairground Archive, which was inaugurated in 1994; see www.shef.ac.uk/nfa (accessed 14 April 2004).

most frequently playing a role, being represented by outsiders whose knowledge may be gained from extensive fieldwork, but who lack the insider perspective. Arguably, they appear as nebulous and as stylized as the bird (supposed to be a wagtail) that formed the emblem for the Gypsy Lore Society's stationery.

Continuing with the historicist approach to Romany Studies and its parameters, Ken Lee, himself of Romany origin, takes issue with the Orientalism that implicitly underpins much of the methodology of the Gypsylorists and founders of the Gypsy Collections. The 'colonial subjects' without a colony are seen as victims of imposed discursive misrepresentations, and these misrepresentations in turn lead to forms of selective amnesia on the part of supposed experts.

In his critical reassessment of Groome's Danubian hypothesis of 1898 regarding the question of Romany migration Lee illustrates some of the ideological factors that determine whether certain discourses are kept alive or forgotten. He then focuses on the largely forgotten challenge that the Gypsy and Folklore Club (GAFLC) represented to the Gypsy Lore Society from 1911 to 1914. At the time of its founding the GAFLC had almost as many members as the GLS, and had Augustus John as its prestigious president. Lee does not offer a defence of the GAFLC, but indicates that, had it been successful, its more practical approach to Romany rights might have produced better results than that of the more scholarly GLS, and the role played by the Romanies in real life might have evolved very differently.[5] Rather than seeing the Gypsies as players of roles selected for them by *gadzos*, Lee, the first example in the volume of the Romany voice, urges that the forgotten discourses of the Romanies themselves be heard.

2. Constructions and Concoctions of Romany Culture

Constructions of Romany culture and identity are at the heart of the following four chapters. For Yaron Matras Romany identity is embodied in the language spoken by the 'Gypsy', whether defined as a member of a peripatetic community or as a person speaking a form of the Romani language. Matras disentangles the two threads and demonstrates how and why they have been interwoven in the past. European scholarship focused on the linguistic-ethnic identity of the Gypsies as part of the wider group of people leading a nomadic life, a typically Orientalist outsider construction. Matras shows how twentieth-century scholars such as Okely and Willems interpret the work of Rüdiger, Grellmann and the

---

[5] *The Journal of the Gypsy Lore Society* changed its name in 2000 to *Romani Studies*. See the website at http://www.gypsyloresociety.org/journal.htm (accessed 14 April 2004).

mainstream linguists of the nineteenth and early twentieth century.

The warrior origin theory is a case in point, where Romany activists appear, as Matras puts it, to want 'package-Gypsies which sell better on the human rights market'. He concludes that the construction of Gypsy history is generally subordinated to an ideological or moral agenda, with much of the received wisdom on the interpretation of Romany origins based on pseudo-scientific linguistic 'arguments'. On balance the process of reviewing scholarly knowledge and approaching linguistic and ethnographic issues relating to the role of the Romanies has paid off, since the central conclusions of two centuries of Romani-related research have withstood the rigours of this prolonged and intricate debate.

Like Matras, Donald Kenrick looks at those who have allocated roles to the Romanies in the past. He examines the beginnings of anti-Gypsyism in fifteenth-century Western Europe as manifested in historical chronicles and town council records. Although there are no claims made that the activities of the Romanies who feature there are representative, it is precisely because the role played by each Gypsy mentioned subsequently becomes metonymic for the behaviour of all Romanies that the stereotypes begin to emerge, stereotypes that present a world with no gradations. Kenrick identifies five different groups into which the Romanies in his sources fall: religious refugees, genuine pilgrims, acrobats, horse-traders and bogus pilgrims, of which the latter are the most frequently mentioned and attracted most attention. Despite the existence of the different roles, Gypsies are labelled by outsiders as petty criminals, spies or quite simply dishonest, images that begin to circulate and proliferate over the centuries and become the stock-in-trade for producers of works of literature and other forms of representation. Labels are stuck on by outsiders without regard for how those in question perceive the given labels.

Reading labels carefully can be fruitful. Ian Hancock, himself a Romany, traces back the vicious circle of constructed and indeed concocted roles of his own ethnic group. He exposes faked stories of the Romany religious tradition, in-group derogatory language describing Romanies, scholarly fabrications and inaccurate presentations of alleged Romany customs and spiritual beliefs. The case of Gypsy Manfri Fred Wood's autobiography, his sources, and the books that in turn used Wood's account as a source is indicative of the ways in which hypotheses about the Romanies enter circulation and gain a momentum of their own, regardless of their accuracy or reliability.

The representation of the Romanies is closely linked to the glimpses caught of the Romani language by non-Romanies. The supposedly 'secret' language of the Romanies is treated differently from other languages, the perpetuation of inaccuracies about the Romani language itself being a function of sloppy investigative techniques and the reliance on second-, third- or fourth-hand accounts. Thus the origins of words, their meanings, usage and cultural connotations may be misinterpreted and add to the growing body of material by writers who are not special- ists. It is this colonialist, cavalier attitude to sources that Hancock rightly attacks. He is concerned not only for the academic field of Romany Studies, but for the Romanies themselves, who lack a voice and cham- pions.

Distinguishing the true from the false accounts is the central issue tackled by Thomas Acton, who wonders whether the Gypsies in fact only exist as staged role-players. He scrutinizes the ways in which we per- ceive the role of the Gypsies, who are themselves staged by others. Despite the variously legitimated claims to authenticity of some schol- arly approaches, the existence of a series of roles within roles within roles has repercussions for the authenticity of representations.

How accurate can representation be? Using illustrations from the world of music, Acton points out the differences between domestic and professional musical production, introducing the 'wild card' of religion as transcending individual cultures, yet still necessarily a relative factor. He then traces the trajectories of the work of four Dutch scholars, namely Lucassen, Willems, Cottaar and van de Port, showing that their metaphysical approach leads them to find what they expect to find in the evidence available. Even positive stereotypes, as seen in Kusturica's film *Time of the Gypsies* (1988), remain stereotypes, roles imposed by outsid- ers, and few scholars succeed in deconstructing the self-fulfilling proph- ecies surrounding expected Romany roles.

Although the majority of scholars do not harbour malicious intentions towards the Romanies, misrepresentation is avoidable. Acton makes a strong case for higher academic standards and greater commitment to Romany Studies, but most particularly argues the need for heightened awareness of the rights and actual role in society of the Romanies them- selves.

3. Orientalism and Gender Issues in Literature

Up to now the concern has been with the ways in which people first began to form impressions of the Romanies and to ascribe certain attrib- utes to them. There have been various attempts to use this evidence to justify particular academic approaches, and some of these issues are reflected in literary works. In the following three chapters the emphasis is on specific nineteenth- and twentieth-century literary constructions of Romany identity, whether from a *gadzo* or a Romany perspective.

Nicholas Saul explores the ways in which Wilkie Collins subverts

Orientalist discourse on Gypsies in his detective novel *The Moonstone* (1868). As Hancock and Acton point out, there is a tendency for representations of Gypsies to be adopted and reconfigured without any insistence on establishing the authenticity of the original representation, but Collins is consciously playing with and transcending stereotypical images. Yet even here the question is raised as to whether the reader, despite the deliberate intertextuality, is merely confronted with images of the Gypsy as the eternal outcast wanderer, one of the most persistent of all stereotypes. Within the novel the provenance of the enigmatic half-Gypsy Ezra Jennings is never quite established. Just as Thomas Acton begins to wonder whether the Dutch actually exist, so Collins poses a multitude of questions about identity in the single figure of Jennings. The latter appears to be both *gadzo* and Gypsy, light and dark, male and female, young and old, and Saul argues that he represents a 'paradoxical wholeness'. Does this have implications for the identity of the Gypsy? Is it only complete when combined with that of a *gadzo*? Although Saul sees the hybrid character as representing a doomed Romantic synthesis, he also conjectures that Jennings may have a mediating role to play between *gadzo* and Gypsy.

Collins is one of many nineteenth-century European authors to portray the role of the Romany as an outsider. By the end of the twentieth century strikingly few authors had transgressed this unspoken norm. Claudia Breger points out that even when the voice of the Romany is heard, the words may not necessarily represent reality. Different strategies towards the reader will influence the process of reading about the roles that authors have devised for the Romanies. Breger analyses how Dutch author Margriet de Moor in her novel *Hertog van Egypte* (1996) challenges and reworks existing stereotypical roles, interweaving them with racially loaded metaphors relating to the concept of hybridity.

Here the Romanies are very clearly 'staged', presented with the proviso that this is one person's interpretation of their character. The very description of non-identity underlines postmodern notions of difference, but underneath this signalling of heterogeneous or multiple identities there is neither confirmation that the Romany history is authentic nor definitive evidence that it is a literary fabrication. The novel breaks the silence, allowing the Romanies who survived the Holocaust to talk about their experiences. De Moor employs the unusual narrative device of the spectre to provide memories and to allow the Romany experience to be heard. With some reservations Breger commends the result as a significant contribution to the dialogue about memory and the 'forgotten Holocaust', the genocide of some half a million European Romanies.

For Nicholas Saul and Claudia Breger the intersection of identity and the otherness of the 'Gypsy' in literature is linked to Orientalism and strategies of representation. In the final chapter in this section Carmel Finnan not only introduces a further dimension, namely that of gender, but broadens out the study of Romanies to look at the Yenish people of Switzerland, a people claimed by some to be Gypsies who migrated from India many centuries ago. Like the Romanies, they have been systematically persecuted for no crime other than their ethnic affiliation. Although Switzerland enjoys the reputation of being a tolerant multicultural society, twentieth-century state-endorsed assimilation and settlement programmes were characterized by oppression and abuse, particularly at the hands of the supposedly children-oriented organization Pro Juventute. This remained unchallenged until Yenish writer Mariella Mehr, who herself suffered from this brutality and alienation, highlighted the long-term impact on the individual. Mehr struggles to raise awareness within Switzerland and beyond of the violence perpetrated against the vulnerable and marginalized Yenish minority. The fragmentation of language in her work echoes her inner suffering as a woman, as the vicious circle of violence envelops both perpetrator and victim.

There is clearly still a need to address the status and vulnerability of the Yenish minority within Switzerland. In the autumn of 2002 Mariella Mehr was herself injured in an attack on her during a reading from her works. This highlighted the immediacy and specificity of the experience of female 'Gypsies', which has until recently remained unexplored.[6]

4. Memory, Records and the Romany Experience

How is the role of the Romanies remembered, recorded and commemorated? The final four chapters revolve around confronting the past, coming to terms with the past, indicating lacunae. The shadow cast by the past over the present is ubiquitous.

Susan Tebbutt examines the contrast between images of Gypsies produced by *gadzo* European artists over the centuries and those created by Romanies themselves. The former give disproportionate weight to the tiny majority of the ethnic group who may in fact be thieves, tricksters and criminals. Furthermore, the overemphasis on the exotic, erotic and nefarious reinforces other existing cultural and literary stereotypes. Nineteenth-century images of Gypsies as synonymous with 'Bohemians' featured Gypsies as outsiders rather than as members of a separate ethnic group. The concept of the amorphous but different mass of nomads or fortune-tellers gave artists scope to recreate and reinforce

---

[6] Amesberger and Halbmayr (2001) published two volumes documenting their interviews with survivors of the women's concentration camp at Ravensbrück.

images of Gypsies as colourful extras, projections of Orientalist fantasies.

A more authentic image of Romanies can be seen in the work of Expressionist artist Otto Pankok, who intervened on their behalf after the end of the Second World War, and was acutely aware of their suffering at the hands of the Nazis. But Pankok did not experience the concentration camps himself. Of the few artworks depicting the genocide of the Gypsies, those by Austrian Romanies Karl and Ceija Stojka are arguably the most striking. They attempt the impossible, to capture in art some of the horrors, abuse and indignity suffered by Romanies in concentration camps. Spelt out here are graphic images of a strong people reduced to the role of numbers and statistics in the balance books of the Nazis.

What other images remain of the Romanies during the National Socialist period? There are some photographs, relatively few of which can be accurately accredited and documented. Eve Rosenhaft presents a case study of photographer Hanns Weltzel, whose images of Romanies taken in Germany in the 1930s were instrumental in his being arrested and executed in 1952 by the Soviet military authorities. The role of the photograph within the quasi-colonialist relationship between subject and photographer is seen by Rosenhaft as paradigmatic for *gadzo* constructions of Romany identity.

The relationship between Hanns Weltzel and Lamperli, a German Sinto, is marked by fragility and ambivalence. The ethnographic interest heightened as Lamperli requested Weltzel's material support in the Gypsies' struggle with the Magdeburg authorities, but Weltzel was more concerned with the role of the Romanies in furthering his scholarly work, and later was to be accused of complicity in deportations of Romanies.

Yet how 'authentic' were his photographs? It emerged that Weltzel was not the only *gadzo* to record the role of these particular Romanies, some of whom had willingly acted as extras in film studios and posed in 'Gypsy-like' dress, thus themselves complicit in the staging of their own lives. The representation of this period of the history of the Sinti and Roma in Germany raises questions about the framing of reality and the negotiating and renegotiating of identities presented to the outside world.

Moving to the end of the twentieth century and the interface between the past and the present, Slawomir Kapralski looks at the ways in which cultural tradition may be associated with memories of the Holocaust. He looks at the 'Romani Caravan of Memory', an annual pilgrimage made by Polish Romanies to the sites where Romanies were murdered. Kapralski explores the politicization of the process of remembering. As opposed to the backward-looking preservation of tradition, the new emancipatory movement towards reconfiguring an identity that acknowledges the political dimension means that the chronology of the racial persecution of the Romanies must be reviewed.

The chronotope, or transhistorical, symbol-laden site of memories, functions to construct the group identity. Auschwitz may be seen as one such chronotope, with awareness of the racial motives of the Nazis tied in to an awareness of contemporary manifestations of anti-Gypsyism. For the Romanies the act of remembering gives a heightened sense of a common shared past, and also a better understanding of the significance of the site for all humankind. The ritual of memory transforms the individual memory into part of a collective memory, with the reconstruction of the 'caravan' involving religious and commemorative ceremonies marking the sites of atrocities committed against Romanies. The event shows how tradition and modernity can converge and complement one another in reinforcing the political and politicized identity of the Romanies.

In the final chapter Colin Clark moves the debate back towards its starting point, the first Gypsylorists and their perceptions of Gypsies. He looks at more general questions concerning the representations of Gypsies as seismographs of the ideologies out of which they emerged. Literary and cultural stereotypical images are disseminated relating to blackness, internal nobility and occultism, crime and sexuality. Clark shows how these images of 'pretend' Gypsies fuel further images produced by the so-called 'experts' and are perpetuated right up to the present day.

So just as Clark's article begins and ends with the arrival of Gypsies in Liverpool, site of the arrival of real Gypsies and the collections of materials by and about real Gypsies, so the volume ends between the constructions of images and the ways in which these images themselves have developed stereotype status. The public reactions to migrations of Gypsies within Europe in the late twentieth century bear a striking resemblance to those of nineteenth-century commentators, yet there is little evidence in either case to justify the ascription of 'other'.

Clark points out that the Romanies remain at once individuals and yet also members of an ethnic group. In the former capacity each one by definition plays a unique role, yet as a group they are consistently presented as though they were homogeneous 'extras' on a set built by *gadzos*. Whether the focus is their dark skin, their supposed kings and queens, their perceived links with the supernatural or criminal, or their sexual 'promiscuity', Romanies are squeezed into straitjacketed roles. Yet they have rarely been in a position to counter these myths, which brings us back to the opening chapter and the work of the Gypsylorists.

It becomes harder and harder to see where the images end and the counter-images begin, where the Romanies are playing a role imposed by the *gadzos* and where they have a role to play in their own right. And there is not one definitive answer. Yet this too achieves a kind of clarity, the kind that emerges when the ground has been cleared and the true questions can be put. The role of the following chapters is to open up the debate and encourage further research.

References

Amesberger, Helga, and Halbmayr, Brigitte. 2001. *Vom Leben und Überleben: Wege nach Ravensbrück; Das Frauenkonzentrationslager in der Erinnerung*, Vols 1 and 2. Vienna: Promedia.

Bradbury, Malcolm, Heading, Bryan, and Hollis, Martin. 1972. 'The Man and the Mask: A Discussion of Role-Theory', in Jackson (ed.) 1972: 41–64.

Giddens, Anthony, and Birdsall, Karen. 2001. *Sociology*. Cambridge: Polity Press, 4th edn (1st edn 1989).

Jackson, John A. (ed.) 1972. *Role*. Cambridge: Cambridge University Press.

Popitz, Heinrich. 1972. 'The Concept of Social Role as an Element of Sociological Theory', in Jackson (ed.) 1972: 11–39.

Part I

Romany Studies and its Parameters

John Sampson and Romani Studies in Liverpool

Anthony Sampson

Dr John Sampson, the leading British authority on Gypsies in the early twentieth century, was essentially the product of Victorian Liverpool in its heyday, when it was the crossroads between the regions of the British Isles, the meeting-place of Irish, Scots, Welsh and English, and the chief link between Britain and America. Every year hundreds of thousands of Europeans sailed from Liverpool: whole communities of Germans, Dutch and Scandinavians settled in the city to profit from the trans-atlantic trade. The growth of the docks along the Mersey, with miles of quays, forests of masts and queues of sailing ships and steamships, pro-vided, as the French historian Hippolyte Taine wrote, 'one of the great-est spectacles of the whole world'. The docks provided all kinds of unconventional jobs and opportunities, legal and illegal, regular or fitful, and attracted every variety of human flotsam and jetsam, includ-ing tinkers, mumpers and Gypsies. The chaos and squalor of nine-teenth-century Liverpool – 'that black hole', as the American consul Nathaniel Hawthorne called it – became notorious. The contrast between rich and poor was shocking to visitors from the south of England. In 1884 a correspondent from *The Times* described 'the hordes of the ragged and the wretched men and women in the cruellest grip of poverty, little children with shoeless feet, bodies pinched'. At the same time 'the superb carriages of the rich, and their freights of refined and elegant ladies, threaded their way among sections of the population so squalid and miserable that my heart ached at the sight of them' (cited in Sampson 1997: 12).

It was in this city of contrasts that my grandfather, John Sampson, was brought up, in a middle-class family struggling on the edge of poverty. He had been born in 1862, in Schull in County Cork, Ireland. His father James Sampson, a prosperous and cultured Cornish mining engineer, had married a formidable Irishwoman, Sarah Macdermott. But soon after John's birth, James lost all his money when a bank in which he was a shareholder crashed with unlimited liability. He came to Liverpool in 1871 but fell ill and died the next year, leaving very little money: his widow had to care for their nine-year-old son John and three other children.

At the age of 14, John Sampson had to leave school and was apprenticed for seven years to Alexander MacGregor, a lithographer and engraver in Liverpool. John had already developed a passion for poetry, and displayed a retentive mind for languages and grammar. While still an apprentice, and with a determination that amazed his friends, he taught himself at night school and at home, absorbing a wide literature with scholarly accuracy. A family friend, James Crocket, recalled that '[e]ven then he was interested in Gypsies and their language and I have a recollection of him reading poems in Romany between puffs of smoke' (Sampson 1997: 13). His real *métier* was philology, which he pursued with all the energy and passion for scholarship that marked the Victorian autodidacts, spending all his spare time learning about languages and phonetics. And Liverpool offered a ready-made laboratory of words, full of foreign enclaves and strange speech, while the ships brought sailors' stories, rhymes and riddles from all over the world. Sampson would never leave Britain, but he encountered the world and its languages in Liverpool.

The mysterious Romani language became his obsession. It began when at the age of 21 he first read the 'glowing romances' of George Borrow, who had died two years before in 1881. It was then, he wrote, that he 'first sought and cultivated the society of English Gypsies, collecting their language, folklore and superstitions, and comparing them with their Continental kinsmen'. John Sampson was part of a new post-Darwin generation who were scientifically minded, but still longed for some escape from the rule of reason as they surveyed a bleakly rational new world. 'To some peculiarly constituted people,' he wrote, 'the name Gypsy is like that other great name that came as a hot blast from the East, maddening men's minds and constraining them to enroll themselves as followers.' Sampson firmly rejected Christianity, but he would compare it to his own obsession with Gypsies, as he explained later in a somewhat high-flown lecture: 'For we rate it as fair a thing to be a Romani Rai as others a poet or Christian' (Sampson 1997: 26).

Inspired by Borrow, in the 1880s Sampson embarked on his own pursuit of Gypsies and their language. He would never forget the early enthusiasm, he wrote later, with which 'I would hail the thin smoke of a Gypsy wagon curling among the trees in some country lane, or the delight which I experienced when "drawing out" some venerable Gypsy'. He immersed himself in the life of Gypsies, sometimes going native among them, and made close friends including Tom Lee, Lias and Eros Robinson, Florence Lovell and Mackenzie Boswell. Liverpool was a crossroads for many Gypsy clans – Boswells, Lees, Locks, Lovells or Smiths – who camped on the open fields outside the city, at Walton,

Greenlane, Tranmere, Sleeper's Hill or Wavertree Fields, and would make occasional forays into Liverpool. In spring, they would set off on their wanderings – some staying in north-west England to make money from gullible tourists at seaside resorts such as Blackpool or Douglas on the Isle of Man; some travelling as far as Cornwall or the north of Scotland in search of business.

For two years Sampson collected vocabularies from the Gypsies of Lancashire, Yorkshire and Cheshire, tracing their links with oriental words. As he later wrote to a friend: 'It is a beautiful thing to feel the *romance* of the words, to find in them a sort of diary of their wanderings, and as if one were wandering in a strange and exquisite museum' (Sampson 1997: 31). Just at this time, in the late 1880s, two keen British scholars, William Ibbetson and David MacRitchie, conceived the idea of a Gypsy Lore Society as a kind of 'club for Romany Ryes'. The first issue of its journal was published in July 1888 and it gave a new focus to Sampson's Gypsy studies. Soon he was included as one of the club, and his friends and colleagues came to call him simply 'the Rai', the Romani word for a gentleman. The Romani Rais or Ryes shared a fascination with the Gypsies' life and language but they also shared the limitations of paternalism and mutual admiration. As Sir Angus Fraser described them a century later, they 'appeared to be uncompromisingly hostile to any adaption that might draw the Gypsies closer to society'.

It was not Romani that gave Sampson his first entry into academia, but a much more obscure and disreputable language called Shelta, which tinkers used as a secret means of communication. He was urged by David MacRitchie to investigate it further. 'Probably he selected me as the least squeamish of his members,' Sampson wrote. 'But even to me it sometimes occurred that Shelta was a language which no gentleman should be asked to collect.' His real advantage was his willingness to mix with very rough customers in the slums of Liverpool and soon he 'tracked Shelta from one squalid lodging house and thieves' kitchen to another'. At last in the spring of 1890 a friendly knife-grinder (who was later jailed for being a fence) directed him to a 79-year-old tinker called John Barlow, who lived in an Irish slum of Liverpool and spoke Shelta as a distinct language. As Sampson wrote: 'From him I collected a complete vocabulary, and from him, too, I obtained words in their purest form and learned to distinguish Shelta from the other jargon mixed with it by the lower orders of grinders and hawkers' (Sampson 1997: 34–36).

Sampson published a paper on 'Tinkers and Their Talk' in the *Journal of the Gypsy Lore Society* in October 1890. It was a remarkable achievement for a self-taught man of 28, and it brought him into contact with Kuno Meyer, a lecturer at the new University College of Liverpool, who was an authority on the Celtic languages and had already been studying the Shelta language. Sampson introduced Meyer to his source, Barlow, and Meyer agreed that Shelta was a secret language of great antiquity: in his own paper he paid a glowing tribute to Sampson, who had 'succeeded in reading the riddle of Shelta, which had baffled all who appoached it before him' (Sampson 1997: 38).

In 1892, Sampson's printing business failed. Never a good businessman, he now found himself at the age of 30 in the harsh surroundings of Liverpool with neither money nor job. But through the mediation of Kuno Meyer, he was offered a position that suited him exactly – as first librarian of the University College of Liverpool. It was an extraordinary invitation for a relatively unknown man who had left school at 14 with no formal qualifications in bibliography – unimaginable in today's universities. But the new College and its library were also starting almost from scratch and the young Sampson already had a deeper scholarship than most of his colleagues. 'I felt myself in Paradise,' he said later. 'It seemed to me a privilege for which the happy holder of the office should pay the Council generously, instead of being paid by the Council. Here one could live among books, not as a recluse in his study, but constantly meeting the most delightful people on the most delightful terms.'

The College was almost ideally suited to the Rai's qualifications and ambitions, for it had already acquired a reputation in the subjects in which he specialized: philology and English literature. He was able to continue his exotic researches while settling down into a secure job surrounded by congenial and original colleagues.

In the summer of 1894 Sampson went camping in North Wales – whose wild splendours had been brought much closer to Liverpool by the railway – with his new university friends, among them Kuno Meyer. They were in pursuit of Gypsies, and in the middle of this journey, as Sampson recalled: 'Kuno returned one evening to our camp-fire near Bala, bearing with him in triumph a captive Gypsy harper [...] then for the first time I heard [...] the Romani language spoken not as an uncouth jargon, but as a pure Indian idiom, a veritable mother tongue, miraculously preserved from corruption by a single tribe among the hills and fastnesses of Wales, which they had entered two hundred years before' (Sampson 1997: 58).

For the next year Sampson spent as much time as he could with the harpist, Edward Wood, who was his sole instructor in deep Romani. Sometimes Edward would come to Liverpool and play at the Welsh Harp, a basic pub by the docks with wooden tables and benches, where Sampson would sit with his friends. But two years later Sampson discovered a cousin of Edward's who proved still more valuable. In the summer of 1896 he was taken to the banks of Lake Tal-y-Llyn, on the slopes of Cader Idris, to the log cabin of Matthew Wood, an energetic woodcutter of about 50, with glossy black ringlets reaching to his shoulders. Matthew and his

family were all faithful conservers of the pure Romani language and rac-
onteurs of ancient folk tales and they welcomed the Rai as someone who
spoke Romani as deep as their own. The Wood family transformed
Sampson's career, for he was now determined to spend all his spare time
compiling a great dictionary of this pure Romani language, which would
trace its connections with Sanskrit, Persian and the European languages.
He was not to know that it would take thirty years to complete.

Sampson was to spend many vacations with Matthew Wood, recording both words and folk tales 'in a sort of frenzy', as he told his old friend
Francis Groome. 'No work could be more exhausting. To note every
accent, to follow the story and to keep the wandering wits of my Romani
raconteur to the point, all made the work trying' (Sampson 1997: 58).
But Matthew Wood was a shy and reserved man, possessed of a Gypsy
restlessness. One day, having cleared the hillside of trees, he walked away
and disappeared without trace. It was not until nine years later in 1909
that Sampson tracked down Matthew Wood again with the help of the
Liverpool librarian Dora Yates, when they found him in the Welsh village
of Bettws-Gwerfil-Goch. Soon Sampson decided to take a house there
and establish his own family base in Bettws, to pursue his Gypsy studies.
During the holidays he presided there over his family, his Gypsy friends
and his female assistants, extending his Romani vocabulary and
grammar with the help of Matthew Wood, while a succession of scholars and friends from Liverpool would make their way from Corwen
station to the remote village. The first entry in the visitors' book was that
of Augustus John, accompanied by a flamboyant self-portrait.

The First World War shattered many of the assumptions of the Gypsy
dream. The philologists and eccentric amateurs were co-opted into the
war effort, the Gypsies were conscripted and regimented in barracks,
which prevented their wanderings and corrupted their language, while
the internationalism of scholars was torn apart by the rival patriotisms
that divided Europe. But Sampson soldiered on with his giant dictionary, until by July 1917 he had mastered the evolution of Romani from
Sanskrit and sent 'half a hundred-weight of solid philology' to Oxford
University Press – only to hear that they would postpone publication
until after the war.

Once the war had ended Sampson was established as the Rai of Rais, and
a new generation of scholars emerged to pay him respect. The Gypsy Lore
Society was relaunched in a more modest form, with a quarterly journal at
half of its former size. In 1926 Sampson's dictionary was finally published,
with a preface that tried to reconcile his two roles of Scholar Gypsy and
Gypsy Scholar: 'An early interest in the Gypsies originating, it must be
confessed, rather in a spirit of romance than of research, led me while still
a boy to the acquisition of their tongue, the better to gain an inner understanding of this peculiar people' (Sampson 1926: vii). The Gypsy enthu-

siasts rallied behind the book all the more keenly because the language was so rare. As Scott Macfie said in a review: 'Never has such feverish diligence been brought to the collecting of a tongue spoken by only a few score persons. There is something Gypsy-like in the contempt of material wealth that impelled a scholar to devote the best thirty years of his life to research so unremunerative' (cited in Sampson 1997: 151). But the dictionary remains seventy-five years later a standard work on the Romani language.

When John Sampson died at West Kirby, near Liverpool, in 1931 he was honoured and commemorated by Gypsies more than anyone. On the morning of 21 November a motor-coach of mourners set off from Liverpool for Llangwm, just below the mountain of Foel Goch, to find a crowd of hundreds of Gypsies already waiting, including a large contingent from Bettws. The straggling crowd was marshalled to walk slowly up the mountain, led by Manfri, the son of Matthew Wood. Below the mountain top, looking across to Snowdonia, Augustus John recited a tribute and my father scattered the ashes. The mourners chanted a Romani farewell and Reuben Roberts played on the triple harp. Later they all reassembled for the funeral feast at Cerig-y-Drudion, where George Borrow had once stayed, where philology mingled with festivity and the Gypsies mixed with the academics.

It is a world that is difficult to recapture today. When I researched in North Wales for my biography of John Sampson, *The Scholar Gypsy*, I was able to meet grandchildren of Matthew Wood, and to talk with them about their remarkable clan. I also had the good luck to discover and buy the Gypsy wagon that my grandfather had used in Bettws, which now stands in my garden in Wiltshire. But the Wood family no longer speak the pure Romani language that was their special pride; and the wild hinterland of woods, heaths and rough tracks that gave Gypsies the freedom to pursue their own lifestyle has been contained and obliterated by the relentless encroachment of suburbia and local councils' regulations. Nonetheless, John Sampson's legacy has been amply commemorated by Liverpool University, by the library's special collections, which include precious archives that were extended by Sampson's protégée Dora Yates, and by the unique collection of photographs of Gypsy life at the beginning of the century.

References

Fraser, Angus. 1990. 'A Rum Lot', in Matt T. Salo (ed.), *100 Years of Gypsy Studies*. Papers from the Tenth Annual Meeting of the GLS, North American Chapter. Cheverly, MD: Gypsy Lore Society. Publication no. 5: 1–14.

Sampson, Anthony. 1997. *The Scholar Gypsy*. London: John Murray.

Sampson, John. 1926. *The Dialect of the Gypsies of Wales*. Oxford: Clarendon Press.

The Gypsy Collections at Liverpool

Katharine Hooper

The collections of 'Gypsy' materials at Liverpool University Library comprise two separate but interrelated sections: the Gypsy Lore Society Archive and the Scott Macfie Gypsy Collections. The archive of the Society records not only its members' scholarship, but also Robert Andrew Scott Macfie's phenomenal powers of organization and persuasion; Macfie's 'personal' collection, given on his death in 1935, formed a nucleus for continuing donations from members of the Society and later additions. Together they document the interests, research, fieldwork and publications of the main figures in the Gypsy Lore Society from before its revival at Liverpool in 1907 up until the Society's move from Liverpool on the death of Dora Yates in 1974.

The Gypsy Lore Society

In November 1887, W.J. Ibbetson suggested in *Notes and Queries* that 'the Anglo-American Romany Ryes [Gypsy gentlemen] should form themselves into a club or correspondence society, for the purpose of compiling and publishing by subscription as complete a vocabulary and collection of songs as may be attainable at this date, and also of settling a uniform system of transliteration for Romany words, which is a great desideratum' (Ibbetson 1887: 397). In May of the following year, David MacRitchie, a qualified accountant from Edinburgh who had given up his profession in favour of intellectual pursuits, sent out a circular announcing the newly formed Gypsy Lore Society: 'The President is Mr. C.G. Leland, the Vice-President Mr. H.T. Crofton; and the following have already promised their support:- Mrs Pennell, the Archduke Joseph of Austria, Sir Richard Burton, Monsieur Paul Bataillard, Mr. F.H. Groome, Mr. J. Pincherle, Mr. Walter Herries Pollock, and Mr. W.J. Ibbetson'.[1]

---

[1] D. MacRitchie, *Gypsy Lore Society Circular*, 1889, GLS Archive LI.2.

This first period of the Society lasted four years and produced the three volumes of the 'old series' of the *Journal of the Gypsy Lore Society*, but by 1892 lack of funds had paralysed its activities. The Society fell into abeyance for fourteen years and many of the original contributors had died before MacRitchie's determination to revive it, or 'set the old vardo in motion once again', as he put it in a letter of 31 December 1906,[2] began to seem feasible. John Sampson and Robert Andrew Scott Macfie in Liverpool were crucial figures in the revival, the latter bringing to bear on the task 'an unbounded enthusiasm, a capacity for making friends, a keen, scholarly mind and a genius for writing beautiful and nervous English that formed an ideal combination for the undertaking' (Ackerley 1938: 3). Macfie set to work immediately, exploiting the Scottish connection he shared with MacRitchie to get a press notice about the revived Society into the first number of *Scotia* on 2 February 1907. By the end of March, he had arranged for the cover of the *Journal* to be the subject of one of *The Studio*'s design competitions, although he later tired of the resulting prize entries and, with advice from Augustus John, the type-design cover emerged that was used from the seventh volume of the new series to the fifty-second (and final) volume of the third series, sixty years later. Macfie's painstaking concern for presentation also led to changes in the design of the wagtail emblem on the Society's stationery. This was originally modelled on a drawing from a specimen at South Kensington Museum, but was later redesigned to resemble 'the animated and "raffish" wildfowl' that, MacRitchie noted in a letter to Macfie, 'have taken the place of the demure bird which ordinarily heads your letters. Your own are much more Gypsy-like'.[3] The demeanour of these birds in the sketches heading Macfie's letters charts the progress being made by the Society in the weeks leading up to the publication of the first issue of the new series of the *Journal* in August 1907. Macfie's letterbooks and the carefully preserved copies of the circulars and notices he sent out now form a major part of the Society's archive.

Macfie's energies increased the Society's membership from below 100 to over 200 and even made the Society financially viable for a short time, but, on the outbreak of war in 1914, he left to serve as Quartermaster-Sergeant with the Liverpool Scottish Regiment. Without Macfie, the Society languished, but was revived for a third series of the *Journal* in 1922. The 'Introductory Note' to the first issue made a positive start to the series:

[2] D. MacRitchie to R.A. Scott Macfie, letter dated 31 December 1906, GLS Archive A1.205.
[3] D. MacRitchie to R.A. Scott Macfie, letter dated 29 June 1907, GLS Archive A1.251.

In Gypsy folk-tales it is generally the third brother, who, aided by a good fairy, succeeds in making his way in the world after his two elder brothers have failed: and often he is small and mean-looking in comparison to them, until the miracle happens that transforms him into a prince. Between this hero of traditional story and the present series of our *Journal* the analogy is close enough to afford a hope that their fortunes may be the same.[4]

The hope proved well founded, as the third series continued for the next fifty-two years, with Macfie taking a lively interest from a distance, following his retirement to Lunds, until his death on 9 June 1935, which sadly prevented him from celebrating the Society's jubilee in 1938. Other notable contributors to the *Journal* from this period include E.O. Winstedt, T.W. Thompson, F.G. Ackerley, H.J. Francis and Dora Yates, who had assisted Macfie with its editing and production from 1907 and became Honorary Secretary of the Society in 1935. For the next twenty years Dora Yates undertook the majority of the editorial work (see Fürst 1999), but she did not officially become editor until 1955, ten years after her retirement from Liverpool University Library, to which she had brought the Society in a natural continuation of the work of her predecessor there, John Sampson. Dora Yates's death on 12 January 1974 ended the Gypsy Lore Society's association with Liverpool, and the longest run of its *Journal*. A fourth series begun in 1974 with financial backing from American members was sporadic, and the North American Chapter, founded in 1977, became the official US-based Gypsy Lore Society in 1989, providing a secure base for the continuation of more than a century's research. The *Journal*'s fifth series, begun in 1991, was renamed *Romani Studies* in 2000 and relaunched under the editorship of Yaron Matras.

The Gypsy Lore Society Archive

The archive of the Gypsy Lore Society at Liverpool University Library relates mainly to the production of the *Journal of the Gypsy Lore Society* through its 'old', 'new' and third series. It falls into three sections: correspondence, administrative materials, and the papers of individual 'Gypsiologists'. The first section contains more than 25,000 pages of correspondence in 31 bound letterbooks (1907–1926) and 11 boxes (1926–1973), with a further four bound volumes of membership lists, accounts and plans for the *Journal*. The second section consists of 11 boxes of files documenting the administrative history of the Society; they include correspondence with T. & A. Constable, printers of the first four

---

[4] 'Introductory Note', *JGLS*, Third Series, 1 (1922): 1.

series of the *Journal*, MacRitchie's original list of members, material relating to the Gypsy Lore Society Jubilee in 1938, and copy for the *Journal*. The third section contains 36 boxes of incoming correspondence and research papers of members of the Society, including the linguist F.G. Ackerley, D.M.M. Bartlett, the 'Gypsies' Padre' George Hall, William Ferguson, the photographer Fred Shaw and the philologist E.O. Winstedt, in addition to the three main Liverpool figures, John Sampson, Robert Andrew Scott Macfie and Dora Yates, of whom brief biographies follow.[5]

Originally from Cork, John Sampson (1862–1931) was apprenticed at 14, following the death of his father, to a lithographer and engraver in Liverpool. The academic honours he subsequently acquired, including honorary degrees from the universities of Oxford and Liverpool, and his status as a Romani scholar, belie the fact that he was largely self-taught. Sampson began work at University College Liverpool (the present University's predecessor) in 1892, just as the first phase of the Gypsy Lore Society was coming to an end, and it was thanks to his presence that the University circle in Liverpool brought together a number of remarkable scholars who were inspired by his enthusiasm for Gypsy studies (derived originally from his reading of George Borrow) and made Liverpool a nucleus for the revived Gypsy Lore Society. The importance of Sampson's role in the revival of the Gypsy Lore Society is expressed in a letter from David MacRitchie to Macfie in which he says, 'I regard it as settled that you will undertake the Secretaryship, with Sampson as guide, philosopher friend. (He shines in all three capacities.)'.[6] MacRitchie and Macfie also concurred in the view that 'the primary duty of the society should be to publish Sampson's rich store of knowledge'.[7] The success of this aim is apparent in the files of pre-publication material relating to Sampson's publications, *The Dialect of the Gypsies of Wales*, *The Wind on the Heath*, *Romane Gilia*, and *In Lighter Moments*, and to his research on Shelta and the Welsh Gypsies. Letters to Sampson in the Gypsy Lore Society archive (some in Romani) include those from the philologist Bernard Gilliat Smith, from Francis Hindes Groome, from Tom Oakes Hirst with Hirst's manuscripts on Welsh Romani grammar, from the founder of the Gypsy Lore Society, David MacRitchie, from Gypsies including Esmeralda Groome and from Macfie. Among the manuscripts in the Scott Macfie Gypsy Collections there are further letters, lectures and notebooks (containing drafts of

---

[5] For a longer account of Dora Yates see Fürst 1999. There is also an account of the early history of the Gypsy Lore Society in Heijning 2002.

[6] Alexander Pope calls Henry St John, Viscount Bolingbroke, his 'guide, philosopher, and friend', in *Essay on Man*, Epistle IV (1734), line 390; see Pope 1966: 279. D. MacRitchie to R.A. Scott Macfie, letter dated 7 January 1907, GLS Archive A1.207.

[7] D. MacRitchie to R.A. Scott Macfie, letter dated 7 January 1907, GLS Archive A1.207.

articles published in the *Journal of the Gypsy Lore Society* and elsewhere) and 14 volumes of diaries kept by Sampson, while the Scott Macfie Gypsy Collections press cuttings include volumes compiled by Dora Yates of obituaries of Sampson and reviews of his Gypsy anthology, *The Wind on the Heath*. The book section of the Scott Macfie Gypsy Collections includes many of Sampson's publications, from those described by Dora Yates as 'Sampson at play' (for example his *Omar Khayyam* [1902], a translation into Welsh Romani of 24 quatrains of Fitzgerald's famous version of the poem), to *The Dialect of the Gypsies of Wales* (1926), described by Angus Fraser as 'the greatest single linguistic study of Romani ever published' (Fraser 1990: 1).

Robert Andrew Scott Macfie (1868–1935) was educated at Cambridge, Edinburgh and Göttingen universities before joining the sugar refining business which his family had owned and operated in Liverpool since 1788. He spent a short time abroad while serving in the army but returned to Liverpool and was one of the first members of the University Club, formed in January 1896 to provide a common meeting place for people from the College and people from the city. Among his Gypsiologist friends in this group were Kuno Meyer, Consul Harald Ehrenborg, the Swedish Gypsiologist, and John Sampson, as well as the artists Augustus John and Anning Bell. Macfie described himself as 'a man who could get on absolutely well with absolutely anybody' and, as previously mentioned, proved to be the ideal person to revive the Gypsy Lore Society in Liverpool in 1907. Among the different bands of Gypsies from whom Macfie collected material were the Lovari or 'German' Gypsies who visited England in 1906 and the 'Coppersmith Gypsies' who came into the country in 1912, an encounter he wrote up in his *Gypsy Coppersmiths in Liverpool and Birkenhead* (1913). In the summer of 1913 Macfie travelled through Bulgaria in the company of a band of Gypsy horse-dealers and subsequently published *With Gypsies in Bulgaria* (1916) under the pseudonym Andreas (one of several he used). In 1914, Macfie left his duties to the Society to serve with the Liverpool Scottish regiment during the First World War. On his return, he retired from the family business to live at Hawes in the Yorkshire Dales, a move commemorated in the last (1921) of the series of bookplates designed for his collections.

Dora Esther Yates was born in Liverpool on 26 November 1879, the youngest child of a large Jewish family. Having enrolled as an Honours student at Liverpool University College, she became, in 1899, the first Jewish woman to be awarded a BA degree by an English university. Her linguistic abilities included fluent German and French in addition to Hebrew and the Anglo-Saxon and Middle English of her degree course, which formed a firm foundation for her study of Romani dialects under the direction of John Sampson. Dora Yates returned to the University of Liverpool as a member of staff in 1906, after a brief teaching career, and worked there continuously until her retirement in 1945. Shortly after her official 'retirement' the University appointed her curator of the Scott Macfie collection of books on Gypsy lore, which she had been instrumental in obtaining for its library in 1935, and which she catalogued in 1936 (see Yates 1936). She was awarded an honorary DLitt by the University in 1963 in recognition of her numerous achievements in many fields of scholarship.

Dora Yates spent many years recording the speech and folk tales of the Wood family of Welsh Gypsies, whose members spoke the 'deep' inflected Romani, the dialect recorded in Sampson's work. The Welsh village of Gwerfil-Goch, where many of the Woods had settled, became a drawing point for Gypsiologists at this time and it was here that Yates met intellectuals and artists such as the poet Arthur Symons, the artist Augustus John and the Gypsy scholars R.A. Scott Macfie, T.W. Thompson, E.O. Winstedt and George Hall. Dora Yates was a member of the Gypsy Lore Society from 1907, and an officer of the Society for over forty years; her publications include *A Book of Gypsy Folk Tales* (1948) and *My Gypsy Days* (1953).

The Scott Macfie Gypsy Collections

The Scott Macfie Gypsy Collections is really a misnomer for these large collections of photographs, illustrations, manuscripts, press cuttings and books, for although the foundation was the presentation of 'the unique library of Romani and Gypsy Lore [...] collected by Mr. R.A. Scott Macfie' and catalogued by Dora Yates, many other Gypsy Lore Society members also donated Gypsy material to the Society. William Ferguson left his collection of Gypsy books and photographs on his death in 1939; Fred Shaw's widow gave his Gypsy library and photographs to the Gypsy Lore Society on his death in 1950; F.G. Ackerley's own gift of 1951 was supplemented by the remainder of his Gypsy collection, donated by his widow on his death in 1954, and E.O. Winstedt bequeathed his entire library to the Society on his death in 1955. The recycling of their Gypsy collections between members of the Society is recorded in the marked-up catalogue of the sale of John Sampson's books and the lists of Gypsy books from Augustus John's library, but there is also evidence that a certain confusion of identity between private collections and Gypsy Lore Society business resulted in the removal and sale of official Society papers.

The collections are now arranged by genre, of which the main sections are photographs, illustrations, manuscripts, press cuttings and books. The photographs date mainly from 1910–1940 and many were taken by the Gypsy Lore Society members Fred Shaw and Ivor Evans. In addition to 18 boxes of loose prints, there are 17 albums of prints, including two albums arranged and mounted by R.A. Scott Macfie between 1910 and 1931, and also albums from Dora Yates and William Ferguson.

The two bound volumes of illustrations of Gypsies that Macfie compiled between 1907 and 1914 were regarded by him as one of the treasures of his collection: filled with 'photographs of real Gypsies from everywhere on earth, engravings of artists' Gypsies such as have never been seen anywhere in the world, highly coloured illustrations of camps, and ancient woodcuts of the costume Gypsies wore of old' (Macfie 1913: 33). In the chapter 'The Photograph' in his *Gypsy Coppersmiths in Liverpool and Birkenhead*, Macfie recalls producing them to show the visitors. They turned the leaves 'indifferently, punctuating their talk with contemptuous exclamations of "Sinte"', until they reached a 'somewhat mean picture-postcard which had reached me through several hands, but came originally from Lemberg in Galitsia [sic]. It represented a troop of elaborately costumed performers, whom I had always taken for "counterfeit Egyptians", dancing and playing huge accordions on an artistically decorated stage, and the subscription was "Gypsies from the Caucasus" [...] "Our *Roma*", they said, approvingly' (Macfie 1913: 33). The text in Macfie's hand in the otherwise blank space explains that the postcard showed, among others, the brother of Tinka, the Romanian chief's wife, whom she had not seen for more than twenty years. Macfie refused offers of 'first a silver plate a foot in diameter, and then a great gold ring such as she herself wore' and removed the card to give to her, leaving 'a blank space, of which I am prouder than of my rarest Callot' (1913: 36). Taken together with the collection of Gypsy prints in the Gypsy Lore Society Archive (material used for reproduction in the *Journal of the Gypsy Lore Society*, including frontispieces by Augustus John), and the illustrations in the book collections, this section of the Scott Macfie Gypsy Collections provides approximately four centuries of visual representation of 'Gypsies'.

The 63 boxes of manuscripts contain much material intended for publication in the *Journal of the Gypsy Lore Society*, and the publication dates of many pieces are noted, but among these letters, notebooks, drafts and typescripts are also many unpublished items, including ten volumes of the notebooks of H.T. Crofton, with manuscript notes by Macfie. Among the manuscript vocabularies is the duplicated typescript of Antun Medven's *Romani Vocabulary* dated 1941, copied by Rade Uhlik and with his preface signed 'Sarajevo, 5.II.1947': 'Mr. Medven's parish lies in the neighbourhood of Zagreb/Agram. The dialect of his Gypsies is rather similar to the Bosnian Romani, but it is more roumainized. This poor Gypsy tribe is fully eliminated by the Hitlerites' (SMGC MS 2.6).

The press cuttings section contains 41 bound volumes and 14 boxes of newspaper and magazine cuttings compiled by Macfie and many other members of the Gypsy Lore Society. These cover a period from approximately 1860 to the removal of the Society from Liverpool, with the larger part dating from the first half of the twentieth century. The earliest volumes were compiled between 1873 and 1879 by H.T. Crofton, first vice-president of the Society and president in 1908–1909. Those compiled by Macfie between 1907 and 1914 include a volume concerning the Gypsy Lore Society and its *Journal*, while Dora Yates compiled volumes containing obituaries of Sampson and reviews of his Gypsy anthology, *The Wind on the Heath* (1930). Further volumes were collected by other members and officers of the Society, including Ivor Evans and E.O. Winstedt.

Particular rarities among the 2500 items in the printed collections include 'poster' edicts against Gypsies from 16 different localities and, among the many Romani versions of the Gospels, the dated page-proofs, with marginal corrections in George Borrow's autograph, of the 1872 revision of his translation of the Gospel of St Luke into Spanish Romani. Macfie was an exemplary book collector, and the books acquired by him bear his signature and date of purchase, often noting the cost not only of the item itself, but of associated binding and even postal charges. The familiar blue linen boards with Macfie's gold crest and monogram, by Fazakerley of Liverpool, stand out on many of the articles and pamphlets, but the bindings also include pictorial boards and Romany colours and motifs – the most striking being perhaps Lord Lilford's Borrow vocabulary, printed for private circulation, bound in stripes of 'the old Romany-Zingari colours' of red, yellow and black.[8] Many of the works were presented to Macfie by their authors, and the evidence of his critical attention remains in the notes, word lists and indexes he added, for example the manuscript Romani vocabulary at the end of his copy of Bercovici's *A Romany Chai* (1933). There are also manuscript notes by Winstedt and others, and letters to Macfie or between members of the Gypsy Lore Society have been retained in some volumes. The contemporary reception of works of members of the Gypsy Lore Society is recorded in cuttings of reviews, while the list of 300 addresses for offprints in Macfie's 'Gypsy Lore' from the 1908 *University Review* testifies to his energetic efforts to revive the Society. The annotations to the books in the collection, particularly Macfie's own copies, suggest his interest in MacRitchie's original view of the *Journal of the Gypsy Lore Society* as a repository to 'garner the thousand and one stray scraps of curious Gypsy lore now lying scattered through local histories, old newspapers, old magazines, old books of travel, and other works unknown or

[8] SMGC H3.59, annotated to indicate the attribution to Lord Lilford made by Alfred James in *JGLS*, Third Series, 13 (1934): 52.

inaccessible to the general student'.[9] After Macfie's death, the collection continued to grow, with the addition of items presented by many other members of the Society or given to Dora Yates by their authors.

The Gypsy collections at the University of Liverpool as a whole represent the same mixture of erudition and romanticism that characterized the lives of the early members of the Gypsy Lore Society. Their historical focus looks back to sixteenth-century Europe and beyond, but their relevance to current academic research remains, whether for the study of the Society itself, continuing its work on Romani linguistics, or monitoring the long history of Gypsy persecution in literature and other media.

References

References to items in the collections are given in the form 'GLS Archive A1.1' for the Gypsy Lore Society Archive, and 'SMGC MS 2.6' for the Scott Macfie Gypsy Collection.

Ackerley, Frederick George. 1935. 'Friend of All the World: A Memoir of Robert Andrew Scott Macfie', *JGLS*, Third Series, 14 (special number): 6–43.

—1938. 'Longarum haec meta viarum 1888–1938', *JGLS*, Third Series, 17.3 (special Jubilee number): 1–11.

Bercovici, Konrad. 1933. *A Romany Chai*. London: Hurst & Blackett.

Fraser, Angus. 1990. 'A Rum Lot', in Matt T. Salo (ed.), *100 Years of Gypsy Studies*. Papers from the Tenth Annual Meeting of the GLS, North American Chapter. Cheverly, MD: Gypsy Lore Society. Publication no. 5: 1–14.

Fürst, Renée. 1999. 'Dora Yates: Prominent Female Gypsiologist and Liverpool Academic, or "the Wretched Dora"? A Critical View of her Life and Work'. Unpublished MA dissertation, University of Liverpool.

Heijning, Miranda van de. 2002. 'Two Societies: On Rais, Rawnies and the Gypsy Lore Society, 1888–1938'. Unpublished doctoral thesis, University of Nijmegen.

Ibbetson, W.J. 1887. 'Songs of the English Gipsies', *Notes and Queries*, 12 (November): 397.

Kelly, Thomas. 1997. *For Advancement of Learning: The University of Liverpool 1881–1991*. Liverpool: Liverpool University Press.

Lee, Ken. 2000. 'Orientalism and Gypsylorism', *Social Analysis*, 44: 129–57.

Macfie, Robert Andrew Scott [Andreas]. 1913. *Gypsy Coppersmiths in Liverpool and Birkenhead*. Liverpool: Henry Young & Sons.

—1916. *With Gypsies in Bulgaria*. Liverpool: Henry Young & Sons.

---

[9] D. MacRitchie, *Gypsy Lore Society Circular*, 1889, GLS Archive LI.2.

Pope, Alexander. 1966. *Poetical Works*, ed. Herbert Davis. Oxford: Oxford University Press.

Sampson, John. 1902. *Omar Khayyam bish ta dui gilia*. Lundrati: poshe yogesko chiriklo David Nutt.

—1926. *The Dialect of the Gypsies of Wales*. Oxford: Clarendon Press.

—1930. *The Wind on the Heath*. London: Chatto & Windus.

Yates, Dora E. 1936. *A Catalogue of the Gypsy Books Collected by the Late Robert Andrew Scott Macfie*. Liverpool: The University of Liverpool.

—1948. *A Book of Gypsy Folk Tales*. London: Phoenix House.

—1953. *My Gypsy Days*. London: Phoenix House.

Note

I would like to acknowledge the work of former colleagues in Special Collections and Archives, University of Liverpool, who were responsible for creating the web pages and the EAD-encoded finding aids for the Gypsy Collections, particularly Julie Allinson, Paddy Collis, Pete Johnston and Micheál O hAodha.

Belated Travelling Theory, Contemporary Wild Praxis: A Romani Perspective on the Practical Politics of the Open End

Ken Lee

I track the disintegrated tribe, I reconstitute the pulverized dynasty. I swim in the canals of the chronicles, go up the apocryphal torrents, I span both time with milliaries and deserts that frighten.

Tahar Djaout, *L'Invention du désert* (1987)[1]

Some of my earlier work analysed the link between Orientalism and Gypsylorism as discursive formations that constitute the subjects of which they write (Lee 2000). Here I extend that work by examining ways in which Gypsylorists, by suppressing alternative possibilities, reinforced their epistemic control in constituting 'the Gypsies'. I develop the inter-linked notions of travelling theory, belatedness, 'wild praxis' and the possibilities that postcolonial theorizing can offer to examine ways in which Romanies can uncover and re-present amnesiac discourses embedded in Gypsylorism. I use two illustrations: Francis Hindes Groome's hypothesis for the origin of the term 'Egyptian' as applied to early Romani arrivals in Europe, and the existence and operation of the Gypsy and Folklore Club from 1911 to 1914.

Romanies as Colonial Subjects

Pollock has argued that Indological studies in the nineteenth and early twentieth centuries, in terms of investment by the state and volume of output, were dominated by Germany, which 'almost certainly surpassed all the rest of Europe and America combined' (1993: 82). He emphasizes that this occurred 'without [...] any direct colonial instrumentality (1993: 82). Consequently, he argues, the epistemic violence of colonialism can occur without the perpetrator necessarily occupying a colonial territory. Similarly, I argue that while Romanies have never been colonized through dispossession of land in the same way as indigenous

---

[1] *Milliaries*: the ancient Roman miles of a thousand paces.

peoples, in many other respects they can be considered as colonial subjects – victims of imposed discursive (mis)representations and structural inequalities, marginalized, patronized, exploited, stripped of language, culture, dignity. Here I contend that recent developments in postcolonial theory can offer a new perspective on the ways in which 'the Gypsies' have been – and still are – constituted and created as subjects.

The Gypsies and Postcolonial Theory

Edward Said (1983) discussed what he called 'travelling theory', the possibility that theories may lose some of their original force when transposed to other times and situations. He later considered alternative ways in which 'travelling theory' could produce the opposite effect, asking if theory 'flames out so to speak, restates and reaffirms its own inherent tensions by moving to another site?' (Said 1999: 200). This possibility he called 'transgressive theory', illustrating it by showing how Lukacs's theory of reification was used by both Adorno (to examine Schoenberg's place in the history of music) and Fanon (to examine the colonial struggle in terms of a European subject–object dialectic). Said concluded that since '[the] work of theory, criticism, demystification. deconsecration and decentralization [...] is never finished [...] the point of theory is to travel, always to move beyond its confinements, to emigrate, to remain in a sense in exile' (Said 1999: 213). He argues that these theoretical displacements suggest 'the possibility of actively different locales, sites, situations for theory without facile universalism or over-general totalizing', resulting in 'travelling theory and [...] intransigent practice' (Said 1999: 214). Such a different locale for theory was developed when Behdad (1994) argued that Althusser's idea of belatedness was a form of 'travelling theory' that allowed postcolonialism to be examined as a form of 'wild praxis' which tries to connect separate disciplinary areas in alternative ways, thereby rethinking 'relations and distinctions between ideology, history, culture and theory' (Behdad 1994: 4). He also claims that 'the wild praxes of postcolonialism produce the conditions of coevalness and contemporaneity for dialectical confrontations of cultures through remembering; they demystify the allochronic discourse of power while reclaiming the unrepresented history' (Behdad 1994: 7).[2]

The prominent postcolonial theorist Gayatri Spivak dealt in her earliest works with the processes of material and epistemic violence by which the colonial and neo-colonial international division of labour had 'worlded' the earth to produce the First, Second and Third 'Worlds'

---

[2] In this context *coevalness* means 'the condition of existing at the same time' and *allochronic* means 'differently timed'. Fabian (1983) discusses in detail the ways in which allochronic discourse and denial of coevalness have been used to create subjects for anthropological study.

(Spivak 1984, 1988a, 1988b). Subsequently, as Goldberg (1993) has argued, this 'worlding' process has perpetuated racialized relationships in international politics, both symbolically and materially. This process of epistemic 'worlding' began in 1952 when the French demographer Alfred Sauvy identified three 'worlds', and was extended in 1974 by Chief George Manuel, a Canadian First Nations Shuswap, who identified a 'Fourth World' composed of the indigenous peoples of the world (Manuel 1974: 1; see also Dyck [ed.] 1985 and Dyck and Waldram [eds] 1993). The First and Second Worlds are primarily colonizers, while the Third and Fourth Worlds are the worlds of colonial subjects. While the vast majority of Romanies inhabit the First and Second Worlds, they experience their lives in an unnumbered and unnamed 'world' that shares many of the characteristics of the Third and Fourth Worlds.

Spivak's work is valuable, since it resists positioning in a 'world' by contributing to anamnesiac projects. Drawing on Foucault's work (which identified the late eighteenth century as a significant disjuncture in discursive formations in Europe), Spivak (1984) began to 'inspect soberly the absence of a text that can "answer one back" after the planned epistemic violence of the imperial project' (1984: 131). The late eighteenth century was also Said's starting point for Orientalism, and was also the time that 'the Gypsies' were first constituted as subjects by Grellmann in his 1783 *Dissertation on the Gipsies*. Here I apply a similar Foucauldian 'archaeology of knowledge' to Gypsylorism, revealing practices of knowledge-construction in the past that have been suppressed or marginalized by hegemonic discourse. That which is ignored, avoided or deemed unsuitable for examination reveals, *precisely because it is rejected and suppressed*, the system that decides the possibilities of knowledge. I begin by examining the background to Francis Hindes Groome's Danubian hypothesis, first articulated in 1898.

Did the Gypsies Come from Egypt?

Conventional wisdom about Romani arrival in Europe is that they came as bands of cunning rogues carrying fake letters of safe conduct, the first indication of their guile and cunning. Grellmann devoted a chapter of his *Dissertation on the Gipsies* to this matter, pointing out that 'such letters of convoy have been *really granted* to the Gipseys' (1787: 104, emphasis added[3]), but added that after an initial period of reasonable treatment, 'people saw too clearly, that, instead of holy pilgrims, they were the mere

---

[3] All citations from Grellmann are taken from the 1787 English edition; his spelling and word usage have been retained.

refuse of humanity' (1787: 104). The conventional wisdom also holds that the exonym[4] 'Gypsies' as a corruption of 'Egyptian' came from their own accounts of having come from Egypt on a penitential pilgrimage. This too is analysed by Grellmann (1787), who devoted an entire chapter to discussing the alleged Egyptian descent of the Romanies. Similar arguments can be found in many standard texts about 'the Gypsies', such as Hancock 1987, Liégeois 1981 and Fraser 1992. I see two problems with this conventional view.

First, although some of the Romanies' letters of safe conduct were genuine and others may well have been fraudulent, neither of these was necessarily a result of a specifically Romani cunning. Rather, it was an adaptation to a widespread existing practice. The medieval world was replete with pilgrims, who had to obtain both permission and letters of safe conduct from ecclesiastical authorities in order to travel in other countries (Hoade 1970 [1952]). Again, Grellmann recognized this, stating that Romanies 'were looked upon as pilgrims; and it was quite conformable to the custom of those superstitious times to grant to pilgrims, as holy people, all sorts of passes, and safe conducts' (1787: 121).

Secondly, what is not remembered, and which I now wish to recall to memory, is an alternative hypothesis that may have provided a more plausible explanation of Egypt as a source for the early Romani groups in Europe. I wish to draw attention to the amnesiac qualities that surrounded the presentation of this alternative hypothesis and the epistemic disjuncture and subsequent trajectory that this created. I do not wish to argue for the truth of this hypothesis, but simply to indicate that it has been suppressed and avoided – and thus constitutes a discontinuity in the archaeology of knowledge.

The Alternative to Fraudulent Passports: Francis Hindes Groome's Danubian Hypothesis

On 30 June 1898, Francis Hindes Groome, one of the founders of the Gypsy Lore Society and a major figure in early Gypsylorism, wrote a letter to John Sampson, another major figure in early Gypsylorism, in which he states:

> In the Itinerarium of Symon Simeonis, an Irish Franciscan who went in 1322 on pilgrimage to Jerusalem (ed by Nasmith 1778) is the well-known passage relating to Gypsies in Crete. There is also in his description of Egypt, a very suggestive passage on pp. 57–58:
> *'be it also known that in the cities of Alexandria and Cairo men, women giving*

[4] *Exonym*: a name given to a group by outsiders, as opposed to an *ethnonym*, a name a group gives itself.

suck, youths and greybeards, are shamefully exposed for sale like beasts & especially the Indians, schismatics and Danubians (danubiani) who all of either sex have much share as to colour with crows and coals. For the Egyptians are constantly at war with the Arabs and Danubians & when they take them prisoners either make them redeem themselves or else sell them into bondage.' [this last is rather a para-phrase than a translation of: 'Iuia hii cum arabio et danubianis semper guerram continuant, atque cum captiuntur [? ie Arabi vel Danubiani] redemtione vel ven-ditione evadunt'] Now the before mentioned Danubians, though not distinguishable from the Indians in feature or hue, yet are distinguishable & recognizable by the long scars on their face. For they burn their miserable faces with a red-hot iron drawn lengthwise, believing that thus they are baptized with fire as the saying is, & purged by fire from the corruptions of sins. Who when converted to the law of Mahomet are worse to the Christians than the Saracens, as also are the renegade Radiani [?]& do them much harm, because like ravening wolves they strive inhumanly to devour the Christians & to rejoice in their blood. Be it known that in the above mentioned cities there is such a multitude of them as cannot be numbered.'

It is sufficiently vague but full of suggestions. In 1322 there seem to have been a great number of prisoners of war in Egypt, Danubians, natives that is of the Danube territories, very black and indistinguishable from Indians. Tattooed, or something of the kind apparently;? compare the Gypsies at Paris in 1427, who had 'le visage deplaie' their faces covered with wounds (GLJ ii: 30). Now if these were Gypsy prisoners (slaves) in Egypt in 1322, & if some of these bought back their liberty & returned to their families in the Danubian territory, there we get an explanation of 'Egyptian' 'Gypsy' 'Gitano' etc & of the story told by the Gypsy immigrants of 1417–35. Have you at Liverpool any competent historian who will face the pathless wilderness of Howarth's History of the Mongols & seek for any corroboration of this guess? I believe it is worth following up.[5]

I can find nowhere in Sampson's published work or correspondence any indication that he took up this hypothesis and examined the possibil-ities that Groome had outlined. However, the amnesia does not stop with Sampson. In his *Gypsy Folk-Tales*, Groome points out that a passage 'on p.57 of the Itinerarium has hitherto escaped Gypsiologists' (Groome 1899: xix). He then proceeds to give the passage (as in italics above) in the original Latin, and adds substantially the same speculation as in his letter to Sampson, concluding:

Were these Danubians, or at least some of them, Gypsies, prisoners of war, from the Danubian territories? And did some of them buy back their freedom and return to Europe? If so, perhaps one has here an explanation of the hith-erto unexplained names 'Egyptian', 'Gypsy', 'Gitano' etc and of the story told

---

[5] GLS Archive C 2 (23), Groome to Sampson, 30 June 1898. Square brackets, punctuation, abbreviations and spelling as in original.

by the western immigrants of 1417–34 of renegacy from the Christian faith. (Groome 1899: xix)

Most Gypsylorists should be familiar with Groome's text. However, I can find no serious examination of Groome's suggestion. Why? Is this because the 'epistemic violence' that constituted the Romanies as cunning nomads had already become sedimented as conventional wisdom in the hundred years since Grellmann first presented 'the Gypsies' as subjects? Would a serious examination of Groome's hypothesis thereby have undermined and destabilized an already established hegemonic edifice of Gypsylorism? Had the late nineteenth-century Gypsylorists already forgotten that Grellmann a century earlier had clearly identified Romanies as slaves in Moldavia and Wallachia, and thus a possible source of prisoners of war from the Danubian area, as Groome had suggested? Grellmann states that 'there is not a single bojar in Wallachia but has at least three or four of them [Gypsies] for slaves, the rich have often some hundreds each, under their command' (Grellmann 1787: 6).[6] As part of an anamnesiac project, I offer the following data that could be brought to bear on Groome's century-old hypothesis.

It is generally accepted, first, that Romanies migrated from India through Anatolia and Armenia, entering Europe from the western end of present-day Turkey, and, secondly, that there is no specific documentary evidence for this migration trail. How then could Romanies reach the Danubian provinces, be enslaved there and later be found in Egyptian slave markets? What data could indicate any possible linkages?

Lewis (1990) has shown that there was a well-established system of slavery in the medieval Islamic world, including trade in slaves from Europe, and a well-developed slave trade with Egypt. He has also argued that during the early centuries of Islamic conquest and expansion, capture of prisoners of war was the most important source of slaves in the Islamic world, and that 'Central and East European slaves [...] were mostly *but not exclusively* Slavs' (1990: 18, emphasis added). Lewis also notes that slaves were also supplied by 'the Tatar Khanate of the Crimea [some of whom had converted to Islam by the late thirteenth century] whose raiders every year rode far and wide in *Central and Eastern Europe*, carrying off great numbers of male and female slaves. These were brought to the Crimea and shipped thence to the slave markets in Istanbul and other Turkish cities' (Lewis 1990: 18, emphasis added). Supporting these arguments, Beck (1989) has argued that the Romani slaves in Romania were acquired as prisoners of war, while Chirot (1976) on the other hand argues that they were already held as slaves by the nomads of the Khanate, although they may already have been taken as prisoners of war.

---

[6] The *bojars* were the landholding aristocracy of Moldavia and Wallachia, which were combined to form present-day Romania.

There was considerable European complicity in the slave trade with Islam, with the Genoese controlling the European slave trade in the Black Sea. To add to this general material, there is an intriguing four-teenth-century Islamic traveller's account that may illuminate Groome's hypothesis, linking Danubian slaves with Egypt.

The Travels of Ibn Battuta

Ibn Battuta came from the north of Morocco, and started travelling in 1325 when he was 20 years old to complete the Hajj (the pilgrimage to Mecca), but continued to travel for a further thirty years, covering about 75,000 miles and visiting the equivalent of 44 modern countries which were then mainly under Muslim rule, including the countries of North Africa, Egypt, Syria and Palestine, Saudi Arabia, Persia and Iraq, the Arabian Sea and East Africa, Anatolia (Turkey), the steppes of Central Asia to Astrakhan and Samarkand, India, the Maldive Islands and Sri Lanka, Malaysia and China, eventually returning to Morocco. He later travelled to Andalusia and the southern parts of Morocco and on to West Africa, before finally returning home, where he recorded his experiences in a *rihla*, or travel book.

Between 1330 and 1333, Ibn Battuta visited Anatolia, and crossed the Black Sea to Kaffa, the Genoese colony on the southern shores of the Crimea. His accounts of Kaffa are interesting, since they record that traders from Genoa, Venice, *Egypt*, Russia and elsewhere lived in the town. He also noted the slave trade from Kaffa. Dunn discussed Ibn Battuta's travels, noting that

> [at] these Black Sea ports they [Battuta and his fellow travellers] could see the trade goods of the steppe: grains, timber, furs, salt, wax, and honey. There were also the trade goods that had come along the Silk Road from Persia or China. And there were *slaves, too: war captives* and the sad children of poor parents who sold their children in order to survive. *They would be sold in the slave markets of Cairo*; others would be sent to work in the sugar plantations of Cyprus or in the rich households of Italy. (Dunn 1986: 163–64, emphases added)

Kedar also discussed the role of Genoese slave-traders in the Black Sea, arguing that the effects of the Black Death had enhanced Venetian and Genoese trade, in that '[the] depopulation certainly furthered the export of Black Sea slaves to the manpower-hungry cities of Italy' (1976: 14). Furthermore, he also makes an explicit link between the Genoese slave trade and the Mameluke rulers of Egypt: 'The Mameluke army of Egypt was severely hit by the recurrent outbreaks of the plague, and it stands to reason that the sultans asked their Genoese suppliers of slave-soldiers to rush in replacements' (1976: 14).

Ibn Battuta also provides evidence of a possible link between these European slave-traders and India. He recorded a regular trade in horses between the nomads of the Khanate of the Golden Horde (whom he called the Turks) and India: 'The horses in this country are exceedingly numerous and their price is negligible. [...] These horses are exported to India (in droves) each one numbering six thousand more or less' (Gibb 1962: 478–79). He also points out that these horses were traded not for their speed, but because '[the] people of India [...] themselves wear coats of mail in battle and they cover their horses with armour, and what they prize in these horses is strength and length of pace' (Gibb 1962: 479). That is to say, the horses were specifically traded as cavalry mounts. This offers a possible link that supports Hancock's Rajput warrior hypothesis for the origin of Romanies (Hancock 1993).

Ibn Battuta also gives an account of his travels overland from Astrakhan to Constantinople, as part of the entourage of a princess of the Khanate. He describes the extent of the retinue – the troops, the slaves, the wagons, horses, oxen and camels. He also records that the princess had 'ten Greek pages with her, *and the same number of Indian pages*', providing another tantalizing link with India (Gibb 1962: 498).

To reach Constantinople the retinue traversed present-day Romania, which the Khanate effectively controlled at the time. Ibn Battuta's account of this section is sketchy: he describes passing through 'an uninhabited waste, for eight days of which there is no water', but no further details are provided (Gibb 1962: 186).

Was Groome Correct?

From all these documentary fragments we can infer some possible links between India as a source of Romani slaves, and the Danubians of Groome's hypothesis. As Ibn Battuta noted, Indian military units traded cavalry mounts with the Turkic horse-traders of the Asiatic steppes. These horse-traders themselves had slaves, both Greek and Indian, and in turn conducted slave-trading with Genoese slave-traders on the northern Black Sea littoral. In turn, the Genoese slave-traders supplied slaves to the Egyptian Mamelukes. It is possible, then, that Indian slaves could have been moved from India, via the Turkic steppe-lands and the Black Sea to Egypt.

All this points to the speculative possibility that Francis Hindes Groome's suggestion may have had an element of truth. It is possible that Romanies had entered the Danubian provinces, been captured as prisoners of war by the Tatars of the Khanate, shipped from Kaffa to Cairo and sold as slaves, but may have purchased their freedom and set about a journey to return to the Danubian provinces, and could quite reasonably and correctly have claimed to be coming from Egypt.

I do not claim that this is a robust new hypothesis of Romani migration, particularly in this sketchy form. I merely wish to present these fragments of data to emphasize the fact that a hypothesis that could have produced a significantly different trajectory in twentieth-century Romani studies was effectively forgotten – or actively rejected – by Sampson, one of the founding heroes of Gypsylorism, and by most subsequent practitioners.

I now turn to another example of amnesiac discourse in Gypsylorism, which suppressed the existence of an alternative organization that took 'the Gypsies' as its subjects.

The Fractured History of Gypsylorism and the Challenge of the Gypsy and Folklore Club

The conventional wisdom of the history of the Gypsy Lore Society is roughly as follows. In 1887, in *Notes and Queries*, William John Ibbetson wrote:

> I would venture to suggest that the Anglo-American Romany Ryes should form themselves into a club or correspondence society, for the purpose of compiling and publishing by subscription as complete a vocabulary and collection of songs as may be attainable at this date, and also of settling a uniform system of transliteration for Romany words, which is a great desideratum. (Ibbetson 1887: 397)

As a result of Ibbetson's suggestion, the Gypsy Lore Society (GLS) was formed in 1888 by a handful of enthusiasts, to whom approximately another 60 members were added, including a considerable number of university and public libraries and learned societies. Once founded, the GLS began publication of the *Journal of the Gypsy Lore Society* (*JGLS*). After a brief life from 1888 to 1892, the GLS wound up and the *Journal* ceased, only to be reincarnated in 1907, extinguished again in 1916 by the impact of the First World War, and reincarnated again in 1922, continuing an uninterrupted output until 1974, ending only with the death of the indefatigable Honorary Secretary, Dora Yates. The Society then languished until 1978, producing only four issues of the *JGLS* and eventually fading out of existence in the UK. In the meantime, the small but dedicated North American Chapter of the GLS continued the sterling work, and in 1991 again reincarnated the Society, incorporating it in the United States under the original name of the Gypsy Lore Society and reviving the *Journal*, publishing the continuing Fifth Series of *JGLS* (under the original name, but later changed to *Romani Studies*). This stylized account is, of course, too neat a mythology, and gives a spurious and seamless precision to what was a much more complex and fractured evolution of Gypsylorism. Here I present an anamnesiac account of alternative possibilities by examining a challenge to the epistemic dominance of the GLS by the Gypsy and Folklore Club.

The Gypsy Lore Society – The Early Years

The original GLS of 1888–1892 was a small and exclusive group of people, never exceeding 75 members, including institutional subscriptions.[7] In fact, the aim was to restrict membership: 'membership we propose to increase to, and *limit* to, 150'.[8] David MacRitchie financially supported the GLS, underwriting the costs of producing the *JGLS*, which was printed privately for members. When MacRitchie could no longer afford this, the organization ended, a point that he reiterated when the GLS was revived: 'the fact remains that when I threw up the sponge, the journal ceased to appear'.[9] With the end of the first GLS in 1892 there was no guarantee that the organization would ever revive. In fact, members were advised that if they continued to work in the area of Gypsylorism, they should submit their material either to the English *Journal of Folklore*, or to the Hungarian *Ethnologische Mitteilungen*.

In 1907 the GLS was revived, again under the presidency of David MacRitchie, based on 'the mass of new information which has accumulated [...] and the growth of interest in Gypsy studies', and 11 members of the original GLS rejoined and promised papers for the new *Journal*.[10] The revived GLS aimed to attract 'every amateur of Gypsy Philology, Folk-lore, and Ethnology, and every student of Sanscrit and Indian Languages'.[11] However, the revived GLS, like the original, depended directly on the support of a single financial benefactor, Robert Andrew Scott Macfie, who undertook to run and support the small-scale organization. MacRitchie himself recognized the dangers inherent in this situation: 'our dear old G.L.S. has always been a one man concern. [...] In short Macfie & I are in the same boat, except that he is working on a larger scale. The gist of this is that, hitherto the Journal has depended upon one man for its existence, myself first and then Macfie'.[12]

What has been effectively forgotten and suppressed, and which I am now recalling to memory, is that during the second revival of the GLS from 1907 to 1916, there was an alternative organization that took as its subjects 'the Gypsies', thereby challenging the dominance of the GLS, namely the Gypsy and Folklore Club (hereafter GAFLC). Although the

---

[7] GLS Archive LI 38–40, GLS receipt books 1888–1892.

[8] GLS Archive LI (2), 1889 flyer, emphasis added.

[9] GLS Archive letter 136, D. MacRitchie to John Sampson, 18 May 1909.

[10] GLS Archive LI (5) 1907.

[11] GLS Archive LI (43) 1907.

[12] GLS Archive letter 136, D. MacRitchie to John Sampson, 18 May 1909.

level of scholarship in the GAFLC was never as rigorous as that in the GLS, the GAFLC was nevertheless *at the time* seen as a considerable challenge to the GLS, and in particular was a source of considerable personal vexation to Macfie. Relations between the GLS and GAFLC ranged from an initial enthusiastic assistance through a subsequent exasperated dismay to a final open hostility, culminating in a rancorous legal entanglement. Here I sketch some of the relationships between the GLS and GAFLC to indicate the extent to which the amnesia or erasure of this history has occurred, and thereby to illustrate the ways in which the current privileged epistemic position of the GLS has been constituted.

The second phase of the GLS ended in 1914, when Macfie enlisted and went to war in France. From 1914 to 1916 the GLS continued to publish the *JGLS* with material that Macfie had already collected. After the *JGLS* ceased publication, the organization became moribund, and again, as at the end of the first phase, there was no guarantee that the Society would survive at all. It was not until a third philanthropic benefactor, William Ferguson, was located in 1922 that the GLS was revived.

The Rise and Fall of the Gypsy and Folklore Club

William Townley Searle, an illustrator and graphic artist, journalist, bit-player actor, bookseller, curio dealer in London, and, according to Macfie, 'a chartered libertine of impecuniosity', had joined the GLS in late 1911.[13] He quickly curried favour with Macfie, sympathizing with the lack of GLS members and the poor state of finances, and suggesting a possible solution:

> It seems to me that an increased membership would be a distinct advantage. Now, I am pretty certain that among my Folklore friends, and customers, I could get a few new members. I think that if you could appoint me London correspondent it might help me, and I should be pleased to put my Gypsy collection at the disposal of London members for lending free of charge.[14]

Macfie agreed to this:

> It would be delightful if you would be the missionary with any title you like. Could you start a Gypsy 'salon' in Hand Court, where Gypsies and their admirers could meet on equal terms? The more ruffianly and Bohemian could frequent a pub round the corner, and the superfine could play guitars and 'peruse' morocco bound editions of Leland.[15]

[13] GLS Archive A 34: 418–19, 7 October 1913.
[14] GLS Archive A 20: 27, no. 392, 6 November 1911.
[15] GLS Archive A 32: 458–59. Hand Court was a mews off Old Holborn in London. It was destroyed during the Blitz.

However, Macfie's motives in this were less than genuine, as he admitted to H.T. Crofton:

> Townley Searle's form of madness is so amiable and so amusing that I have done all I could to egg him on to further lunacy [...] If I could succeed it might be a useful preparatory school for the GLS. [...] I sort of hope that Searle may discover a few Romane Raia we have missed. [...] if he puts two or three really good clean men into the way of becoming Romany Rais he may do good.[16]

The unsuspecting Searle quickly set up the GAFLC in late 1911: 'I have now talked the matter of the Gypsy Salon over with a few people, you will see that I think of calling it the Gypsy and Folk Lore Club'.[17] Macfie even assisted Searle by providing a motto and logo for the newly founded club: ' "Work is for fools"! In deep Anglo Romani it would be *Butsi si dinilenge*. The hedgehog makes a fine badge'.[18]

The GAFLC continued until about 1914. It was based in London, with its own club premises, a well-publicized lecture series, a library, and a journal that ran for three years under the following three different names: *Romanitshels', Didakais' and Folklore Gazette. Reflecting also the opinions of Tinkers, Travellers, Gawjos, Show-Folki and Posh-rats* in 1912; *Gypsy and Folklore Gazette* in 1912 and 1913; and *The Journal of the Gypsy and Folklore Club* in 1913.

The challenge to the epistemic dominance and hermetic dilletantism of the GLS by the GAFLC was made clear when Inglis (1912: 47) pointed out that both 'Gypsy-Lore' and 'Folk-Lore' 'have remained a closed study' and that the *JGLS* 'was a "sealed" publication to most people, for, to obtain it one had to become a member of the GLS'. He added that while the *JGLS* 'met the demands and wants of what may be considered a select "few" [the study of Gypsies] is no longer the private study of a few, but [...] a national topic of interest' (Inglis 1912: 47).

A list of members of the GAFLC (a total of 93 – almost as many as the GLS at the time) appeared in the first issue of Searle's journal, including several members of the GLS; in fact Macfie was member no. 1. Many of the GLS members also contributed to Searle's journal, including Macfie himself and the Rev. George Hall. In 1913 H.T. Crofton gave Searle permission to reprint his *English–Gypsy Vocabulary* in the *Gypsy and Folklore Gazette*. In a letter to John Sampson, Searle boasted: 'All the best-known member of the GLS are with us while the Club owes its being to Macfie. We have a weekly Romanes [i.e. Romani language] class and have now 140 members – the largest Gypsy library in the world, and have had 25 lectures in less

---

[16] GLS Archive A 32: 647, 4 December 1911.
[17] GLS Archive A 20: 30, no. 400, 23 November 1911.
[18] GLS Archive A 32: 613, Macfie to Searle, 22 December 1911.

than six months on Gypsy Lore and Folk Lore'.[19] Searle, seeking a suitable president for his club, consulted Macfie, who suggested 'Why not have Augustus John? He is unconventional enough in all conscience'.[20] Searle did so, a move that was later to produce several unintended and unwanted consequences.

Searle was a shrewd publicist in promoting his alternative organization. Emphasizing the exotic sensuality of 'the Gypsies', he arranged a visit from a snake charmer, who 'promises to tell us some interesting facts in connection with the Gypsies' and who is 'really interested in – phallic worship'.[21] During this visit, the snakes escaped, and the resulting 'snake stampede' was widely reported in the London press. Searle admitted to Macfie that 'of course the snake stampede was arranged in advance'.[22]

The inaugural issue of Searle's journal in 1912, however, created a serious division between the GLS and GAFLC, since for the first time there was a tangible competitor to the discursive control of the *JGLS*. Macfie was shaken by the lack of scholarship and editorial sloppiness in Searle's journal, describing it as 'like a jumble sale and most carelessly corrected, and [with] almost nothing about Gypsies in'.[23] More importantly for my argument, though, Macfie was concerned about the possible impact of Searle's journal on the position and status of the GLS, stating 'we must be careful just now for fear of being confused with Townley Searle's journal'.[24] By mid-1913, though, after Searle's second issue was published, Macfie had radically changed his views about the value of Searle's club and journal:

> I thought a year ago, that Searle's Gazette might be a useful medium for the publication of the more popular type of article for which the JGLS has scarcely room [...] I have changed my mind with middle aged caution and *ratvalo* [bloody] slowness. However, it <u>is</u> changed; and I am convinced that no good can come from a club managed by so vulgar and dishonourable a man as Searle.[25]

A little later in 1913, Macfie, seeking to distance the GLS from the GAFLC, published material in the *JGLS* that Searle thought defamatory, and he sued Macfie for libel. The events leading up to this were as follows. In the *JGLS* Macfie had published a notice that welcomed the establishment of the GAFLC:

[19] GLS Archive B 2 (93), Searle to Sampson, 15 June 1912.
[20] GLS Archive A 32: 706, Macfie to Searle, 19 January 1912.
[21] GLS Archive A 22: 52, no. 476, 9 February 1912.
[22] GLS Archive A 22: 54, no. 478, 18 February 1912.
[23] GLS Archive A 32: 886, 5 March 1912.
[24] GLS Archive A 32: 740, 26 January 1912.
[25] GLS Archive A 32: 690, 16 January 1912, underlining in original.

THE GYPSY- AND FOLKLORE CLUB.

To the GAFLC the GLS extends a hearty welcome. Founded by Mr W.
Townley Searle, and under the Presidency of Mr Augustus John, it proposes
to promote the cultivation of Gypsies, and the collaboration and conviviality
of their admirers, by social methods which the older society, with its world-
wide membership, cannot adopt. Although situated in London, its appeal is
not only to Londoners; for Mr Searle intends to publish a monthly magazine
which will represent gypsy life and thought in a spirit less scientifically severe
perhaps, but also more romantic – possibly even more humourous – yet not
necessarily less illuminating, than is possible in this journal. (Macfie 1911:
234)

At this stage, Macfie clearly envisaged the GAFLC as a complementary
organization to the GLS, rather than as a competitor.

Following this notice in the *JGLS*, Augustus John had an argument
with Searle over the loan of a painting, resulting in John smashing the
windows of Searle's club-rooms. Searle in response turned John's anger
to advantage by displaying a notice at the club, reading: 'These windows
broken by the celebrated impressionist artist, Augustus John, in his
eagerness to enter the club'.[26] In a subsequent issue of the *JGLS*, Macfie
inserted this notice:

In the JGLS (p. 234) it was stated that Mr Augustus John was President of
the GAFLC. As this statement, if uncorrected, might lead friends to suppose
that he was still a supporter of that institution, he has requested that the following notice should be published at once:-
'Mr Augustus John repudiates all interest in, or connection with, the Gypsy
and Folk Lore Club, Hand Court, London. In view of an entirely erroneous
announcement, he wishes it to be known that he is not, nor ever would be,
President, or even a member, of that assemblage'. (Macfie 1912a: 145)

Searle promptly responded with a letter to Macfie:

Mr W. Townley Searle requests the insertion of the following reply to a note
which appeared on p. 145 of this volume of the JGLS.
'On December 31 1911 Mr Augustus John joined the GAFLC as an ordinary
member, paying the ordinary subscription. On April 13th 1912, he accepted
the position of President. On June 3rd he "reluctantly relinquished the
honour" owing to his "lack of social attainments" (I quote from the correspondence before me as I write). Moreover, it was Mr Augustus John who
suggested the name of the Club publication. From this you will judge that this
gentleman's statement that he "is not, nor ever would be, President, or even
a member of this assemblage" is entirely erroneous, for at the date your paragraph was written he was both.'

---

[26] GLS Archive A 34: 418–19, 7 October 1913.

[The paragraph to which Mr Augustus John referred appeared in the Daily Sketch on Dec 10 1912, and included him among 'Friends of the movement or members of the Club'. The methods of the GAFLC have won the indignant disapproval of members of the GLS who have attempted to support it. Among others Mr Augustus John gave the new venture his willing aid at the beginning, and was unluckily persuaded to become its first President. When personal experience had convinced him that it was undesirable to be connected with the Club in any capacity whatsoever, he sent his resignation to Mr Searle in the polite terms quoted above. -Ed]. (Macfie 1912b: 330–31)

Searle then issued a writ against Macfie in October 1913, on the grounds that publication of the above items in the *JGLS* was detrimental to his Club and his reputation. He also threatened to sue T. & A. Constable, printers of the libel. Since Searle was more skilful at manipulating the press and creating publicity than the GLS, the GAFLC also challenged the privileged epistemic position of the GLS, and apart from the threat of the libel case, what Macfie feared was that the position of the *JGLS* as discursive controller of Gypsylorism would be compromised, since 'Searle would do his best (and being unscrupulous, possibly succeed) to make the affair appear to be a case of jealousy *between two rival institutions of equal merit*'.[27]

Macfie became increasingly agitated about the libel case, while Searle continued to publish his journal, shamelessly plagiarizing accounts of the Coppersmith Gypsies from the GLS, and even an entire issue of another journal, 'stolen from the "Folklore Journal, edited by the Working Committee of the South African Folklore Society", Cape Town 1879–80'.[28] Throughout 1913 and most of 1914, Macfie continued to be worried by the legal wrangle, not sure he could win, irritated by the distraction as well as the personal and financial costs, but particularly concerned about the effect it might have on the position of the GLS. The last reference to the Searle case was in August 1914, when Macfie had engaged a firm of London solicitors and was more optimistic about the progress of the case. However, with the outbreak of war, Macfie (who had been a volunteer in the Liverpool Scottish Regiment) enlisted and passed over the running of the GLS to other members. With the end of Macfie's financial support and editorial control, the loss of members and consequent lack of material for the *JGLS*, the second revival of the GLS ended in 1916. After Macfie's return from the war, no more was heard of the libel case, and he retired a semi-invalid to the Yorkshire Dales.

The important thing about the conflict between the GLS and the GAFLC is not so much the hypocrisy and farcical antics that resulted from Macfie's, Augustus John's and Townley Searle's respective

[27] GLS Archive A 34: 520, 27 October 1913, emphasis added.
[28] GLS Archive A 34: 880, 16 January 1914.

behaviours, but the fact that during the second phase of GLS there was an alternative organization, which took as its subjects 'the Gypsies', and actively challenged the hegemonic position of the GLS. The dispute between the GLS and the GAFLC, with the real fear of a challenge to discursive domination, has been suppressed in recounting the history of the GLS. The only public traces of this conflict are the three short entries in the *JGLS* cited above. To make sense of these requires excavation and analysis of the archival material of the GLS – a Foucauldian archaeology of knowledge which recalls to memory that which has been suppressed or forgotten, thereby allowing an alternative reading of this period of Gypsylorism. This amnesia is not merely a matter of historical interest, for it continued to influence the running of the GLS. In 1931, when 'Prince Gypsy Petulengro' appeared, Macfie wrote to Dora Yates: 'We shall have to ignore the author of Romani Remedies ('Gypsy Petulengro'). We could only mention him to expose him, and that would probably mean a libel action by a man of straw, a costly business as I know from Searle's case'.[29] The GLS, though claiming to control scholarly discourse on 'the Gypsies', by 'ignoring' Petulengro, signalled its unwillingness to insert itself into the public arena to challenge an individual its members believed to be a fake.

Conclusion

As Edward Said (1978) pointed out, the discursive construction of a privileged epistemological position involves controlling not only what is written, but what is not allowed to be written. My illustrations show how two potential trajectories for Gypsylorism were rejected in favour of an established hegemonic discourse. If Gypsylorists had seriously considered Groome's Danubian hypothesis in 1899, then possibly Gypsylorism would have developed differently. For example, the fact of Romani slavery in Moldavia and Wallachia might have occupied a more prominent position in the understanding of Romani histories, or the possible entry of Romanies into Europe across the Black Sea might have been given earlier consideration. Similarly, if Searle had been adept enough to wrest the public focus of Gypsylorism from Macfie, then the position of Romani studies today might have been very different. Unlike the overtly scholarly GLS, Searle supported advocacy on behalf of Romanies, telling Macfie that the GAFLC was 'now forming a Gypsy Protection Society, and getting a list of *atchintans* [camping sites], Gypsy

---

[29] GLS Archive D 1 (235), 16 March 1932.

Lawyer etc.'.[30] Searle later suggested that '[if] only legislation could be made with the protection of the Gypsy as its object a great thing would certainly be accomplished' (Searle 1912: 36). Had such protection occurred in the 1910s, then the position of Romanies in Britain today might have been very different.

The anamnesiac speculations and archaeological analysis outlined above offer a contemporary wild praxis as a counter to the hegemonic dominance of Gypsylorism. Such wild praxis, I argue, shows how an analysis of amnesiac discourse can contribute to the small-scale deconstruction of a major discursive formation.

References

Bakhtin, Mikhail M. 1981. *The Dialogical Imagination*, ed. M. Holquist, trans. C. Emerson and M. Holquist. Austin: University of Texas Press.

Beck, Sam. 1989. 'The Origins of Gypsy Slavery in Romania'. *Dialectical Anthropology*, 14.1: 53–61.

Behdad, Ali. 1994. *Belated Travellers*. Durham, NC: Duke University Press.

Chirot, Daniel. 1976. *Social Change in a Peripheral Society*. New York: Academic Press.

Clifford, James (ed.). 1988. *The Predicament of Culture: Twentieth-Century Ethnography, Literature, and Art*. Cambridge, MA: Harvard University Press.

Clifford, James, and Marcus, George E. 1986. *Writing Culture: The Poetics and Politics of Ethnography*. Berkeley: University of California Press.

Djaout, Tahar. 1987. *L'Invention du desert*. Paris: Seuil.

Dunn, Ross E. 1986. *The Adventures of Ibn Battuta, a Muslim Traveler of the Fourteenth Century*. Berkeley: University of California Press.

Dyck, Noel (ed.). 1985. *Indigenous Peoples and the Nation-State: 'Fourth World' Politics in Canada, Australia and Norway*. St John's, Newfoundland: Institute of Social and Economic Research: Memorial University of Newfoundland.

Dyck, Noel, and Waldram, James B. (eds). 1993. *Anthropology, Public Policy, and Native Peoples in Canada*. Montreal: McGill-Queen's University Press.

Fabian, Johannes. 1983. *Time and the Other: How Anthropology Makes its Object*. New York: Columbia University Press.

Fonseca, Isabel. 1995. *Bury Me Standing: The Gypsies and their Journey*. New York: Alfred A. Knopf.

Fraser, Angus. 1992. *The Gypsies*. Oxford: Blackwell.

Gibb, Hamilton A.R. 1958. *The Travels of Ibn Battuta A.D. 1325–1354*, I. Translated with revisions and notes, from the Arabic text. Ed. C. Defrémery and B.R. Sanguinetti. Hakluyt Society. Cambridge: Cambridge University Press.

---

[30] GLS Archive A 22: 81, no. 509, 14 June 1912.

—1962. *The Travels of Ibn Battuta A.D. 1325–1354*, II. Translated with revisions and notes, from the Arabic text. Ed. C. Defrémery and B.R. Sanguinetti. Hakluyt Society. Cambridge: Cambridge University Press.

Goldberg, David T. 1993. *Racist Culture: Philosophy and the Politics of Meaning.* Oxford: Blackwell.

Grellmann, Heinrich M.G. 1787. *Dissertation on the Gypsies: Being an Historical Enquiry, Concerning the Manner of Life, Family, Oeconomy, Customs and Conditions of These People in Europe, and their Origin.* London: G. Bigg (trans. Matthew Raper).

Groome, Francis H. 1899. *Gypsy Folk-Tales.* London: Hurst and Blackett.

Hancock, I.F. 1987. *The Pariah Syndrome.* Ann Arbor, MI: Karoma Publishers.

—1993. 'India's Forgotten Warriors', in Jagat Motwani, Mahin Gosine and Jyoti Barot-Motwani (eds), *Global Indian Diaspora: Yesterday, Today and Tomorrow.* New York: Global Organisation of People of Indian Origins.

Hoade, Eugene. 1970 [1952]. *Western Pilgrims: The Itineraries of Fr. Simon Fitzsimmons (1322–23), a certain Englishman (1344–45), Thomas Brygg (1392), and notes on other authors and pilgrims.* Publications of the Studium Biblicum Franciscanum, No. 18. Jerusalem: Franciscan Printing Press.

Ibbetson, William John. 1887. 'Songs of the English Gipsies', *Notes and Queries*, 12: 397.

Inglis, Cyril. 1912. 'The Folk-Lore Revival', *Romanitshels', Didakais' and Folklore Gazette. Reflecting also the opinions of Tinkers, Travellers, Gawjos, Show-Folki and Posh-rats*, 1.2: 47.

Kedar, Bernard Z. 1976. *Merchants in Crisis: Genoese and Venetian Men of Affairs and the Fourteenth Century Depression.* New Haven, CT: Yale University Press.

Lee, Kenneth W. 2000. 'Orientalism and Gypoylorism', *Social Analysis*, 44/2: 129–56.

Lewis, Bernard. 1990. *Race and Slavery in the Middle East: An Historical Enquiry.* Oxford: Oxford University Press.

Liégeois, Jean-Pierre. 1987. *The Gypsies.* London: Al Saqi.

Macfie, R.A.S. 1911. 'Notes and Queries No 28', *JGLS*, New Series, 5.3: 234.

—1912a. 'Notes and Queries No 27', *JGLS*, New Series, 6.2: 145.

—1912b. 'Notes and Queries No 50', *JGLS*, New Series, 6.4: 330–31.

Manuel, Chief George. 1974. *The Fourth World: An Indian Reality.* New York: The Free Press.

Pollock, Sheldon. 1993. 'Deep Orientalism? Notes on Sanskrit and Power beyond the Raj', in Carol A. Breckenridge and Peter van der Veer (eds), *Orientalism and the Postcolonial Predicament.* Philadelphia: University of Pennsylvania Press.

Porter, Dennis. 1994. 'Orientalism and its Problems', in Patrick Williams and Laura Chrisman (eds), *Colonial Discourse and Post-Colonial Theory: A Reader.* Hemel Hempstead: Harvester Wheatsheaf.

Said, Edward. 1978. *Orientalism.* New York: Vintage.

——1983. *The World, the Text, and the Critic*. Cambridge, MA: Harvard University Press.

——1999. 'Travelling Theory Reconsidered', in Nigel C. Gibson (ed.), *Rethinking Fanon*. Amherst: Humanity Books.

Searle, William T. 1912. 'Editorial', *Romanitshels', Didakais' and Folklore Gazette. Reflecting also the opinions of Tinkers, Travellers, Gawjos, Show-Folki and Posh-rats*, 1.2: 35.

Spivak, Gayatri C. 1984. 'The Rani of Sirmur', in Francis Barker, Peter Hulme and Margaret Iversen (eds), *Europe and its Others*. Colchester: University of Essex Press.

——1988a. *In Other Worlds: Essays in Cultural Politics*. London: Routledge.

——1988b. 'Subaltern Studies: Deconstructing Historiography', in Ranajit Guha and Gayatri C. Spivak (eds), *Selected Subaltern Studies*. New York: Oxford University Press.

——1990. *The Post-Colonial Critic: Interviews, Strategies, Dialogues*, ed. Sarah Harasym. New York: Routledge.

——1993a. *Outside in the Teaching Machine*. London: Routledge.

——1993b. 'Can the Subaltern Speak?', in Patrick Williams and Laura Chrisman (eds), *Colonial Discourse and Post-Colonial Theory: A Reader*. Hemel Hempstead: Harvester Wheatsheaf.

Willems, Wim. 1997. *In Search of the True Gypsy*, trans. D. Bloch. London: Frank Cass.

Worsely, Peter. 1984. *The Three Worlds*. London: Weidenfeld and Nicolson.

Young, Robert. 1990. *White Mythologies: Writing History and the West*. New York: Routledge.

Part II

Constructions and Concoctions of Romany Culture

The Role of Language in Mystifying and Demystifying Gypsy Identity

Yaron Matras

'Gypsy': A Double Signifier

No discovery has been as significant to the understanding of the history of the Gypsies as the illumination of their linguistic connection with India. Having said this, there arises immediately a need to clarify. For the connection between the Romani language and the languages of India has no bearing at all on the history and origin of the Irish Travellers, and probably little and only indirect significance for an understanding of the culture of the German or Swiss Yenish, to name but two examples out of many. At the same time it is impossible to understand the Rom, Romacel, Romanichel, Sinte, Manush or Kaale without knowing something about the origins of their language – *romani chib*, or *romanes*, or, as it is referred to in modern linguistics, Romani. How might we resolve this contradiction? The answer is very trivial: two separate signified entities are captured by the term 'Gypsy'.

GYPSY 1 denotes the social phenomenon of communities of peripatetics or commercial nomads, irrespective of origin or language. Whether or not the diverse communities that fall under GYPSY 1 have much in common is the subject of occasional discussions among members of these groups, and of intense research among social scientists describing their cultures. Let us accept both that members of these distinct groups often show interest in one another and may at times feel a sense of common destiny, and that at the scientific level comparative research into diverse peripatetic communities is now an established discipline.

GYPSY 2 is as it were a popular English translation for a set of ethnonyms used by those groups whose language is a form of Romani. Despite the diversity of its dialects, Romani can be clearly defined as an entity. Indeed, since it is an isolated language, being the only Indian language spoken exclusively in Europe (and by emigrants from Europe, in the Americas, for instance), the boundaries between Romani and surrounding languages are much more obvious than, for example, the boundary between dialects of Dutch and German, Swedish and Norwegian, Italian and Spanish, or Polish and Slovak. I will not enumerate the features that are shared by the dialects of Romani, or the isoglosses that separate them, and I refer the reader instead to my recent book, which deals with those in great detail (Matras 2002).

To some extent, there are challenges in the definition of both notions. Social scientists must come up with a set of features that are found throughout the diverse communities that constitute GYPSY 1 if they are to justify comparative research on them as a distinct phenomenon. These features are usually sought in the social and economic relations with outsiders to the community, and sometimes in folklore (e.g. origin myths; cf. Casimir 1987). For GYPSY 2 or the *Rom* – for reasons of convenience I will be using this term for all speakers of Romanes or Romani, regardless of their own self-ascription – there is a long history of attempts to generalize about various aspects of culture and social organization, which however vary considerably (and one should not forget that the customs of various groups of Jews, Indians or Germans vary as well). The one feature that stands out as a common denominator of the Rom is, by definition, their use of the Romani language.

Nonetheless, one might argue that linguists also encounter a transitional zone as far as the linguistic definition is concerned, notably in the margins of Romani, where the language itself is not spoken, but communities are familiar with Romani-derived vocabulary which they may use occasionally. However, such use of selected items of Romani vocabulary – now termed 'Para-Romani' in the linguistic literature – is marginal to the study of the dialects of Romani itself. Whether Para-Romani vocabularies testify to the use of inflected Romani in the respective community at an earlier time (the retention of a small number of lexical items having followed language shift), or whether they represent instances of vocabulary borrowings from Romani by people whose ancestors were not Romani speakers, is an interesting question, but not one that bears on the definition of the Rom. The fact that so-called 'mixtures' (better: patterns of insertion of foreign lexicon) exist does not in any way relativize the coherence of Romani itself, and does not pose, for linguists, any difficulty in recognizing what is and what is not a dialect of Romani. It is obvious from a linguistic viewpoint that the mere insertion of occasional words such as *gorgio* or *vardo* or *grai* does not qualify as use of the Romani language itself, any more than saying 'I survived the Blitz' qualifies as speaking German or the exclamation 'What a tasty vindaloo!' is a sample of Hindi.

It is a matter for speakers who use just the occasional Romani word to decide whether they choose to refer to such a style through their interpretation of the term 'Romany', as many do. It is similarly a matter for individuals who do not speak Romani, but whose ancestors did speak it, to choose whether they identify with their roots in such a way as to wish to refer to themselves as Rom. This applies in some cases to entire communities, where Romani is not spoken, but appears to have been spoken in the past (for instance among the Gitanos of Spain), or where Romani-derived lexical items may have been acquired, or where encounters with the Romani language or indeed with the Romani political movement may evoke identification with the Rom (such as among the Yenish). These are the so-called 'test cases' where one might argue that being Romani or claiming to speak Romani is a 'representation' or 'construction', rather than a verifiable descriptive account. The fact that there are margins, however, does not in any way suggest that there is a void in between those margins.

The historical complexity of 'Gypsy' representations and images derives from the potential interface of what I referred to above as GYPSY 1 and 2. GYPSY 2 – the Rom – are unique in having a language that is originally Indian, and so they also have an Indian origin. At the same time, GYPSY 2 is a sub-set of GYPSY 1, i.e. the Rom are, historically at least, one of numerous peripatetic communities, who happen to be of Indian origin and speak an Indo-Aryan language. This leads to real-life encounters between the Rom and other peripatetics, and to a very concrete reality for those travelling in the present or past – sharing caravan sites, sharing a destiny, creating social and economic bonds and even family bonds, and borrowing from one another's cultures. There is, in my view, neither a theoretical nor a practical problem in understanding and accepting a complex set of historical interrelations between the Rom and other peripatetics. And yet modern Gypsy/Romani Studies is haunted by a controversy among two circles at its opposite ends, a controversy that revolves around the distinction between these very two entities. My paper is devoted to this controversy.

The first side, best represented by anthropologist Judith Okely (1983), and more recently by the 'deconstructionist school' of Leo Lucassen (1996) and Wim Willems (1997), denies any kind of division between what I am here calling GYPSY 1 and GYPSY 2. More specifically, it recognizes only GYPSY 1 (peripatetics as a social phenomenon), and denies GYPSY 2 (Rom of Indian origin), claiming that it is no more than a social construction by outsiders, in an attempt to exoticize or romanticize GYPSY 1. Since the 'anti-Indianists', as Okely (1997) herself terms them, reject a division between GYPSY 1 and GYPSY 2, they are unable to accept that the so-called 'Indianists' make their own assertions about an Indian origin only with reference to GYPSY 2 (the Rom), and not to GYPSY 1 (peripatetics in general). The division, claim the 'anti-Indianists', is not an attempt at a historical-linguistic taxonomy, but amounts to a potentially racist division between 'pure' ('Indian') and 'impure' ('non-Indian'). Willems (1997) indeed goes as far as asserting that it was the postulation (i.e. the scientific recognition) of GYPSY 2 by scholars in the eighteenth and nineteenth centuries that formed part of the ideological justification behind the persecution of Gypsies under the Nazis in the Second World War.

At the opposite end, there is by contrast a denial that there is or was any historical interface at all of GYPSY 1 and GYPSY 2. This view is best represented by Romani linguists and activists Ian Hancock (2000), Vania de Gila Kochanowski (1994), and their followers. Any actual, real-life connection between the Rom and GYPSY 1 (peripatetics), they claim, results from oppression through European society, which marginalized the Rom and forced them to bond with indigenous peripatetics. Moreover, European scholarship projected its biased social attitudes onto its own investigations of Romani history, creating a one-sided narrative according to which the Rom had been originally peripatetics. Thus, in their view, the position that GYPSY 2 (the Rom), a distinct linguistic-ethnic entity, is a sub-set of the more global phenomenon of GYPSY 1 (peripatetics), is a social construction by outsiders, who project their stereotypical and romantic images onto the Rom.

My interest in this debate is twofold. First, however marginal the positions might seem in relation to the bulk of work carried out in the various fields of Gypsy and Romani Studies, they are being expressed by some rather prominent scholars who have made some very influential contributions to the discipline. Moreover, it is by taking positions with regard to the margins that the mainstream discipline can define itself. Secondly, the arguments put forth by both groups are attempts to construct, deconstruct, or reconstruct a linguistic argument which has been accepted by mainstream Romani studies for over two centuries. Their arguments revolve around analyses and alternative analyses of language. It is hard for a linguist interested in an interdisciplinary approach to Romani studies to resist the temptation to review the role that language and attitudes to language play in the construction and deconstruction of identities and images. I begin with a discussion of the discovery of the Indian origin of Romani, followed by a very brief review of the linguistic arguments put forth by the Old School – the school whose conclusions are being challenged at both ends of the debate.

Johann Rüdiger and the Indian Origin

Clearly, interest in the Gypsies (that is, all 'Gypsies') and their origins and speech habits had been motivated well into the eighteenth century by a passion for exotic peoples, as well as by the practical consideration of authorities and law enforcement officers eager to penetrate the protective shield of social and cultural isolation that surrounded the Gypsies. But the late eighteenth century saw not just the emergence of

Romanticism, but also of a scientific methodology in comparative philology. It was in this latter context that Rüdiger (1990 [1782]) postulated the Indian origin of the Romani language.

Rüdiger's work, though a rather short essay, is a strikingly impressive document of originality and personal integrity. Rüdiger had exchanged ideas with other colleagues, to whom he gives credit. He did not claim to have been the first to notice a connection with Indo-Iranian languages, but he was the first to display the evidence and the analysis. Rüdiger was thus both a pioneer – his publication of the Indian origin of Romani pre-dated that of all other scholars, including Grellmann, and he was original – he collected his Romani data directly from a speaker of the language, and he extracted the Hindustani data that he used for comparison from a manual of the language composed by a missionary. Moreover, Rüdiger was sympathetic to the Gypsies, and very critical of society's treatment of them. Elsewhere (Matras 1999a) I have discussed Rüdiger's essay at length. I shall therefore only summarize in brief his linguistic procedure and findings, and document a few statements that are representative of his overall approach, both social and linguistic.

Rüdiger proceeded as follows. From his colleague and teacher Christian Büttner he heard the viewpoint that the 'Gypsy' language (*Zigeunersprache*) might be of Indian or Afghan origin. He was further encouraged by Hartwig Bacmeister to participate in a collective scholarly effort to determine its origin through comparison with other languages. He located a speaker of Romani, whom he asked to translate sample sentences and grammatical paradigms into her language, which he then compared with the Hindustani manual at his disposal. The display of the linguistic material begins with a series of sentences, in both languages, with a German gloss. It then surveys the major domains of nominal and verbal morphology, some function words, and some remarks on syntax. Rüdiger thus presented the scholarly community with the first ever sketch of Romani grammar. The dialect documented is that of the German Sinti-Manush-Kale, still very close to the Romani spoken today in Germany and surrounding regions. What makes Rüdiger's essay a methodological breakthrough is the fact that it not only shows the similarities in vocabulary and structure between Romani and Hindi/Urdu, but that it also discusses and explains the differences.

Thus Rüdiger points to changes in the syntactic typology of Romani, which, he correctly hypothesizes, are the result of language contact. He is able to relate this to a more general methodology in comparative linguistics, reminding the reader that in other language families (Germanic, Romance) vocabulary is more stable than inflection or syntax. Nonetheless, he recognizes the Indian roots of Romani grammatical items as well, such as nominal case endings or personal pronouns. With the knowledge of the time, had Rüdiger attempted to compare Danish and Dutch, or Russian and Bulgarian, or Arabic and Hebrew, or any other pair of genetically related languages, he could have followed a very similar layout. There are some naive statements in the grammatical discussion (see Matras 1999a: 102–103), but this is dwarfed by the significance of the achievement.

Nominally, Rüdiger is one in a series of scholars who speculate on the origin of the Gypsies. But in examining language he is certainly doing more than demonstrating mere fascination with the exotic. Rather, he takes a methodological approach to language as a stable indicator of origin and affinity, knowing that languages are usually not invented by populations, and that populations do not simply adopt foreign languages unless there has been some obvious motivation to do this, for instance colonial rule by another nation. Naturally, there had been no Indian colonial rule in Europe and so no reason for a (largely illiterate) population to adopt an Indian language. The fact that they do speak one is thus indicative of their foreign origin: 'none of the distinctive characteristics of a people is as reliable, long-lasting, crucial and unchanging as language. Form, practices and customs change because of climate, culture and mixing with others, however amid all this change language remains identifiable from one pole to the other' (Rüdiger 1990 [1782]: 59).[1] Not only is he not pursuing the exotic, Rüdiger also takes a very sympathetic position towards the Gypsies, and one that is critical of mainstream society. Commenting on their status, he says:

> The Gypsies are respected and protected by the laws, as long as they do not cause offence to anyone. Nonetheless I have the impression that even in the most skilfully governed lands the survivors among this unfortunate people have not yet fully received compensation for the injustice that had been committed against their ancestors. For nowhere have they obtained full civil status and equality with the rest of us humans – to which they are naturally entitled. (Rüdiger 1990 [1782]: 47)

And he continues further: 'This is still a political inconsistency, which our enlightened century should be ashamed to tolerate. For, the mistreatment of the Gypsies has no other cause but deeply rooted xenophobia [*Volkshass*]' (Rüdiger 1990 [1782]: 49). Finally, although Rüdiger offers a number of speculations and possible scenarios in respect of the Gypsies' motivation to leave India, he remains modest in his conclusions:

> I dare not give a more detailed description of the reasons that motivated their migrations. However, I am, even without the use of supportive tools too much

---

[1] Translation based partly on a version by M. Priego-Timmel, U. Bernhardt and A. Monreal (University of Manchester, 1996).

of an outsider to this particular field of history in general and will leave it therefore to the actual historians. I hereby give in modestly before them not only being content but feeling amply rewarded if my small investigation proves to be of any help to them and might give rise to further discoveries in the future. I hope that by using the plumb line of philology I was able to facilitate and safeguard the journey across the history of the Gypsies. (Rüdiger 1990 [1782]: 84)

Note that, as a trained philologist, Rüdiger does not equate 'vocabulary' with 'language'. Rather, 'language' for him includes by definition the grammatical paradigms of inflection, function words, and syntax. Thus, Rüdiger explicitly makes his statements based on a study of grammar, and not just words. This point has been consistently ignored by the 'deconstructionists' of the Okely school, who refer to 'language' as though the discussion revolves around mere vocabulary. In fact, a number of sources even preceding Rüdiger were very much aware of the distinctness of secret lexicons as used by peripatetics (GYPSY 1), and the fully-fledged language used by the Rom or GYPSY 2. Items from the respective speech forms are consistently identified as separate entities already in the Waldheim Glossary of 1726 (cited in Kluge 1901: 185–90), a vocabulary collected at an institution that served as a prison, an orphanage, and a shelter for the poor in Waldheim between Leipzig and Dresden in Upper Saxony. The *Rotwelsche Grammatik* of 1755 has separate vocabulary lists for *Rotwelsch* or 'cant' (also 'argot' or 'jargon') and *Zigeunersprache* or 'Gypsy language', and documents a two-page text in the latter. The Sulz List of 1787, a report on interrogations and court hearings authored by police chief Georg Schäffer, also separates the two. On p. 10 Schäffer presents a number of German sample sentences each translated separately into both *Jaunersprache* or 'thieves' jargon' and *Zigeunersprache* (see Matras 1999a: 111). Wim Willems ignores this aspect of the Sulz List, saying only that '[for] the compact typology of groups which Schäffer prefixed to his compilation of names of undesirables, he based his text primarily on Fritsch and Thomasius. This explains why many of their ideas about this subgroup are recognisable in his characterizations. Gypsies are said to have a secret language (*Rotwelsch*) of their own and possibly a foreign origin, but nevertheless they were Germans and as such a segment of the larger category of itinerants' (Willems 1997: 16). In fact, Schäffer writes that 'according to Fritsch, they [i.e. their language] is not related to any other language, rather, it is only through words that Gypsies and vagabonds [*Jauner*] can communicate among themselves. Fritsch calls this Gypsy language "Rotwelsch"' (Sulz List 1787: 10, my translation). But Schäffer is quoting Fritsch, and he himself documents a different reality, namely the existence of two separate speech forms, on the very same page of the List.

Rüdiger's contemporary was Heinrich Grellmann, who was wrongly given credit for discovering the Indian origin of Romani. Grellmann was hostile in his attitudes to Gypsies, and propagated enforced social and cultural assimilation. Ruch (1986) has shown that Grellmann plagiarized most of his ethnographic chapters from a series of publications in the *Wiener Anzeiger* (Vienna Gazette). He also argued that Grellmann is likely to have plagiarized parts of his chapter on language as well, and that the ideas he presents there were in any case not his, but were taken from Büttner and possibly also from Rüdiger. I have further shown (Matras 1999a) that Grellmann cited Romani data from different dialects and so quite obviously from different sources, and that his Romani vocabulary was in large part plagiarized from the *Rotwelsche Grammatik*, including a number of items that were, in fact, not Romani but *Rotwelsch* or cant.

Willems (1997) dedicates the most important chapter of his book to Grellmann, celebrating the fact that the author who was most success-ful in broadcasting the Indian origin theory was also a cheat and a racist. Willems' argument disputing an Indian origin rests almost entirely on discrediting Grellmann. On the other hand, Willems's attitude to Rüdiger is a combination of mockery and downplaying:

> he included a long article wherein, on grounds of some linguistic compari-sons, he believed he was able to show that Gypsies originally came from India [...] The development of comparative linguistics during the second half of the eighteenth century pointed naturally to the East, the cradle, to be sure, of all European languages. In Rüdiger's single substantial article about Gypsies, he revealed that he was of the romantic school which would come to maturity only decades later and then especially in England. (Willems 1997: 80)

While Willems's case against Grellmann is, essentially, the latter's aca-demic discredit and hostility to Gypsies, he does not have a single point of substantial criticism against Rüdiger. His 'deconstruction' of Rüdiger's work relies on inappropriate understatement: referring to 'some' linguis-tic comparisons (but not mentioning which, and whether they were correct or incorrect), distancing himself from the conclusion ('he believed'; but was he wrong?), suggesting that the conclusion (rather than the method applied) was predetermined by *Zeitgeist*, and associating Rüdiger with a hitherto unnamed 'romantic school' that would evolve only decades after his passing away. This is the essence of Willems's argu-ment against the Indian origin of the Romani language and people.

The Emergence of the Mainstream Narrative

In the century-and-a-half that followed the publications by Rüdiger and Grellmann, Romani philology became an established discipline, with a periodical that served as a principal forum for discussion (the *Journal of the Gypsy Lore Society*), and with the participation of numerous prominent Indologists. I shall give a very brief summary of the major developments of this period. In 1844–45, August Pott published a comparative grammar and a comparative lexicon of two dozen Romani dialects that had been documented since Rüdiger. He elaborated on the origins of both grammar and vocabulary. One of his most outstanding achievements was to point out a layer of pre-European loan words from Armenian and Persian, which he suggested were acquired during a gradual migration from India to Europe.

Between 1872 and 1880, Franz Miklosich published a series of papers which together constituted a further comparative study of the dialects, based largely on first-hand documentation. Miklosich identified a Greek layer of loans, and concluded that the Gypsies must have stayed in Greek-speaking territory for a considerable period before dispersing throughout Europe. He then attempted to trace the migration routes of individual groups of Romani speakers throughout Europe by analysing the layers of borrowings from other European languages. Both Pott and Miklosich were pioneers of language contact studies, applying a methodology that is now commonplace, namely to relate lexical and structural borrowings into a language to a period of cultural contact with the so-called donor language and culture. Okely however polemicizes against this method:

> Studies of the language or dialects of Gypsies in Europe in the late eighteenth and early nineteenth centuries revealed a connection with a form of Sanskrit said to have evolved around or before 1000 A.D. The different forms of 'Romany' found throughout Europe have also many words from Persian, modern and Byzantine Greek, Slavic, and Rumanian. These other ingredients have been perceived by scholars as 'corruptions' of a once 'pure' Indian Gypsy language. (Okely 1983: 8)

Okely does not specify to which 'scholars' she is referring, and leaves the reader to infer that the same scholars who studied the language and dialects of the Gypsies also viewed loan elements as 'corruptions'. In none of the linguistic studies, however, does one find any evaluative judgements of this kind, alluding to either 'corruptions' or 'purity'. Rather, the statements are always of a descriptive nature and are part of a historical reconstruction of linguistic and cultural contacts. It is Okely who is constructing an image – the image of a conspiracy among biased, Romantic, even racist philologists.

Both Pott and Miklosich also included in their surveys data on a dialect spoken in the Middle East by a group of peripatetics who referred to themselves as Dom, and were known in the region by a variety of names. Recognizing the Indic origin of this language (later to be known as Domari; see Matras 1999b), and the similarities in social organization between the Dom and the European Rom, both authors regarded the Dom and their language as one of the sub-branches of Romani and the Rom. The similarity in the names – Rom and Dom – had prompted Pott to consider that both groups might be descendants of the Domba, a caste of service-providers mentioned in medieval texts from Kashmir. The position was thus gradually emerging in nineteenth-century philology that the Rom had always been a peripatetic community (part of GYPSY 1), albeit one that originated in India and emigrated westwards, retaining its socio-economic profile as a peripatetic group but also its Indian language. Although the catch-all term used for them was still the ambiguous 'Gypsies' (German *Zigeuner*), an understanding of GYPSY 2 as a sub-set of GYPSY 1 was evolving. This track was also pursued by Grierson (1888) in the *Journal of the Gypsy Lore Society*, where he pointed out that low castes of peripatetic service-providers known as 'Dom' were still in existence in India. Since commercial nomads are known to migrate, the question of why and how the 'Gypsies' migrated to Europe did not seem to pose a problem.

There were other hypotheses. Pischel (1883), for instance, suggested that war surrounding the Islamic conquests of northern India may have driven the ancestral population of the Rom out of the area, and de Goeje (1903) proposed that the Rom might have been camp-followers of the Jats, a group of warriors who served under the Sassanide armies. The hypothesis of a connection with other populations of Indian origin was strengthened through descriptions of the Indian-derived vocabulary of a further population of commercial nomads in Armenia, called Lom (Finck 1907). All three names – Rom, Dom, and Lom – could easily be proved to be connected etymologically through regular sound changes. Furthermore, all three groups had cognate terms for outsiders: *gadjo*, *kacca*, *kadja*. Grierson (1922) pointed out further cognates among the terms for outsiders used by Dom castes in India itself. The fact that there was evidence of linguistic ties with India and cognate group names in all three populations led Sampson (1923) to assume that all three groups were sub-branches of one single population, who left India together and then split while in Iranian-speaking territory.

This hypothesis does not seem likely, for, as Turner (1926) pointed out, although both Romani and Domari are originally Central Indian languages, some of the linguistic differences between them are rather old, and seem to have pre-dated the exodus from India. The evidence seems to point in the direction of several distinct populations sharing a caste background, or rather, sharing the socio-economic profile of commercial nomads or peripatetics, migrating from India possibly at different times, and speaking different Indian languages. While the linguistic evidence clearly points to India, as Rüdiger had already proved, the case for an origin in peripatetic populations cannot be made on linguistic grounds. Rather, it relies on piecing together the linguistic and ethnographic evidence. There are other populations of commercial nomads north and west of India (in Central Asia and the Near East) who speak Central Indian languages. Most have ethnonyms deriving from Indian caste-names (Jat, Parya, Dom), and some share specific ethnonyms and names for outsiders, as mentioned above. Although no direct connection with any of the groups can be established, the phenomenon of westward migration of Indian commercial nomads is historically well attested. Any alternative interpretation of the origin of the Rom would need to explain the combination of circumstances as a historical coincidence: a Central Indic language; ethnonyms that are cognate with caste-names and shared with other commercial nomads; and a socio-economic profile as a peripatetic population.

The division of Romani into dialects can be reconstructed on the basis of comparative data from the dialects as having emerged following the immigration into Europe of a more or less uniform linguistic entity. The structural similarities make it highly unlikely if not impossible that any of the Romani dialects of Europe formed a separate linguistic entity in pre-European times. This can be seen in the shared development of the pre-European component, as well as in the shared layer of Greek lexical and grammatical loans. In some areas of Europe, mainly in the northern, western and southern peripheries, Romani is no longer spoken, but we find populations that make use of a Romani-derived vocabulary ('Para-Romani'). It is assumed that this is due to a shift into the majority language, retaining lexical items that were functional as an in-group register or style. It is possible, and has been suggested, that such shifts took place as a result of merger between peripatetic populations of Romani and non-Romani origin. It has, however, never been argued in the linguistic literature that the use of individual words of Romani origin constitutes proof of Indian descent, but rather that it proves connections with a Romani-speaking population.

'Deconstruction': No 'Rom', Just Gypsies

Nevertheless, Okely, in a monograph that has become a standard textbook in British anthropology, questions not just the Indian origin but even the existence of a Romani language. Without making any direct references to the linguistic literature, she writes:

> By the nineteenth century, the theory of an Indian origin emerged, thanks to diffusionist ideas and to studies of the dialects or 'secret' languages used by Gypsies mainly among themselves. [...] Today, the extent to which Indian origin is emphasised depends on the extent to which the groups or

individuals are exoticised and, paradoxically, considered acceptable to the dominant society. (Okely 1983: 5)

Okely thus equates dialects (of Romani) with secret languages, a view that does not reflect even the discussion in eighteenth-century compilations by law enforcement officers, let alone the serious academic sources of the nineteenth century. She further suggests that contemporary scholars choose to define a language as Indian by origin not according to its structures, but according to their political interest in the population of speakers. No evidence for this is cited, however.

In one of his earliest papers on Romani, Hancock (1970), writing in the *Journal of the Gypsy Lore Society*, speculates on the emergence of what is called in the linguistic literature 'Angloromani', and which in fact is a Para-Romani style, i.e. the insertion of Romani-derived vocabulary into English discourse. Using a term from a field in which Hancock himself had been trained, and which was attracting interest in linguistics at the time, Hancock referred to Angloromani as a possible 'creole': a simplified mixture of two languages, English and Romani, which had become the regular in-group language of a population mixture. Inspired by this article, Okely ventures to suggest her own hypothesis:

> I suggest that the so-called 'pure' Anglo-Romany recorded by Sampson among some families in Wales at the beginning of the twentieth century could also have been imported by Gypsies who migrated from Europe more recently than the sixteenth century. In any case, Hancock's suggestions that Anglo-Romany is a creole could be extended beyond the British Isles. Further research is needed here. Perhaps many forms of Romanes might be classified as creole or pidgins which developed between merchants and other travelling groups along the trade routes. These served as a means of communication between so-called Gypsy groups. (Okely 1983: 9)

What Okely refers to as 'so-called pure Anglo-Romany' of Wales is however a separate phenomenon, notably an inflected dialect of Romani, which in the linguistic literature has never been referred to as 'Anglo-Romany', and has only been referred to as 'pure' in the sense that it preserves Romani inflection paradigms, unlike Angloromani, which is based on English (cf. Sampson 1968 [1926]). There are indeed other Para-Romani varieties outside the British Isles, but they do not shed any new light on the development of Romani. What Okely failed to understand was the fact that there is a difference between Romani as a language and the use of Romani-derived vocabulary in the grammatical framework of other languages. Elsewhere she writes: 'By definition Romanes cannot stand as a language once the non-Indian words are screened out' (Okely 1984: 65). The archaic inflection paradigms of Romani – the language preserves for example the Middle Indo-Aryan present verb conjugation, which has been lost elsewhere in Modern Indo-Aryan – could not have evolved (and could not have been revived from Prakrit) as a result of traders and merchants seeking a common form of communication along the trade routes.

The denial of the language is a necessary tool to be able to deny the immigration of a population from India. Okely rejects both as a Romanticist fantasy:

> It may be the case that groups of people brought or appropriated some linguistic forms, creole or pidgin related to some earlier Sanskrit in the movements along the trade routes between East and West, but it does not follow that all 'real' Gypsies or Travellers are the genealogical descendants of specific groups of persons allegedly in India nearly a thousand years ago. It is of course exciting that such linguistic links can be made between some Gypsies and 'magical' Asia. The Gypsiologists have thus given exotic status to persons who labour also under negative and banal images. (Okely 1983: 13)

The construction of an abstract adversary, termed 'Gypsiologist' by Okely, turns the argument into a self-righteous crusade. Okely nevertheless tries to offer a quasi-sociolinguistic argument against the possibility that a Romani language could ever have existed:

> Given the special economic niche of all Gypsies who can never approximate to economic self-sufficiency, but must always trade with outsiders in the surrounding society, their language usages have to be consistent with their positions. In order to earn their living, the Gypsies need to be fluent in the languages of non-Gypsies. It would be of little use for Gypsies to tell fortunes in Romanes to non-Gypsies, their major clients. Thus, any forms of Romanes used between Gypsy groups cannot and can never have been the sole nor necessarily the dominant language of a Gypsy group. (Okely 1983: 9)

The statement however is rhetorical: nobody has ever claimed that the Rom were monolingual. On the contrary, all studies of Romani, beginning with Rüdiger (1782), have stressed the centuries-old multilingual reality of Romani communities. Nobody has ever denied that Gypsies are, and in all likelihood always were, fluent in the languages of non-Gypsies, and nobody has suggested that they once used Romanes to tell fortunes to non-Gypsies. None of this detracts from the recognition that they speak Romani among themselves. Indeed, the claim is similar to asserting that Chinese Britons couldn't possibly speak Chinese, since in order to run Chinese restaurants in England they must be able to speak English. Yet Okely's narrative, which ignores two centuries of serious scholarship from different parts of Europe, has been celebrated as a breakthrough in the ethnographic study of foreign cultures.

Contrary to Okely's understanding of the linguistic argument, the retention of an Indo-Aryan language does not mean that no Europeans have been absorbed into the Romani population since its arrival in Europe (although a massive sign-up is unlikely to have occurred). Nor does it mean that the Rom were once a self-sufficient sedentary group, and not part of an Indian caste of commercial nomads. It also does not mean that there are no commercial nomads of indigenous European origin, who coexist alongside the Rom in Europe (our GYPSY 1). There is therefore no basis at all for Okely's claim that '[the] fixation upon the distant place of origin diverts attention from the circumstances in which the Gypsies first appeared in Britain and elsewhere in Europe. With the collapse of feudalism, many persons were uprooted and took to wandering' (Okely 1984: 64).

Furthermore, the Indian origin of Romani does not mean that all commercial nomads in India speak Romani. This would not have been the case after one thousand years of separation even *if* all commercial nomads in India had originally spoken the same language. Okely had devoted so little time to reading the actual work of the infamous 'Gypsiologists' that she failed to notice long discussions comparing very distinct languages. Okely the anthropologist could nonetheless be expected to know that several hundred different languages are spoken in India. However, commenting on Irving Brown's observation that the language of the Dom of India was different from that of the Rom of Europe, she says: 'Thus the original search for Indian links based on language links is turned on its head when it suits the Gypsiologist!' (Okely 1983: 11).

Okely's 'deconstructionist' narrative has in more recent years inspired the works of Lucassen and in particular Willems, who sets out to expose the alleged myth of an Indian origin. As alluded to above, Willems even draws a connecting line between interest in the origin of the Romani language and the Nazi genocide: 'Again and again, in popular criminological writing, we find Grellmann's vocabulary list of "Gypsy words" recurring – to which every writer tried to add a number of words that he himself had noted down – printed together with an ethnographic portrait of the group, and with comments on the Gypsies' occupational activities'. He goes on to name some of these writers, concluding that '[they], in turn, exercised considerable influence on criminological biologists during the Nazi regime' (Willems 1997: 22).

Like Okely, Willems is drawn to the linguistic argument, and equates Romani language with Para-Romani vocabularies:

His [Miklosich's] linguistic research brought him to the conclusion that Gypsies left India in groups somewhere between the eighth and tenth century – without his venturing to establish the reasons why – a standpoint which continues to win supporters even today. There has been an ongoing interest in the study of Gypsy language, with the idea of an umbrella parent language as a continuous thread, even though social reality presents the more differentiated picture of many dialects and mixed languages – with a Romani vocabulary, true, but the grammar of another language. What has been noted recently is that some Gypsy groups adapt their core vocabulary to the grammar of the country in which they are living so that to outsiders it appears as if they are listening to their own language without their being able to follow the words actually spoken. (Willems 1997: 82–83)

And, showing little originality, he also repeats Okely's alternative scenario for the evolution of Romani as a so-called trade language:

It is possible [...] that linguistic influence made itself felt through trading outposts or cultural transmission and that thus the speakers of an Indo-European language in Europe did not migrate in the remote past from Central Asia but perhaps made the language of others their own. Research into these matters has still not generated conclusive answers, which prompts the question whether in the case of so many diverse Gypsy groups a similar process may not have taken place, i.e. that certain groups between the eighth and eighteenth centuries came, as a kind of group ritual, to adopt a dialect of the Indian Romani. (Willems 1997: 83)

Contrary to Willems's impression, research into these questions is very conclusive indeed, and rules out the idea that archaic inflections and regular sound changes could have been acquired by illiterate merchants on trade routes as a 'group ritual', especially since there is no known precedent for such an occurrence anywhere in the world.

Willems also copies Okely in his polemical style: 'Folklorists carry on with their search for authentic traces of Gypsy culture with undiminished zeal, including linguists who have elevated Romani-philology to a special status' (Willems 1997: 305). Without analysing any of the texts actually produced by linguists studying Romani, Willems purports to be able to detect their hidden passions and questionable motives. Willems even argues that linguistics is irrelevant to the study of Romani history, since Gypsies are not persecuted because of their language (as though linguistics were the study of a cure against discrimination): 'Linguistics will never be able to give conclusive answers to all such questions concerning the reconstruction of the Gypsies' history. Moreover, the criterion of language is utterly inadequate for explaining why people were (or still are) defined as Gypsies. Where governments were busy stigmatizing Gypsies, language appears never to have been utterly of decisive importance' (Willems 1997: 308). Finally, Willems too regards the Indian narrative as part of a political campaign (a point also emphasized by Okely [1997]):

Since, for some Gypsy groups in western European countries, the process of emancipation has only commenced recently, hardly any revaluation of extant historical knowledge has yet taken place. It remains questionable, moreover, whether corrections are to be anticipated from this corner since the intelligentsia in Gypsy circles are not likely to profit very much by challenging the core concepts of Gypsy studies. For political and pragmatic reasons they will sooner close ranks in support of the idea of a *collective* Gypsy identity, including a language that belongs to them. (Willems 1997: 307)

According to Willems, then, Gypsy activists are pretending to be speaking a language of their own, for political reasons.

To summarize the arguments of the Okely–Willems school (see Lucassen 1996 for similar conclusions): there is no Romani language for which an Indian origin can be postulated. What there is amounts to the use of individual words, i.e. an in-group vocabulary among diverse groups of Gypsies. Since there is no language, there is also no evidence to link Rom to an emigration from India. The fact that so much attention has focused on Indian origins derives from the need that scholars felt to exoticize Travellers, and to interpret their forms of social organization and ethnic identities in terms familiar to mainstream society – that is, in terms of race, territorial origins, and language. In modern times, this image of the Rom as, historically, an immigrant group of non-European origin is useful to campaigners seeking to promote their political ideas, since recognition is more easily granted to groups that fit a territorial-linguistic definition, and who are or were at some point in their history self-contained and self-sufficient, that is, with a language, economy, and land of their own.

I have clarified why most of these claims must be rejected. In the next section I shall explain why I nevertheless agree with the final observation, namely that campaigners seek to promote a historical narrative which they believe can help them mobilize their own people as well as outsiders who are sympathetic to their cause in a more efficient and more convincing way.

Neo-Construction: Romani Warriors, not Romani Gypsies

During the time I served as press officer and assistant to a well-known Romani civil rights campaigner, in the early 1990s, I was instructed to prepare a paper claiming that the Rom originated not in a caste of musicians and metalworkers, but in a population of captives who were taken prisoner in India, and brought to Europe as slaves. The search for a historical narrative of this kind was inspired by a feeling that there were similarities between the status of the Rom as the pariahs of Europe, and that of the African-Americans. The concrete trigger was the release of the film *Malcolm X* (dir. Spike Lee, 1992), some parts of which were a source of political inspiration to the campaign I worked for. I searched the libraries and was able to find evidence of Indian warriors who were taken prisoner and brought to Mesopotamia during the Umayyan dynasty. I also came across the well-known text by At-Tabari describing the capture of Zott at Ain-Zarba by the Byzantines. None of this, however, was conclusive proof that this was indeed the origin of the Rom. In the pamphlet that was then produced, I wrote that the ancestors of the Rom 'may have been brought to Asia Minor against their will'.

The argument reminded me, however, of the logic of Zionist analysis of Jewish presence in Europe, which I had been taught at school in Israel. It seemed to agree with the anti-Semitic viewpoint, which regarded Jews as a parasitic nation since they lacked a territory, and denigrated them as moneylenders and merchants, which of course were judged dishonourable occupations. In adopting these aspects of anti-Semitic thinking, Zionism, as is well known, sought to remove the Jews from the Diaspora, and to change their socio-economic profile, turning them into an 'industrious' and 'productive' territorial nation. But it also sought to create a historical narrative. And so we were taught at school that Jews first arrived in Europe as captives of the Romans, who had crushed their uprising and destroyed their Temple. From slaves building roads for the Romans in Europe, they then mysteriously worked their way up to become pharmacists, merchants, scholars and moneylenders in Spain, France and Germany. Official textbooks taught us that they were forced into these trades, since they were not allowed to cultivate land (which implies that, had they been allowed to purchase and cultivate land, they would have happily become farmers). Since Zionism accepted the anti-Semitic premise that continued Jewish diasporic presence was an anomalous condition, it needed to restore pride to its people by developing an argument according to which Jews had been reluctant to move away from their homeland in the first place. They therefore could not have emigrated to Europe, as Roman citizens, of their own free will, in order to promote their careers or businesses. The captives-narrative served to underline the consistency of the victim role throughout Jewish history.

Romani activists have been searching for an escape from the postulated origin of the Rom as a caste of commercial nomads, or Dom, for a number of years now. The idea of a warrior origin of the Rom was first put forth by Kochanowski (1968), inspired by de Goeje's idea of the Jats and their camp-followers, in a paper called 'Black Gypsies, White Gypsies'. This was then picked up by Rishi, a retired Indian diplomat who published a magazine on Romani issues, who writes:

Roma, the so-called Gypsies of Europe [...] are the descendants of the Rajputs and Jats of Northern India, to be precise, the Greater Punjab [...] The ancestors of the Roma left their mother country India (they call it Baro Than – the land of their ancestors) to foreign lands about a thousand years ago during the Muslim invasions of India. In foreign lands they were victimised not only by governments but also by industrial and trade guilds and the church. They were forced to live a non-sedentary life. (Rishi 1983: 1)

This line of argument was then continued by Kochanowski, now referring to 'interdisciplinary collaboration between European and Indian scholars':

> En effet, en collaboration avec les savants de l'Europe et de l'Inde, nos études interdisciplinaires où sont comparés les systèmes et non pas les faits séparés nous ont permis d'apporter les solutions à ces questions qui peuvent être réduits aux trois principales:
> 1. Origines exactes des Romané Chavé en Inde? Etat de Delhi et ses environs, en particulier le Rajasthan.
> 2. Castes originelles? Environ 90% de Kshatriyas et de Rajputs; 10% de Brahmanes.
> 3. Dates et causes de leurs exodes? – 1er exode au VIIIe siècle après J.C. dû au débordement du fleuve Sindh; – 2e exode à la fin du XIIe siècle après J.C. dû à la défaite de la dernière bataille de Teraïm (1192). (Kochanowski 1994: 146)

Kochanowski thus suggests two waves of migration from India. The first was of Kshatriyas (a warrior caste) from the province of Sindh, the 'Sindhiens', whom Kochanowski brings into connection with the 'Sinti' – a popular notion among the Sinti themselves, but one that lacks any foundation whatsoever, since the term 'Sinti' is a European loan word adopted by the population in or around the eighteenth century, possibly a borrowing from a German-based secret language (see Matras 1999a: 108–11). Kochanowski explains that the Sinti left Sindh for Mesopotamia due to climate changes, and later journeyed to Greece together with the Roman legions. Four centuries later, the Rajputs (another warrior caste) were defeated at the battle of Teraïm by a coalition of Muslims. Some of them fled through Kashmir and Afghanistan, and arrived in Greece, only to meet their compatriots and unite with them there: 'C'est ainsi que les Kshatriyas sindhiens et les Rajputs de Delhi et de ses environs (en particulier du Rajasthan) formeront ensemble un seul et même Peuple: le Peuple romano dont les membres s'appellent eux-mêmes les *Romané Chavé* (litt. 'Fils de Ram')' (Kochanowski 1994: 41). Kochanowski's fantastic story – attributing the name Rom to the 'Sons of the God Ram' – was now presented again by Rishi as a case of international research collaboration, in the following 'Appeal':

> An appeal. Roma – Descendants of Warrior Classes of India. Interdisciplinary research in India and abroad by prominent linguists and scholars has proved beyond doubt that the Roma are, mainly, the descendants of people of warrior

classes of North-India – Kshatriyas, Rajputs and Jats. [...] Please do not repeat not connect them with the *Doms*, a lower caste in India. (Rishi 1995: v)

The 'proof' provided by Kochanowski amounted to a discussion of the Rom's care for horses (which supposedly links them with ancient warriors), accounts of their service in European armies and the fact that they made 'good soldiers', and alleged comparisons of blood groups between descendants of the Kshatriyas in India and the European Rom.

Proof of a different kind for a warrior origin is sought by Hancock. Having cited the warrior origin hypothesis in his earlier works (1988, 1991, 1992), Hancock has now adopted it, basing it on linguistic arguments. In his entry on Romani in the *Encyclopaedia of European Languages*, Hancock writes:

> In its lexicon and phonology in particular, it [Romani] demonstrates a Central Indian core, but with greater evidence from North-western Indian and to some extent Dardic. Such linguistic clues support the most current theory of the origin of the population itself, which is that the ancestors of the Roma descend from a composite population assembled as a military force at the beginning of the 11th century to resist Islamic invasions led by Mohammed of Ghazni. (Hancock 1998b: 378–79)

That Romani has a Central Indian core and some north-western and Dardic features was demonstrated by Turner (1926), and little fresh evidence has been cited since (but see Matras 2002, ch. 6 for an analysis of the Dardic origin of the Romani past-tense conjugation). But this evidence merely lends linguistic support to an immigration from the centre to the north-west, which makes sense geographically, in terms of the route taken towards Europe. It does not amount to any proof of a warrior origin.

Hancock is more explicit in other contributions, however. His evidence is lexical, and is based on an interpretation of lexical items as reflecting a military culture:

> If we look at the vocabulary of Romani, we find indications of a specifically military history. For example, the most common word for someone who is not a Rom is *gadjo*, and this comes from an old Indian word *gajjha*, meaning 'civilian' or 'non-military person' ('civilians' is still used by Roma to refer to non-Roma in parts of Europe, e.g. in Slovenia and Italy). Another word for a non-Rom is *das*, which originally meant a prisoner of war, and which means 'slave' in modern Hindi and Panjabi. [...] The words for 'sword', 'battlecry', 'spear' and 'gaiters' are also all Indian, and all belong to the military semantic domain. (Hancock 1999)

But this is inaccurate, to say the least. There is no Old Indian word *gajjha* meaning 'civilian'. The attested form is the Old Indo-Aryan word *garhya* meaning 'domestic', from which Pischel (1900) hypothesized an unattested Middle Indian sound form **gajjha*, which could have developed into the Romani word *gadjo*. Pischel thus argues for an etymology that supports a dichotomy between settled outsiders and Rom as Travellers or peripatetics. Hancock is merely reversing the argument, in a rather playful manner. The word *gadjo* is of course used by Rom today, not just in Slovenia and Italy. Its general meaning is 'non-Rom', though some groups use it in a more specific meaning, namely 'farmer', which tends to support Pischel's hypothesis. As for *das*, it does indeed mean 'slave' in Indo-Aryan languages, and presumably it meant that in Early Romani too, but there is no evidence whatsoever that it ever meant 'prisoner of war'. Only the Balkan Rom use *das* as a term for foreigners or non-Rom, though not just for any foreigners, but specifically for the Slavs (as opposed to the Turks/Muslims of the Balkans, called *xoraxane*, and the Greeks, who are called *balame*). The origin is in a wordplay, modelled on the similarity between Greek *sklavos* 'slave', and *slavos* for 'Slav'. It has nothing to do with viewing all outsiders as 'prisoners of war' or even 'slaves', and so it provides no evidence that the Rom regarded themselves as warriors, as Hancock suggests.

Some of the alleged 'military' vocabulary is commented on in Hancock's (1998a) unpublished manuscript, to which the author also refers in Hancock 2000. Glossed as 'gaiters' we find the word *patavo*, which in fact simply means 'clothes'. And glossed as 'battlecry' we find *chingaripe*, which simply means 'shout'. Hancock further suggests that the lack of Indo-Aryan terms for smithery and metals, and use of Greek-derived items instead, indicates that the relevant concepts were unknown to the Rom's ancestral population before they reached Europe, and that therefore the Rom could not have been metalworkers.

These statements are based on the mistaken and misleading assumption that lexical borrowing is always motivated only by cultural and conceptual renewal, and that by contrast the stability of inherited vocabulary is a reliable indicator of an ancient, original culture. Romani borrows the numerals 'seven', 'eight' and 'nine', and the words for 'flower', 'bone' and 'road' from Greek, which does not in any way indicate that the relevant concepts were unknown to the Rom prior to their immigration to Greece. Romani also borrows words for 'grandmother' and 'grandfather' from Greek, and the word for 'family' from European languages – none of which suggests that the ancestors of the Rom did not have tight family structures before arriving in Europe. On the other hand Romani has Indo-Aryan words for 'to beg', 'to steal', 'to tell fortunes', 'to sing', and 'to play music', though this in itself does not at all suggest that the ancestors of the Rom were thieves, beggars, fortune-tellers, or musicians. Hancock further maintains that the fact that some Romani words have surviving cognates in distinct Indo-Aryan languages suggests that

Romani was a koïné, i.e. a language of diverse origins spoken by a composite population. Split cognates however are a trivial phenomenon among related languages, which does not prove a koïné origin, especially since sound changes from Old Indo-Aryan to Romani are on the whole extremely regular (cf. Matras 2002, ch. 3). Moreover, a koïné does not prove a military origin.

Nonetheless, the mere suggestion, by a distinguished linguist, that there is linguistic 'evidence' of a warrior origin is sufficient for the new narrative to become adopted by followers of the political cause. Romani activist Ron Lee argues on the email discussion list Patrin for what he calls 'Scenario 1': 'The ancestors of the Roma were the defeated army of an Indian kingdom who left their original homeland in Gurjara and made their way north up the Indus valley into the Dardic speaking regions. They remained here after forming a new kingdom until driven out later by Ghaznavids.' Challenged to cite the evidence for the theory, he responded:

> We all have the right to our theories but academic theories will not give pride to young Roma searching for their identity. Scenario 1 makes sense and with further research I am sure it will be verified. No other theory even makes sense. In the meantime, like the Jewish scribes who wrote the Old Testament, people like Ian [Hancock] and I and others are trying to create Romani history. (Ron Lee, Patrin email discussion list, 14 August 2000)

In a further posting, Lee went on: 'Roma nationalists and intellectuals are doing what is necessary to create a Romani nation and a Romani history and like Zionists, some of us want to see our people survive with pride in their origins' (Ron Lee, Patrin email discussion list, 17 August 2000).

Referring to Hancock (2000), Acton and Gheorghe (2001) similarly accept that 'recent linguistic arguments suggest that the Romani language and identity derive from a relatively late twelfth century emigration, distinct from the earlier eighth century migration which created the Dom or Nawar and similar groups of the Middle East' (Acton and Gheorghe 2001: 59).

The warrior origin theory is gaining ground, because Romani activists and others sympathetic to their cause wish to see the Rom they sympathize with in a consistent, smooth and indisputable victim role throughout history. They want, in a sense, package-Gypsies who sell better on the human rights market. Moreover, like the Zionist movement in its relation to anti-Semitism, they have internalized the anti-Gypsyist point of view that self-employed musicians, fortune-tellers and scrap-metal dealers are a nuisance to society and a source of shame rather than pride. Having accepted this viewpoint, the only way they can protect themselves from the supposedly shameful image is to replace it by a proud ancestry: to postulate, namely, that they have been turned into what they are reluctantly, having held a prestigious and honourable social position before being victimized.

Good Guys, Bad Guys

Although their respective viewpoints differ, there are some similarities between the type of discourse employed by Hancock, Lee and Acton and that used by Okely and Willems. I see similarities in three principal areas.

First, both circles present a narrative of Gypsy history that is subordinated to an ideological agenda. The picture they depict of early Romani history and origins is, to use a common term, a 'construction'. In Okely's writings, the agenda is to relativize the European notion of ethnicity by questioning the link between ethnicity and language and territory. In fact, one might interpret Okely's work similarly to the way in which she herself interprets the work of others: Okely sets out to maintain the image of Gypsies as 'free' of the conventional baggage of nations and modern nation-states – 'free' of a state and a territory, but also 'free' of a language and an origin. This is an image that matches the stereotype of the 'Gypsy' who allegedly wanders aimlessly about throughout history, 'free' of the worries or awareness of a past or a future.

While Okely may be correct in recognizing the social and political functions of the Indian narrative and its adoption by some Romani communities, the fact that the Indian origin is used in such a way does not mean that it is fictitious. Willems's agenda, however, is to expose a fallacy, a hoax, by criticizing text. His political agenda is to trace the roots of racism to the Enlightenment, and so enlighten us in respect of our naive acceptance of the Romanticism of that period, the beliefs that were formed in that time, which we still hold on to. To prove his point, Willems needs to demonstrate that there was no Indian origin, and that there is also no Indian language, at least not one that could only have been brought to Europe by an immigrant population.

Hancock, finally, and with him Kochanowski, Rishi, Lee, and other activists, view the historical discourse as an instrument for changing the image of the Rom and their status in present-day society. Through the constructed narrative of the warrior-turned-victim they highlight the oppressive role that outside society has played in relation to the Rom, hoping to strengthen the legitimacy of their claim to be able to influence and shape the destiny of their people.

This brings me to the second point of similarity. In order to challenge the mainstream view on Romani origins, both sides need to take up the central argument on which this view is based – language. We therefore find on both sides attempts at a linguistic discourse, which however is stripped of all the technical and established methodological notions that are normally part of linguistic analyses. At the centre of the linguistic 'arguments' put forth by both sides is the notion that language equals words or lexicon; the analysis of grammatical structures, which is the essence of comparative and historical linguistics, is lacking entirely, not just from the active discourse (granted, only Hancock and Kochanowski are linguists by training), but also from the reception of mainstream philological literature. Okely, and in her footsteps Willems, both equate the Romani language with the odd word, and come up with the theory of vocabularies picked up along the trade routes – an unscholarly idea, inspired by disconnected impressions of the emergence of trade pidgins and the spread of Indo-European languages following the spread of agriculture (rather than through population migrations), as well as by a fairly deep layer of Romanticism (see Willems's notion of Romani as a 'ritual' language). Hancock plays word games, attaching to words unattested meanings that support his argument, and claiming, in relation to methodology, that ancient culture is reconstructable through an analysis of vocabulary – an outdated notion in historical linguistics, which if pursued consistently might backfire severely.

Thirdly and finally, both sides assert a moral agenda, claiming to expose racist, conservative and biased adversaries. In the foreground we find less deconstruction of the actual arguments that are being criticized: Willems has no debate with Rüdiger, for instance, or with any subsequent philologist, about the Indian origin of Romani inflectional paradigms, Okely does not discuss the westwards migration of Indian peripatetics, and Hancock downplays the socio-economic profile of the Rom, Dom, Lom and Indian Doms. Instead, the focus is on discrediting the authors who represent the mainstream viewpoint. In the writings of Lee (and to a lesser degree also Hancock), there is recurrent reference to 'European scholars' who supposedly represent the oppressive point of view. Okely has coined the terms 'Gypsiologist', which apparently represents all those who have studied Gypsy language and culture pre-Okely, as well as 'Indianist', which appears to denote a person who adheres to the view that there is a connection between Romani and India, and perhaps also between Gypsies and Romani. This personification of the argument serves as an implicit intimidation of the readers, who must constantly reassure themselves that they stand on the right side of the debate, lest they too should be exposed as part of the system of oppression. The individual concept of any given adversary, however, usually remains undefined.

A blend is offered by Actons, who relates to both Willems and Hancock, and baptizes the adversary as 'Gypsylorist'. Acton states that he, together with the International Romani Union, represents Romani nationalism, which 'developed in dialectical opposition to an earlier discourse of European states and scholars about the "true Gypsy" which formed a variant of European "scientific racism", well analysed from different points of view by Hancock, Mayall, and most recently, Willems, and which has been called "Gypsylorism" (after its flagship publication, the *Journal of the Gypsy Lore Society*)' (Acton 1998: 6). For Acton, then, the *Journal of the Gypsy Lore Society*, to which both he and Hancock have contributed, represents a variant of European 'scientific racism', which is why he joins forces against it – a case of 'dialectical opposition' indeed.

The ideological commitment, the lightweight linguistic arguments, combined with the negative personification of the 'adversary', give the impression that the neo-construction of Rom/Gypsies serves the purpose of ideological or intellectual mobilization, rather than academic investigation. As a result, the gaps between positions and interpretations are widening. The ideological baggage complicates the dialogue and debate between the various approaches considerably. Nonetheless, the fact that such different directions are being pursued results in new and divergent models, especially models of interpreting language. Overall this poses a very healthy challenge to the 'mainstream' interpretation of the linguistic and ethnographic facts, a challenge that it cannot afford to ignore entirely, and as a result of which it must review the structure of its argument continuously. It is thanks to this review procedure, invoked by the debates, that the 'mainstream' approach can, on the whole, look with satisfaction at the achievements of two centuries of Romani-related research; for, so far, none of its central arguments has been convincingly refuted.

References

Acton, Thomas. 1998. *Authenticity, Expertise, Scholarship and Politics: Conflicting Goals in Romani Studies*. Inaugural Lecture Series, University of Greenwich.

Acton, Thomas, and Gheorghe, Nicolae. 2001. 'Citizens of the Worlds and Nowhere: Minority, Ethnic and Human Rights for Roma', in Will Guy (ed.), *Between Past and Future: The Roma of Central and Eastern Europe*. Hatfield: University of Hertfordshire Press: 54–70.

Casimir, Michael J. 1987. 'In Search of Guilt: Legends on the Origin of the Peripatetic Niche', in Aparna Rao (ed.), *The Other Nomads: Peripatetic Minorities in Cross-Cultural Perspective*. Vienna: Böhlau: 373–90.

De Goeje, M.J. 1903. *Mémoire sur les Migrations des Tsiganes à travers l'Asie*. Leiden: Brill.

Finck, Franz Nikolaus. 1907. *Die Sprache der armenischen Zigeuner*. St Petersburg: Kaiserliche Akademie der Wissenschaften.

Grellmann, Heinrich M. 1787. *Historischer Versuch über die Zigeuner, betreffend die Lebensart und Verfassung, Sitten und Schicksale dieses Volkes seit seiner Erscheinung in Europa und dessen Ursprung.* Göttingen: Dietrich, 2nd edn (1st edn 1783).

Grierson, George A. 1888. 'Doms, Jats, and the Origin of the Gypsies', *JGLS* 1: 71–76.

——1922. *Linguistic Survey of India. Vol. XI: Gipsy Languages.* Calcutta: Superintendent Government Printers.

Hancock, Ian F. 1970. 'Is Anglo-Romanes a Creole?', *JGLS*, Third Series, 49: 41–44.

——1988. 'The Development of Romani Linguistics', in Mohammad Ali Jazayery and Werner Winter (eds), *Languages and Cultures: Studies in Honor of Edgar C. Polomé.* Berlin: Mouton de Gruyter: 183–223.

——1991. 'Romani Foodways: The Indian Roots of Gypsy Culinary Culture', *The World and I* (April): 12–26.

——1992. 'The Social and Linguistic Development of Scandoromani', in Ernst Håkon Jahr (ed.), *Language Contact: Theoretical and Empirical Studies.* Berlin: Mouton de Gruyter: 37–52.

——1998a. 'The Indian Origin and Westward Migration of the Romani People'. Unpublished MS, University of Austin, Texas.

——1998b. 'Romani', in Glanville Price (ed.), *Encyclopedia of the Languages of Europe.* Oxford: Blackwell: 378–82.

——1999. 'The Roma: Myth and Reality', *The Patrin Web Journal*, http://www.geocities.com/Paris/5121/mythandreality.

——2000. 'The Emergence of Romani as a Koïné outside of India', in Thomas Acton (ed.), *Scholarship and the Gypsy Struggle: Commitment in Romani Studies.* Hatfield: University of Hertfordshire Press: 1–13.

Kluge, Friedrich. 1901. *Rotwelsch.* Strasburg: Trübner.

Kochanowski, Vania de Gila. 1968. 'Black Gypsies, White Gypsies', *Diogenes*, 43: 27–47.

——1994. *Parlons Tsigane: Histoire, Culture et Langue du Peuple Tsigane.* Paris: L'Harmattan.

Lucassen, Leo. 1996. *Zigeuner: Die Geschichte eines polizeilichen Ordnungsbegriffes in Deutschland 1700–1945.* Cologne: Böhlau.

Matras, Yaron. 1999a. 'Johann Rüdiger and the Study of Romani in Eighteenth-Century Germany', *JGLS*, Fifth Series, 9: 89–106.

——1999b. 'The State of Present-Day Domari in Jerusalem', *Mediterranean Language Review*, 11: 1–58.

——2002. *Romani: A Linguistic Introduction.* Cambridge: Cambridge University Press.

Miklosich, Franz. 1872–1880. *Über die Mundarten und Wanderungen der Zigeuner Europas X–XII.* Vienna: Karl Gerold's Sohn.

Okely, Judith. 1983. *The Traveller Gypsies.* Cambridge: Cambridge University Press.

——1984. 'Ethnic Identity and Place of Origin: The Traveller Gypsies in Great

Britain', in Hans Vermeulen and Jeremy Boissevain (eds), *Ethnic Challenge: The Politics of Ethnicity in Europe.* Göttingen: Herodot: 50–65.

—1997. 'Some Political Consequences of Theories of Gypsy Ethnicity: The Place of the Intellectual', in Allison James, Jenny Hockey and Andrew Dawson (eds), *After Writing Culture: Epistemology and Praxis in Contemporary Anthropology.* London: Routledge: 224–43.

Pischel, Richard. 1883. 'Die Heimath der Zigeuner', *Deutsche Rundschau,* 36: 353–75.

—1900. *Grammatik der Prakrit-Sprachen.* Strasburg: Trübner.

Pott, August. 1844–45. *Die Zigeuner in Europa und Asien: Ethnographisch-linguistische Untersuchung vornehmlich ihrer Herkunft und Sprache.* Halle: Heynemann.

Rishi, W.R. 1983. 'Roma – A Study', *Roma,* 7.2: 1–10.

—1995. 'Appeal', *Roma,* 42–43 (January–July): v.

Rotwelsche Grammatik. 1755. *Beytrag zur Rotwelschen Grammatik, oder Wörterbuch von der Zigeuner-Sprache, nebst einem Schreiben eines Zigeuners an seine Frau (Contribution to the Grammar of Cant, or Dictionary of the Gypsy Language, along with a Letter by a Gypsy to his Wife).* Frankfurt.

Ruch, Martin. 1986. 'Zur Wissenschaftsgeschichte der deutschsprachigen "Zigeunerforschung" von den Anfängen bis 1900'. PhD thesis, University of Freiburg.

Rüdiger, Johann C. C. 1990 [1782]. 'Von der Sprache und Herkunft der Zigeuner aus Indien', in *Neuester Zuwachs der teutschen, fremden und allgemeinen Sprachkunde in eigenen Aufsätzen,* I. Leipzig, repr. Hamburg: Buske: 37–84.

Sampson, John. 1923. 'On the Origin and Early Migrations of the Gypsies', *JGLS,* Third Series, 2: 156–69.

Sampson, John. 1968 [1926]. *The Dialect of the Gypsies of Wales, being the Older Form of British Romani Preserved in the Speech of the Clan of Abram Wood.* Oxford: Clarendon Press.

Sulz List. 1787. *Sulz. Zigeuner-Liste und genaue Beschreibung […].* Tübingen: Balz.

Turner, Ralph L. 1926. 'The Position of Romani in Indo-Aryan', *JGLS,* Third Series, 5: 145–89.

Willems, Wim. 1997. *In Search of the True Gypsy: From Enlightenment to Final Solution.* London: Frank Cass.

The Origins of Anti-Gypsyism: The Outsiders' View of Romanies in Western Europe in the Fifteenth Century

Donald Kenrick

In this chapter I shall concentrate on the years 1400–1450 when Gypsies[1] in large numbers first arrived in western Europe. The generally held opinion in the field of Gypsy Studies is that there then occurred an invasion of a large group of Romanies, who pretended to be refugees while indulging in pickpocketing and shoplifting. This view is based on a variety of sources reproduced in the pages of the *Journal of the Gypsy Lore Society* during the last century. But if historians of the future based their research on the popular press, we might get a similar impression of the situation today. In both cases we are in fact looking at a situation where the largely misreported behaviour of a small minority outweighs the generally unreported un-newsworthy lives of the majority – at that time the thousands of Romanies working as craftspeople and fieldworkers in central and eastern Europe.

This is a period in which we have no poems, plays or fiction mentioning Gypsies. The literary stereotype of Gypsies had not yet evolved. We have to wait until 1450 for the first Gypsy character in literature, when a foolish (*närrisch*) male fortune-teller appears in a Swiss play (see Gilsenbach 1994: 86), while the first picture – a simple portrait of a couple and their children – dates from 1480 in Amsterdam (Gilsenbach 1994: 100). The image of the Gypsy in this period is, rather, to be found in historical chronicles and town council records. These created an image – based on a select minority – that has survived to the present day. As sources of this image I am considering only contemporary writers and the records made by council clerks of their 'emergency payments' to indigent visitors to their towns. Chroniclers describing contemporary events of which they were first-hand observers are rare – four, in fact: Conrad Justinger (d. 1426), Clerk to Berne Council; the monk Hermann Korner (d. c. 1437); a 'Gentleman of Paris' writing in 1427; and an anonymous chronicler from Bologna (see Gilsenbach 1994: 57, 49, 62, 68–69). A second cleric, Andreas (Gilsenbach 1994: 65),

---

[1] I use 'Gypsies' and 'Romanies' as synonyms.

belongs to the period, but seems to have written partly what he was told by someone else rather than what he himself had seen. His transcription of a letter of safe conduct given to the Gypsies by Emperor Sigismund is, however, probably authentic.

We have to be careful of taking as true accounts written some years later. The oft-quoted Fabricius, writing in 1560, refers to an incident 134 years earlier (Gilsenbach 1994: 46). Angus Fraser has given one example of how history can be twisted. A German translation of Aventinus published in 1566 says that Gypsies are allowed to steal. The original Latin, however, says that the citizens 'suffer them to steal and cheat'. And even the Latin version was written in 1522, many years after 1439, when the incident it refers to is supposed to have happened (see Fraser 1997: 295).

Together with the town clerks' reports we have in total some 62 contemporary records for the period in question (1400–1450) (see De Meneses 1971, Gilsenbach 1994, *JGLS* Series 1 and 2 [passim], Van Kappen n.d. and Vaux de Foletier 1970). It is from these early chroniclers, copied and exaggerated over the centuries, that the literary image of the Gypsy was to emerge. The popular image is more likely to have come from actual observation, again repeated and exaggerated over the years.

All are agreed that the newcomers are black and ugly,[2] with long hair, thick beards and earrings. An earlier Gypsy coppersmith, visiting northern Europe, also aroused attention because of his dark colour (Ehrenborg 1910–11: 73–74). The Gentleman of Paris says: 'The women were the ugliest and darkest-skinned anyone has seen' (Gilsenbach 1994: 69).[3] It is not until 1488 that we get the first mention of a beautiful Gypsy woman – a later stereotype – in the shape of a Maria Cabrera who has a relationship with a Spaniard (see Gilsenbach 1994: 106).

The Gypsies who come to western Europe in this period travel in large groups – up to 300 – with a leader or nominal leader mounted on horseback. Often this leader is lodged in a hotel by the town council, while the rank and file sleep in a field. Horses and tents are rarely mentioned, and there is only one reference at this time to a wagon – yet there must have been more, as the Romani word *vurdon* would hardly travel from the Middle East to western Europe without the vehicle itself. The vast majority of the Romanies apparently made their journeys on foot.

The Gypsies concerned fall into several groups when defined on an economic basis:

1. *Religious refugees*. This group stated that they were fleeing from the

---

[2] German: *greulich, häßlich* (see Gilsenbach 1994: 56).
[3] See also Tuetey, 1881.

Turks. Not only Romanies but also other peoples fled, as the Muslim Turks conquered eastern Europe. The defeat of the Serbs at the Battle of Kosovo in 1389 marked the start of Turkish rule over the Balkans. Bulgaria fell in 1393, although it was not until 1453 that Constantinople was captured, having been bypassed during the invasion of Europe. It is likely that these refugees were fleeing not so much from the Turks as from a region where it was impossible to earn money as an itinerant trader or craftsman and where even the serfs felt unsafe. Be that as it may, they were accepted – alongside other refugees – as Christians fleeing the Muslim advance. But there are in fact very few references to Gypsies claiming to be religious refugees. There are examples at Zurich in 1418 and Deventer in 1420 (Gilsenbach 1994: 55, 58). When arriving at the latter town the leader of the company, Duke Andrew, said that he had been driven out of his country because he was a Christian. More common, however, are the pilgrims (see below), whose story arises from the Turkish invasion but is distinct from that of the refugees.

2. *Genuine pilgrims.* Pilgrims – genuine or bogus – form the largest group, with the highest number of references in our sources (52 out of 62). As Romanies today make pilgrimages to Lourdes, Saintes Maries de la Mer and elsewhere, there seems no reason to doubt that some of the pilgrims were genuine – particularly those who were on their way to Santiago de Compostela, a popular pilgrimage site then as now. Such perhaps was 'Count' Thomas, who was recorded on his way to Santiago in 1425 (Gilsenbach 1994: 67).

3. *Acrobats.* A group of acrobats came to Magdeburg in 1417. Although they too said that they were refugees, they paid for their stay in the town for two weeks, performing in the Fish Market, balancing on one another's shoulders and dancing. They performed conjuring tricks for the town council, and were rewarded with a barrel of beer, a cow and bread (Gilsenbach 1994: 47). This professional troupe should not be confused with the reports of children performing acrobatic tricks in Paris. The same travelling group, judging from the description, continued touring and performed in Meiningen in 1435. After 11 days, however, a local priest forced them to leave the town (Gilsenbach 1994: 76). These were, however, probably not successors to the 'Egyptian' circus troupe in Constantinople around 1300 (Soulis 1961: 147), as the latter's show included walking the tightrope and tricks on horseback, neither of which is mentioned in the German records.

4. *Traders in horses and cross-border dealers.* I class in this group the two companies who are reported as having plenty of money and paying for their own food and lodging. The only references we have to actual trading mention horse-dealing. The cross-border dealer in question is Count Thomas, referred to earlier, who seems to have completed his pilgrimage to Santiago and moved on from seeking alms to buying and

selling on either side of the French–Spanish frontier (De Meneses 1971).

5. *Bogus pilgrims*. This is the group that has attracted the most attention from the historians and the Gypsylorists, who were fascinated by the stories told about them. One group (recorded by Andreas) said that they were travelling in respectful memory of the flight of the Holy Family to Egypt, but the rest had a different story. In general, the essence was that they had been Christians but had converted to Islam under Turkish rule. Returning to the Christian faith, they had been given a penance which involved them wandering for seven years, during which time they were to be supported by alms.

Whether they believed the stories or not, the townsfolk in France and the Netherlands in particular were relieved to find that this band of dark-skinned people had come in peace, unlike the companies of Routiers or Dravanten (see Van Kappen n.d.: 212), bands of demobilized mercenary soldiers who pillaged the countryside from 1370 onwards. They were happy to give them some food and drink, lodging for a night and speed them on their way.

Sifting through the records, we also come across a small number of petty criminals as well as some men accused of passing false currency (Gilsenbach 1994: passim). As today, these aroused more coverage in the reports than did the law-abiding groups. One wonders if much of the reported pickpocketing was not done by locals mingling with the crowd, rather than by the Gypsy fortune-tellers themselves, who would have been the obvious suspects. The Gentleman of Paris says that, although he heard many reports of this crime, he never witnessed it himself (see Tuetey 1881: 219–21). Surprisingly perhaps, we do not meet a musician in western Europe until 1469, in the shape of a zither player in Italy (Gilsenbach 1994: 96).

Welcome at first as a harmless diversion from everyday life, the tide – to use Angus Fraser's phrase – turned against these strangers from around 1450. Refugees and pilgrims from then on were refused entry to towns, given money to go away, or worse. In 1453 one Gypsy (Martin de la Barre) was killed by armed citizens of La Cheppe in France, who drove the company out of their town. Count Jehan was told in the Belgian city of Damme in 1460 that he would be killed if he reappeared within a year (Gilsenbach 1994: 87, 91).

The term used by Vaux de Foletier for this period is 'conflicts with the sedentary population' (Vaux de Foletier 1970: 58). We can only speculate on the reason for the change in attitude which led to these conflicts. Was it simply that the citizens had tired of seeing the same faces reappear year after year demanding money? Or was it because there was a new large influx of Romanies from eastern Europe – as seems to have been the case in Spain? In 1496 the German Parliament (the Diet of the Holy Roman Empire) discussed the Gypsy problem and decided to devote a day to the issue in the next parliamentary session – the following year. The discussion that ensued is rather surprising. There is no mention of bogus refugees, bogus pilgrims, petty crime or defecating in public, for all of which accusations some justification could have been found. None of these. Rather, out of the blue, the Gypsies were accused of being spies for the Turks. In 1498 the Parliament ordered their expulsion from Germany, and any who remained were to be classed as outlaws (Fraser 1992: 89) and could be killed at will. This was the foundation for what Thomas Acton has suggested (in his inaugural address as Professor of Romani Studies at the University of Greenwich in 1998) could be called the first genocide, which was to begin around 1550.

In contrast to the German law the contemporaneous Spanish law, the so-called *Pragmatica* of 1499, refers specifically to nomadism and not working – wording that could have been taken from speeches by many a British politician 500 years later. There is reason to believe that this was inspired by a new wave of Gypsies after 1450 coming by sea from Greece to Spain, as opposed to earlier visitors who had crossed from France (De Meneses 1971: 1–24):

> To you the Egyptians who vagabond through our kingdoms and domains with your wives, your children and your houses, Grace and Health. Know that we have been informed that you have been going from place to place for a long time without any profession or other manner of living which could feed you except by asking for alms and stealing, in trading and in making yourself sorcerers and diviners and doing other things which are not permitted and dishonest. (Leblon 1964: 3)

This, then, was the image – rather than that of the spy[4] – that was to be repeated and exaggerated by historians and politicians in the sixteenth century and that would endure to the present day.

References

Acton, Thomas. 1998. *Authenticity, Expertise, Scholarship and Politics: Conflicting Goals in Romani Studies*. Inaugural lecture series: University of Greenwich.

De Meneses, Amada Lopez. 1971. 'Noves Dades sobre la immigració gitana a Espana al segle XV', in *Estudis d'Historia Medieval*. Barcelona: Institut de Estudis Catalans: 1–24.

Ehrenborg, H. 1910–11. 'Magnus the Tinker', *JGLS*, New Series, 4: 73–74.

Fraser, Angus. 1992. *The Gypsies*. Oxford: Blackwell.

---

[4] This accusation was not revived until the Nuremberg Trials of those who had taken part in the Nazi massacres of Jews and Romanies in eastern Europe.

—1997. 'Juridical Autonomy among Fifteenth- and Sixteenth-Century Gypsies', *American Journal of Comparative Law*, 45: 291–304.

Gilsenbach, Reimar. 1994. *Weltchronik der Zigeuner*. Vol. I. Frankfurt am Main: Peter Lang.

Leblon, Bernard. 1964. 'Les Gitans dans la Peninsule Ibérique', *Etudes Tsiganes*, 1.2: 1–24.

Soulis, G.C. 1961. 'The Gypsies in the Byzantine Empire and the Balkans in the late Middle Ages', *Dumbarton Oaks Papers*, 15: 143–65.

Tuetey, Alexandre (ed.). 1881. *Journal d'un bourgeois de Paris, 1405–1449*. Paris: Champion.

Van Kappen, O. n.d., *Geschiedenis van de Zigeuners in Nederland*. Amsterdam: Van Gorcum (circa 1960).

Vaux de Foletier, François de. 1961. *Les Tsiganes dans l'ancienne France*. Paris: Société d'Editions Géographique.

—1970. *Mille ans d'histoire des Tsiganes*. Paris: Fayard.

Acknowledgement

My thanks are due to Claire Paul for trawling through the *JGLS* and encyclopaedias, and to Antonio Gomez Alfaro for directing me to the literature on Spain.

The Concoctors: Creating Fake Romani Culture

Ian Hancock

To be fair, not all fake Romani culture has been faked deliberately; more often it is simply the result of misguided or misinformed hypotheses finding their way into the conventional account, and being repeated by subsequent writers unchecked. A prime example of deliberately faked tradition, however, is found in Manfri Fred Wood's much-publicized *In the Life of a Romany Gypsy*, which appeared in 1973. Here, he summarized (1973: 65–69) what was allegedly remembered of the original Romani religion. He begins: 'Now, as to Romany religion, there is not much anybody remembers of it today. There was a prophet called Soster, and a lot of the stories had to do with him'. Wood then goes on to relate the story of the creation of the universe and the world out of a burst of fire, and of the two gods Moshto and Arivell, and Moshto's three sons, and the ginko or maidenhair tree, and of the two clay figures into whose mouths Moshto blew its seeds to give them life.

What is curious is that six years later, Leon Petulengro (Leon Lloyd) repeated the story in his own book *Romany Boy*, where on pp. 136–37 the same account – of a void within a void, and the explosion of a ball of fire, and of the two gods, Moshto and Arivell, and Moshto's three sons, and the two clay figures, and the ginko tree – is told (Petulengro 1979). But this time the story is attributed to his paternal grandmother Anyeta, who, he says on p. 12, came from Romania. He had already introduced her a decade earlier as 'Anyeta, a Romanian Zingari, and a true Romany herbalist' in his book *The Roots of Health* (1968: 15), though that book makes no mention of Moshto or the old religion. In *Romany Boy* (1979: 24) her membership in a 'tribe' in Romania is referred to, as well as her being the head of her tribe, presumably also in Romania, since Petulengro states that after coming to England she 'did not live with us but with my father's cousin and his tribe, the Lovells'. Oddly, he has her speaking British Romani with native fluency on the same page. In 1936 his father, Gipsy (elsewhere Gypsy) Petulengro, 'King of the Romanies' (1968: 15) wrote a book of his own entitled *A Romany Life*, but his wife Anyeta does not appear in it by name even though she is featured throughout quite prominently. He seems to have first introduced the actual name Anyeta in a chain-letter he circulated in 1940. In *A Romany Life* she is referred to as a 'Berber' (1936: 2, 25 and 162), Petulengro Senior's own peculiar notion of Romani origins which he had already spelt out in *The Listener* (1935a: 649) a year earlier. In an essay there, he wrote that '[the] Romanies are not Egyptians, nor descendants of Egyptians, as many people seem to think. The Romanies are descendants of the Berbers who trekked to practically every country in the world.' There is much else to question in *A Romany Life* – thus the spurious jargon presented as Romani (1936: 33, 49 and passim), and the use of uniquely British forms presented as Romanian Vlax (*boro-roy*, *tarno*, *rokkered*), contrasting with Continental Romani pronunciations presented as the dialect spoken in England (e.g. *yag-kash* for *yog-koshter*, 'firewood') in his *Listener* essays on British Romani life. In *The Roots of Health* the slogan '*kooshti sante!*' appears more than once as Romani for 'good health', though *sante* (*santé*) is a French word.

The question arises: who was the original owner of the Moshto story? Evidently Wood, since his version predates Petulengro's by six years. He linked it to general but fading community memory, while Petulengro on the other hand attributed it specifically to his grandmother from Romania, though in an account so similar to Wood's as scarcely to be coincidence.

The most detailed study of Romani spiritual belief among Romanian (Vlax) Romanies is Chatard and Bernard 1959. Here (1959: 22–26) some of this story appears, although there is no reference to Moshto or Arivell by name. Instead, there are O Pouro Del and O Bheng, which is to say 'the old god' and 'the devil' in Vlax Romani. The two clay figures are mentioned, and called Damo and Yehwah, clearly Adam and Eve. They are brought to life not by the seeds of the maidenhair tree, but by O Pouro Del's touching each of them with his wand. Wlislocki (1890) does not include the story, nor is it found in the imaginative works of Jean-Claude Frère (1973) or Françoise Cozannet (1973). The equally suspect Clébert (1961) relies on Chatard and Bernard, but does refer to a similarity with Zoroastrianism and Manichaeanism, while Elysseeff, summarizing Kounavine's concocted work, wrote that '[the] essence of the primitive beliefs of the Gypsies [is] borrowed from the different religions encountered by the Gypsies on their journey, and particularly those borrowed from the religion of Zoroaster' (1890: 169).

Kounavine was one of the boldest concoctors of fake Romani culture, claiming that he found Brahma, Indra, Lakshmi, Ahriman and other deities being worshipped by name among Romanies in Russia, who (he said) had also retained a number of elaborate Hindu prayers. But we learn about his 'immense store of [Romani] materials' only at second hand in the same article by Elysseeff; none of the material can be examined at first hand since Kounavine says he lost it all in the snows of Siberia. Sampson has already commented on Kounavine as 'not to be taken too seriously' (1907: 7), pointing out that one of the alternative names he gives for Brahma is Khakhava (*XOXABA* in the original, i.e. *xoxavav*) which in Romani means 'I deceive'. Was this given him by a Romani interviewee who was having fun with the inquisitive *gadjo*, or was Kounavine himself having a private joke at the expense of his readers?

Correspondence within its inner circle during the early years of the Gypsy Lore Society contained a number of risqué exchanges, with 'Romani words providing a coded language' (see Sampson 1997: 111, where John Sampson's verses composed for Dora Yates provide just one example). These were not usually meant for its general membership but rather as in-group humour to be understood and appreciated only by the initiates. Did this sometimes deliberately find its way into material for a wider, though unsuspecting, audience, perhaps like Kounavine's Khakhava or Frank Elémeny's heroine Gali Minsh (i.e. *kali mindž*) in his novel *Poor Janos*, thereby compounding the fun?

Some word lists reflect legitimate misunderstandings recorded in earnest, such as Sinclair's (1915) *brokla* for 'cabbage' (actually the English – or rather Italian – word 'broccoli'), or *karri, korri* listed to mean 'cock, domestic fowl' (the actual meaning is 'penis'); Prince (1907), probably lifting from Smart (1863: 7) where the same mistake occurs, has *kovaskaruk* 'willow, laurel' when this is simply *kova's a ruk*, i.e. 'that's a tree'. Even Manfri Fred Wood, in the word list at the end of his book (1973: 122), lists *becker* as 'fruit', evidently a misreading of the entry in a lexicon he had of English Romani collected by a site worker called Alice Bartlett, where she had it correctly glossed, though poorly handwritten, as 'frog'. But sometimes these collectors were the innocent dupes of their informants and such errors were deliberately provided: for example, Otto Duhmberg's word list of Siberian Romani (reproduced in Miklosich 1878: 280–81) has the enty *kari* glossed as 'grandson', *chamrimintsch* (i.e. *xa miri mindž*) as 'granddaughter' and *bremintsch* (i.e. *bari mindž*) as 'donkey'.

But to return to Moshto. Given that Clébert's very popular book became widely available in English in a Penguin paperback edition in 1967, the possibility must be considered that Manfri Fred Wood, or else his ghost-writer John Brun, used this as a general source and subsequently sought out some literature on the Zoroastrian religion – and, as a result, on the basis of the original Zoroaster, Ahriman and Mazda created the names Soster, Arivell and Moshto (this last perhaps also influenced by the Romani word *mishto* 'well, good'). Six years later, Leon Petulengro (or perhaps his ghost-writer Betty Messenger) plagiarized it practically word for word.

Leon Petulengro's father was Walter Lloyd, a herbalist from Rochdale, who wrote under the name Gipsy (or Gypsy, and also sometimes Xavier) Petulengro. By his own account (1935b: 80) his family name 'Lloyd' was a re-spelling of the Welsh word *llwyd* meaning 'grey' but which, he maintained, was in their case really an anglicization of the Romani word for horse, *grai*.

For a while he also called himself Walter Smith. A smith is a *petulengro* in Borrovian Romani, more accurately *petalengro* (from *petalo*, 'horseshoe'), and he claimed to be a direct descendant of Borrow's Jasper Petulengro; the information that 'Gypsy Petulengro is the grandson of Tinker Petulengro immortalised by George Borrow' appears under his name in the *Listener* series, and in his book he recounts that '[as a child in Romania] I could not speak English, although my father spoke English and Welsh being the son of Tinker Jasper Petulengro immortalized by George Borrow in his books' (1936: 2).

One wonders how Leon ever communicated with his father if he didn't speak English himself; his father, after all, revealed all of Anyeta's herbal mysteries to him 'when [he] was a boy' (1968: 15). Yet it could not have been in Angloromani, itself a register of English, and spoken very far away indeed from Romania. Furthermore, since Jasper Petulengro (George Smith in real life) was in fact from East Anglia, why would his son, Leon's father, necessarily have spoken Welsh?

Fred Wood's story has been picked up and woven into at least one work of fiction, Charles De Lint's *Mulengro: A Romany Tale* (1985), where Moshto is mentioned on pp. 87 and 277, and it has also found its way into academic treatises and retold as though it were fact. Thus W.R. Rishi in his book *Roma* writes, with his own additions, that 'the supreme god is Moshto (from the Romani word *mishto* meaning good) symbol of goodness, and Arivell (from Sanskrit *ari* 'enemy'), the symbol of evil. Moshto's three sons are the trinity of Hindu gods, Brahma (the creator), Vishnu (the sustainer) and Shiva (the killer of all that is evil)' (1976: 79). In the same section of his book, Rishi also paraphrases and quotes Kounavine extensively as fact. Dennis Liggio treated the Moshto story as a genuine Romani myth in an unpublished essay entitled 'The Influences of Zoroastrianism and Manichaeanism on the Romani Creation Myth' (1996), while John McLaughlin, a professor at the University of Illinois, recounts it in detail in his book *Gypsy Lifestyles* (1980: 4–7). Taking his cue, though maybe unwittingly, from Leon Petulengro, McLaughlin elaborated the story with embellishments of his own, stating that 'Moshto laid down strict rules of cleanliness to ward off disease, and many of these practices are still followed today by the gypsies. [...] As will become clear later, the gypsies believe these stories, and they have a serious impact on gypsy life' (1980: 6–7). At any rate Professor McLaughlin evidently believes that Romanies believe them, and his widely consulted book has certainly helped to entrench this concocted folklore yet more firmly in the ubiquitous and alternative Romani historical identity that continues to misdirect and misinform the interested scholar. I personally have not met or heard of anyone, whether Romanichal or Vlax, who was acquainted with the Moshto story, and there is every indication that it originated with Wood, or more probably with his ghost-writer John Brun.

Romani Studies has lent itself easily to scholarly fabrication, and the literature is replete with it; Decourdemanche's 'Romani script' reproduced uncritically by Clébert is one well-known example. Presumably of much more recent fabrication, and managing to offend women as well as demonstrating no small lack of respect for Romani Studies, are the off-colour sentences that appear inserted into one version of Andrew Borde's 1542 text of early British Romani ('Mayde shew us yr tyttes' – *Achae te sycke vesse meng itirrae berkes*, 'Mayde prythee doff thyn knyckeres' – *Achae te lelle patouty tirrae drawers*, 'Allo darling give us one off ye wrysste then' – *A pirani te des mai cabbe rancke*). These were sent to the present writer by a colleague in France who can himself shed no light on their source, though from the idiom they almost certainly originated in Britain. It is significant that while such sentences would immediately attract the attention of those wishing to avoid any accusations of sexism, statements that are openly 'anti-Gypsyist' do not generally rouse such passions.

Other Romani 'facts' that, once claimed, may get repeated ad infinitum have to do with the vocabulary of the language. These have without exception been made by people who don't speak Romani, but whose authority shows itself in their perceptions of what Romani should or should not be like. Elsewhere I have documented the repetition of the idea that Romani lacks words for 'possession' and 'duty' from ten different sources (Hancock, 1998), each copying from its predecessor over a period of more than a century, and seemingly having originated with statements first found in Grellmann (1807). Eleanor Smith writes that 'in the gypsy language the words "divine" and "devilish" are the same' (1943: 59) – Smith being a novelist, incidentally, whom Angus Fraser called 'desperately fond of inventing fantasies about herself, [and who] liked to claim Gypsy blood' (1994: 29). In fact, the Romani words for 'divine' and 'devilish', both native to the language, could not be more different, viz. *devlikano* and *bengesko*. Similar statements from other writers maintain – wrongly – that Romani does not have words for 'truth', 'beautiful', 'read', 'write', 'time', 'danger', 'warmth' and 'quiet'.

An example of the inaccurate, though probably not deliberately inaccurate, presentation of Romani custom and belief is Barbara Walker's *Women's Encyclopedia of Myths and Secrets*, which appeared in 1983, and which contains many Roma-related references throughout, all written in the past tense and all with a feminist (and often anti-male) bias. For example, Walker states that '[t]he matriarch was the center of Gypsy tribal life; everything that went on around a tribal mother resembled the old pagan sex rites. Her husband was a drone, whose function was to impregnate her [...] if he failed to beget perfect children, the tribe "accidentally" killed him' (1983: 361). Like the other concoctors, Walker based her statements not on first-hand acquaintance with Romanies, but on the writings of others, in this case Derlon (1977). An examination of that book reveals that Derlon's already lurid descriptions had been very freely elaborated on further by Walker, who, like Rishi and McLaughlin, could not resist the urge to editorialize, pad and reinterpret.

Elsewhere Walker states that 'together with "Smith", "Faa" is the most common gypsy surname, and means "fay" or "fairy"' (1983: 361). But this is in fact an old lowland Scottish surname and not Romani in origin at all, and was adopted only after Romanies arrived in Scotland in the late 1400s. Again, 'the popular gypsy surname *Kaldera* or *Kalderas* may have been derived from [the name of the Hindu goddess] Kali-Devi' (1983: 363). The reference given for this is Esty (1969: 67), which, on being consulted, actually says that 'the Kalderaš tribe, that huge group of Gypsies spread halfway around the world [is] governed in patriarchal fashion. There is no king or chief: all the men in the vitsa make all the decisions'. No mention of Barbara Walker's Kaldera, or of popular surnames, although Esty does state incorrectly that Kalderaš Romanies have no leaders.

In 1973, Dodgson drew attention to what he hoped might have been the very first documented sample of written Romani: a rhyme apparently published in 1517, a full quarter of a century earlier than Borde's sentences referred to above. He had come across the following bawdy incantation while thumbing through a recently published book on witchcraft by Peter Haining (1972):

> Dui rika hin mire mine
> Dui yara hin leskro kor
> Avnas dui yek jelo
> Keren akana yek jeles

As his source for this, Haining listed a work of esoterica entitled the *Grimorium Verum*, for which he gave a publication date of 1517. Dodgson was unable to locate the *Grimorium* and so wrote to Peter Haining care of his publisher. Haining replied that he had also been unable to find the book, but had been given the verses and that reference by an (unidentified) colleague. He also failed to provide a return address. Dodgson then passed the task along to the late Angus Fraser, who ascertained that the book is generally believed by scholars to be an eighteenth-rather than a sixteenth-century work, but who was himself also unable to locate a copy.

The rhyme is in a remarkably standardized spelling for a sixteenth-century (or even an eighteenth-century) Romani text, although it contains the misreading *mine* for *minč* in its first line. The dialect is a Central one, probably from the Hungarian-Slovak or the Transylvanian lands, and the orthographic conventions are English, not Continental, to judge from the evident values of the 'j' and the 'y'. Given its form, and that it is an incantation to ensure fertility in women, a few readily available sources from which it might have been lifted come at once to mind. The only one aimed at a popular market, however, is Leland (1891), and sure enough, the verse is to be found on p. 100 of that book, with the following form:

Dui riká hin mire minč
Dui yārá hin leskro kor
Avnás dūi yek jelo
Keren akána yek jeles

Leland made no secret of the fact that many of the rhymes and incantations throughout his book, as well as their orthography, were taken from Wlislocki's various works. Consulting these, the original source for the rhyme in question is revealed in an article by him written in 1887 concerning birth, life and death beliefs among tent-dwelling Roma in Transylvania.

While Leland is known for his creativity where Romani language and culture are concerned, the culprit this time would appear to be Peter Haining, whose lack of familiarity with Romani orthography, and whose failure to identify his source or to provide his own return address, make him another prime candidate for Concoctor of Fake Gypsy History.

Leland himself was probably more guilty of sloppy investigative techniques and an active imagination than of intentionally creating false data. He elicited some of his 'Romani' vocabulary from his informants by reading words from a Hindi dictionary to them and asking whether they sounded familiar. Being paid or treated to food and drink for their time, they clearly didn't want to disappoint their interrogator.

His contemporary George Borrow is also responsible for creating non-existent Romani words, which have been picked up from his books and reproduced elsewhere (for example by Pott [1844–45] and by Miklosich [1878]), and he may well qualify for the category of deliberate concoctor (Hancock, 1997); well over half of the unsubstantiated words in Smart and Crofton's dictionary of English Romani (1875: 157–63) originate with Borrow, who, Smart and Crofton diplomatically suggest, 'procured [them] from various and widespread sources' (1875: xii). These include words from other Romani dialects which he inserted into

English Romani, such as *covantza* 'anvil' or *pishota* 'bellows', as well as words with Continental Romani forms distinct from their English Romani equivalents such as *pindro* 'hoof' and *gulo* 'sweet' (Angloromani *piro, gudlo*), and even words from Spanish such as *mosco* 'a fly' and *vol* 'to fly'. In addition he created words of his own, such as *bollimengreskonœs* 'after the manner of a Christian' and *yeckly* 'only', while at the same time calling such fabrications 'genuine Gypsy [...] clear-sounding and melodious' (Borrow 1874: 11). An excellent extended discussion of this is found in Grant (1994).

Borrow's inventiveness is betrayed by his poor knowledge of Romani grammar in his discussion of a verse he calls 'the oldest specimen of English Gypsy at present extant, and perhaps the purest [...] at least as old as the time of Elizabeth' (1982: 11). The lines in question, with his own translation, are:

> *Coin si deya, coin si dado?* ('who's your mother, who's your father')
> *Pukker mande drey Romanes,* ('do thou answer me in Romany')
> *Ta mande pukkeravava tute.* ('and I will answer thee')

Coin is the form of Common Romani *kon* ('who') that Borrow imported into the Romanichal dialect from his vocabulary of Spanish Romani, though it is not attested in any other dialect; *deya* and *dado* are both vocatives and cannot follow the verb *si*, the former taken from his Lovari word list, and not found in Britain (though he does have the British form *daiya* elsewhere in his book). In the second line, *Romanes* is an adverb, though Borrow does not seem to have realized this; he has it glossed as a noun in his dictionary, and believing it to be a noun has it following the preposition *drey*. In the form *Rumnis* it is a noun today, but it would not have been in the sixteenth century. In the third line, he has the inflected locative forms *mande* and *tute* ('at me', 'at you') functioning as personal pronouns as they do only in Angloromani, while *pukkeravava* is a causative verb form, meaning 'I'm being made to tell'. The verses, in British Romani, ought to have read *kon si tiri daj, kon si tiro dad, phuker mange romanes tha (me) phukerava tuke*. Borrow's contemporary Laura Alexandrine Smith called his work 'most incomprehensible [...] hover[ing] between romance and reality', and noted that it 'can have done but little towards establishing a more friendly feeling between gorgios and Romanies' (1889: 134).

An amusing though unintentional reinterpretation of a word is found in Sutton's 1982 reprint of Borrow's *Romano Lavo-Lil*, where the original *hin* 'to void ordure' is glossed as 'to avoid ordure'. This is modern Angloromani *hingger* or *hinder* 'defecate'.

Roger Moreau (1995) has built an entire thesis around a misinterpretation. On the basis of the word 'Nawar', the place-name Dasht i Nawar is believed by him to mean 'Desert of the Nawar'. According to the standard Nelles 1:1,500,000 map of Afghanistan there is a Lake *Navar* about 90 miles west of Ghazni, and Moreau places his desert next to this. It is posited by him in his book to be the location to which three Indian peoples were taken from India as captives by Mohammed of Ghazni, three distinct ethnic groups who grew together over time to become the ancestors of the Romanies. 'Nawar' is an Arabic name for the Domari-speaking Gypsies in the Middle East. Their eventual date of departure for the West, he maintains, was at the end of the twelfth century:

> 'When do you think they left that terrible place on their journey West, Uncle?'
> 'The year following the Battle of Tarain – twenty-five miles north of Delhi – AD 1193 would be my guess. In fact I'd put Patsi's shirt on it.' (Moreau 1995: 111)

Moreau continues: 'They had entered Dasht i Nawar as three separate peoples. Three and a half centuries later they were leaving as a race, the appellations Lohar, Banjara and Kanjar forgotten. Their "Romany roots" had taken hold' (1995: 116). But that would have been in AD 843, over a century before Mohammed of Ghazni was born.

Nawar is the plural of *Nuri*, elsewhere known as *Luri* and *Luli*, and probably adopted by Arabic from the Indian *luth*, meaning 'plunderer' (cf. *lur* 'robber' in Romani). One would assume, then, that the entire toponym would be Arabic. However, 'Desert of the Nawar' would be *sahra'i nawar* in that language. The word *dašt* means 'rubbish' in Arabic. In Persian, long the lingua franca of Afghanistan, the word for 'desert' is either the adopted Arabic *sāhra* or the native *biaban*, while *Nawar* is an Iranian family name entirely unconnected with the Dom. The indigenous language of the area, however, is Pashto, and here, the word for 'desert' is *dašt*, while *nawār* in Pashto means 'a cultivated place, a habitation' – *Dašt-i-Nawar*, therefore, in the native language of the area, means something like 'inhabited desert' rather than 'desert of the Nawar'. Alternatively, if the lake's name Navar is the source of the toponym, it is hardly likely that a lake in a non-Arabic-speaking country would be named with the Arabic word for 'Gypsies'. *If* the area is called *dašt* today (though Dasht i Nawar does not appear on the Nelles map) this is surely more recent, and refers to the fact that the lake bed is now dry. The very name Lake Navar indicates that it held water in the past, and it is hard to imagine that 1200 years ago the area adjoining it would have been a desert and named as such for the Lohar, Banjara and Kanjar that Moreau believes to have occupied it.

Like the Moshto story, which has been picked up and repeated as fact in works published subsequently, Moreau's account of Roma origins is likewise already finding adherents. Patrick Lee (2000: 27) says that it provides a more feasible solution to the puzzle of the Gypsies' early days. Roger Moreau [...] suggests that the Gypsies were taken from their homeland in vast numbers as slaves in the ninth century AD by the Afghan-Turks who used them to ferry booty out of India into Afghanistan. Three tribes, the Lohar, the Banjara and the Kanjar, who bore a great resemblance to the Gypsies in Europe and who were also at the lower end of the caste system in India, provided easy pickings for these ruthless marauders in their greed for India's vast wealth.

Besides questioning the actual meaning of *Dašt-i-Nawar*, and therefore the entire hypothesis that rests on it, we can also question the date of the exodus proposed by Moreau (the ninth century) and the identity of the ancestors of the Roma (from 'the lower end of the caste system in India'). Regarding the date, the relocation of the Lohar, Banjara and Kanjar into non-Indian-speaking territory in the first half of the ninth century does not coincide with the fact that the language or languages that subsequently developed into Romani were still a part of Middle Indo-Aryan at the time of its development into New Indo-Aryan at the beginning of the eleventh century. We know this because of the redistribution of the original Middle Indo-Aryan neuter gender, which became reassigned to either masculine or feminine when it began to be lost. The redistribution of the nouns in Romani that derive from original Middle Indo-Aryan neuters match those in (for example) Hindi and Panjabi to a degree approaching 100 per cent; if pre-Romani had left India in the 800s it would have done so with three grammatical genders, and the subsequent loss of the neuter would have occurred randomly, outside of India.

Regarding the caste identity of the pre-Roma, Bhalla (1992: 331–32), on the basis of bio-anthropological data comparing Romani and Indian blood groups, concludes that

> the results of the distance analysis clearly refute the Dom theory. The gene pool of East European Gypsies is more in line with the stock of Indian people represented by Jat Sikhs, Panjabi Hindus and Rajputs, who share a common ethnic substratum. The dominant ethnic element in the Doms and Kolis, the two representatives of the low caste population, is Proto-Australoid, which is not reflected in any sizeable proportion in the genetic makeup of East European Gypsies.

This 'common ethnic substratum' is supported by recent and more rigorous serological investigation. A team of researchers at Cowan University's Centre for Human Genetics in Perth, after exhaustive blood samplings from 14 Romani communities throughout Europe, concluded in a report dated June 2001 that

> [a]nalysis of slow-evolving polymorphisms has identified a single paternal and a single maternal lineage of Indian shared by all [Romani] groups [...] these lineages belong to a small subset of the known genetic diversity of the Indian

subcontinent. Thus, Roma descend from a small ancestral ethnic minority in the Indian subcontinent that has subsequently fractured into multiple population isolates within Europe. (Gresham et al. 2001: 1315)

Elsewhere (Hancock 2002), I discuss the need for higher academic standards in treatments of Romanies. That certain authors demonstrate less attention to accuracy may well be a reflection, conscious or not, of the low regard in which they hold Romanies as a people. As controversial as the findings of Bhalla and others may be, like the contemporary linguistic research being undertaken by Boretzky, Bakker, Matras, Halwachs and others, they are the result of scientific investigation and analysis, and contrast as sharply with the non-academic literature as the image of 'gypsies' cultivated by the latter does with true Romani identity. Indeed, a clear parallel is evident here between the two: those writing about Romanies generally maintain scholarly standards; those writing about 'small-g gypsies' see no need to do so. The newcomer to the field has a difficult job discerning the two.

When the Cowan findings were made public (in Gresham et al. 2001), the immediate response from a subscriber to one Romani/Traveller listserve, himself an academic, was that they were a 'newly souped-up version of racialist thought', and 'crap'. Such reaction, and the debate it engenders, is necessary; it moves the discipline forward and separates the useful lines of pursuit from those leading nowhere. But the arena is *not* mostly populated by specialists who are in a position to judge and critique the data. The overwhelming majority of those with even a passing interest in Romanies are the same people who might read Stephen King's *Thinner* or watch Walt Disney's *Hunchback of Notre Dame*.

Working with my own students over the years, I hear from them repeatedly that they cannot tell whether the sources they are consulting for their own research papers are reliable or not. Should a project on Romani religious belief rely on Wood? Should a study of gender roles use Walker as a source? Is Moreau a good book for early Romani history? All have been assumed to be trustworthy by my students. If there is to be a sincere concern for Romani Studies there must be a sincere concern for Romanies too, and the same criticism we do not hesitate to level at the work of our academic colleagues must extend to the popular treatments which, after all, reach a far larger audience and which help to shape the misconceptions and attitudes associated with the Romani people.

References

Bhalla, V. 1992. 'Ethnicity and Indian Origins of Gypsies of Eastern Europe and the USSR', in Singh (ed.) 1992: 324–46.

Borde, Andrew. 1542. *A Caveat for Common Cursetors. Analecta Cartusiana, 92, The Fyrst Boke of the Introduction of Knowledge by Andrew Borde, Former Monk of the London Charterhouse*, with an introductory study of Borde's works by James Hogg, Vol. II: Text. London. (Facsimile copy published by Institut für Anglistik und Amerikanistik, Salzburg, 1979, ed. James Hogg.)

Borrow, George. 1874. *Romano Lavo-Lil: Word-Book of the Romany, or English Gypsy Language*. London: Murray. (Reprinted 1982, Alan Sutton, Gloucester).

Chatard, J., and Bernard, M. 1959. *Zanko – Chef Tribal*. Paris: La Colombe.

Clébert, J.-P. 1961. *Les Tziganes*. Paris: Arthaud.

Cozannet, Françoise. 1973. *Mythes et Coutumes Religieuses des Tziganes*. Paris: Payot.

De Lint, Charles. 1985. *Mulengro: A Romany Tale*. New York: Ace Books.

Derlon, Pierre. 1977. *Secrets of the Gypsies*. New York: Random House.

Dodgson, R. 1973. 'Early Romani', *JGLS*, Third Series, 52.3–4: 87–89.

Elémeny, Frank. 1886. *Poor Janos: A Tale of Hungarian Gipsy Life*. London: Henry Vickers.

Elysseeff, A.V. 1890. 'Materials for the Study of the Gypsies, collected by M.J. Kounavine', *JGLS*, 2: 93–106, 161–71, translated from 'Materialax dlja izučenja Cigan sobrannix M.I. Kunavinom', *Geografičeskije Investija*, 17.5 (1881).

Esty, Katharine. 1969. *The Gypsies: Wanderers in Time*. New York: Hawthorn Books.

Fraser, Angus. 1994. 'George Borrow as a Character in Fiction', *The George Borrow Bulletin*, 7: 27–30.

Frère, Jean-Claude. 1973. *L'Enigme des Gitans*. Paris: Maison Mame.

Grant, Anthony. 1994. 'Plagiarism and Lexical Orphans in the European Romani Lexicon', in Matras (ed.) 1994: 53–68.

Grellmann, Heinrich. 1807. *Dissertation on the Gipseys*. London: Ballantine.

Gresham, David, et al. 2001. 'Origins and Divergence of the Roma', *American Journal of Human Genetics*, 96: 1314–31.

Haining, Peter. 1972. *The Warlocks' Book*. London: Allen & Co.

Hancock, Ian. 1997. 'George Borrow's Romani', in Matras, Kyuchukov and Bakker (eds) 1997: 199–214.

—1998. 'Duty and Beauty, Possession and Truth: The Claim of Lexical Impoverishment as Control', in Tong (ed.) 1998: 115–26.

—2002. *We Are the Romani People: Ame Sam e Rromane Džene*. Hatfield: The University of Hertfordshire Press/Paris: Interface, Centre de Recherches Tsiganes.

Lee, Patrick Jasper. 2000. *We Borrow the Earth: An Intimate Portrait of the Gypsy Shamanic Tradition and Culture*. London: Thorsons (Harper Collins).

Leland, Charles G. 1891. *Gypsy Sorcery and Fortune Telling*. London: Unwin.

Liggio, Dennis. 1996. 'The Influences of Zoroastrianism and Manichaeanism on the Romani Creation Myth'. Unpublished essay. Austin: University of Texas.

McLaughlin, John. 1980. *Gypsy Lifestyles*. Lexington, KY and Toronto: D.C. Heath.

Matras, Yaron (ed.) 1994. *Romani in Contact*. Amsterdam and Philadelphia: John Benjamins.

Matras, Yaron, Kyuchukov, H., and Bakker, P. (eds). 1997. The *Typology and Dialectology of Romani*. Amsterdam and Philadelphia: John Benjamins.

Miklosich, Franz X. 1878. 'Beiträge zur Kenntnis der Zigeunermundarten', *Kaiserliche Akademie der Wissenschaften; Philosophisch-historische Classe*, 4: 245–96.

Moreau, Roger. 1995. *The Rom: Walking in the Paths of the Gypsies*. Toronto: Key Porter Books.

Petulengro, Gipsy (or Gypsy, or Xavier). 1935a. 'Romany', *The Listener* (17 April): 649.

—1935b. 'Romany', *The Listener* (4 September): 80.

—1936. *A Romany Life*. New York: Dutton.

Petulengro, Leon (Leon Lloyd). 1968. *The Roots of Health*. London: The Souvenir Press.

—1979. *Romany Boy*. London: Hale.

Pott, August Friedrich. 1844–45. *Die Zigeuner in Europa und Asien*. 2 vols. Halle: Heynemann.

Prince, J. Dynley. 1907. 'The English-Rommany Jargon of the American Roads', *Journal of the American Oriental Society*, New Series, 2: 271–308.

Rishi, Weer R. 1976. *Roma: The Panjabi Emigrants in Europe, Central and Middle Asia, the USSR and the Americas*. Patiala: Punjabi University Press.

Sampson, Anthony. 1997. *The Scholar Gypsy*. London: Murray.

Sampson, John. 1907. 'Gypsy Language and Origin', *JGLS*, New Series, 1.1: 4–22.

Sinclair, A.T. 1915. 'An American Romani Vocabulary', *Bulletin of the New York Public Library*, 19.10: 727–38.

Singh, K.S. (ed.) 1992. *Ethnicity, Caste and People*. Delhi and Moscow: Manohar.

Smart, Bath C. 1863. 'The Dialect of the English Gypsies', *Transactions of the Philological Society*, 1862–63, as an appendix.

Smart, Bath C., and Crofton, H.T. 1875. *The Dialect of the English Gypsies*. London: Asher.

Smith, Eleanor. 1943. *Caravan*. Garden City, NY: Doubleday.

Smith, Laura A. 1889. *Through Romany Songland*. London: David Stott.

Tong, Diane (ed.). 1998. *Gypsies: An Interdisciplinary Reader*. New York & London: Garland Publishing.

Walker, Barbara. 1983. *Women's Encyclopedia of Myths and Secrets*. San Francisco: Harper & Row.

Wlislocki, H. 1887. 'Gebräuche der transsilvanischen Zeltzigeuner bei Geburt, Taufe, und Leichenbestattung', *Globus*, 51: 249–51, 267–70.

—1890. *Vom wandernden Zigeunervolke*. Hamburg: Richet.

Wood, Fred. 1973. *In the Life of a Romany Gypsy*. London and Boston: Routledge & Kegan Paul.

Modernity, Culture and 'Gypsies': Is there a Meta-Scientific Method for Understanding the Representation of 'Gypsies'? And do the Dutch really Exist?

Thomas Acton

The philosophical problematic of metaphysics dealt with debates around establishing abstract principles of ontology, that is, trying to establish what are the general rules by which we reach decisions about what we shall agree to treat as existent. Much of this debate was abandoned in the second half of the twentieth century under the influence of Wittgenstein's 'dissolution' of metaphysical enquiry as formulated by logical positivists. This dissolution enjoined us all to remain silent about that whereof we cannot speak. We have preferred, instead, more practical and immediate ontologies, direct debate about the existence of contested entities, flurries of construction and deconstruction, which have been pursued, particularly in the byways of intellectual endeavour such as Romani Studies, without much regard to the problem of what the rules for such debates might be, that is, the problems of metaphysics, forgotten and dissolved this past half a century.

It is not my intent in this chapter to make a Strawsonian resurrection of metaphysics (see Strawson 1959), but rather to point out that much recent analysis of representations of 'Gypsies' contains an implicit metaphysics that cannot stand up to sustained scrutiny. This implicit metaphysics has allowed our ad hoc ontologies to become sceptical, and challenging of received wisdom, to the point where a number of writers, especially, it seems, those of Dutch origin, have argued that 'Gypsies' are no more than a series of representations, with only a shifting and tenuous relation to underlying reality, if indeed such a thing may be said to exist. This chapter will argue the contrary: that the Roma are at least as real as the Dutch, and that reality constrains the representations even though it is true that the representations, being themselves also part of reality, may help to reshape reality over time.

The problem of acknowledging this feedback of representations on the reality they purport to represent is, like any problem of a self-fulfilling prophecy, an example of the problem of philosophical relativism for any kind of reflexivity. We can see that representations of the

Roma are conditioned by the prejudices and social context of the writer or artist, which may lead to historical errors; but how do we know that our own perceptions of those making the representations are not similarly conditioned, and thus similarly unreliable?

In pursuit of a way of establishing that they are not subject to the same danger of unreliability, writers often resort to positing various criteria of scientificity or authenticity. Some, such as Barany (2000a, 2000b), have claimed that the normal procedures of validation within scholarly disciplines (in his case, political science) will weed out spurious claims to knowledge in a way that those inter-disciplinary amateurs who concentrate merely on Romani Studies (such as auto-didacts from within the community) cannot appreciate.

By contrast, social anthropologists of the anglophone tradition often suggest that periods of fieldwork of one, two or three years yield a dividend of authenticity that other forms of social enquiry lack: thus Okely argued that 'the holistic and open-ended approach of anthropology has authority. The view from within and below gives voice to those who are not represented in the social circles of the state' (1983: 232). Although she explicitly disclaimed 'any position as spokesperson', she was making a claim to record accurately because 'there is a need for the voices of the minority at the grass roots to be transmitted through the printed word; if only initially via a Gorgio [sic] participant observer and mediator' (Okely 1983: 26).

This neatly tied up with another often-proposed criterion of authenticity, that the experiental knowledge of those claiming Romani ethnicity is to be preferred to the syntheses of non-Romani scholars based on documentary evidence. At the same time, however, there is an implication that any Gypsy who could actually write out his or her own views would be too far from the grass roots to be representative. To be fair, however, in her afterword to a later collection, Okely (1997: 204) says that this situation has changed in the twenty years since her original fieldwork; she asserts that at conferences Travellers may now use their reading of the scholarly texts to elucidate their representations of their own identity in ways that then form part of the general scholarly debate over identity.

This chapter will leave it to the reader to decide on the relative claims of political science and social anthropology to scientific authority. Obviously the claims of Barany (2000a, 2000b) and Okely (1983) are at one level strictly incompatible; what they have in common (although both would be horrified to be accused of positivism) is that they make a claim to scientific authority based on their methodologies. The more mature Okely (1997) puts her finger on the problem of all such claims, which is that because of their reflexivity and constant reference to one another, the very coming into existence of representations changes the thing represented.

A complete agnosticism as to the relative authenticity of representations would, however, render critical thought impossible. If we want, like Heuss (2000), to build an account of 'anti-Gypsyism' that will enable its specificity to be contrasted with that of anti-Semitism, or anti-Black racism, then we have to work with the idea that distortions are distortions of something. Heuss writes:

> Anti-Gypsyism designates a construct which hypothetically assigns social phenomena (mostly of an undesirable nature) to the minority group who call themselves the Roma. A causal relationship is posited between these phenomena and their presumed cause – the 'Gypsies'. This presumptive causal relationship is so firmly anchored that it can neither be changed nor nullified by any empirical evidence. Such explanations derived from the longterm social construction of reality then give rise to bigotry and prejudice of extreme intransigence.
>
> In this paper, the term 'Gypsy' is used either where it is a reference to sources or where the image of 'Gypsies' fabricated by the majority and its institutions is meant. The term 'Roma' is used to denote the actual members of the minority concerned. (2000: 53).

Note that this formulation avoids making claims to absolute truth. Heuss is simply contrasting discourses, although we are left in little doubt which side he is on. But there is still a problem. There are Romani people who refer to themselves as 'Gypsies'. Heuss is a member of the non-Gypsy majority here making a representation about members of a minority he characterizes as 'actual'; there is no philosophical reason to treat this representation as any less of a fabrication than other images of the 'Gypsy', even if I and most of the readers of this article prefer it.

The answer, then, cannot be found in philosophy, or philosophical methodology. I wish to suggest, by contrast, that we can come to a better understanding of how representation works if we look at it sociologically, that is to say if we look (as Heuss does in examining particular German writers) at the actual human activity of making a representation.

Up until 1800 almost all the writing, pictures and transcribed music we have that represent Roma were put on paper by Gaje, some of whom witnessed Roma self-representations themselves, and others of whom worked indirectly from the representations of other Gaje. In the nineteenth century, however, while the direct contribution of Roma to the written record remained small, there was an increasing professionalization of Romani self-representation in Europe, in the sense that musicians, fortune-tellers and hosts of Gypsy balls and spectacles were able to charge Gaje for attending at their own representations of Romani life, thus obliging the Gaje experts to include this Gypsy self-representation. They could do so by representing Romani music as 'folk music' and

Romani verbal accounts as folklore, and Romani-made images as 'folk-art' or 'naive art'. They could thus represent these productions as not being the work of individual authors, but rather as collective facts of nature, which only become a concrete representation when in some way authored by the collector, the folklorist. Only in the twentieth century do we find the individual Romani writer or artist beginning to challenge that easy ascription of cultural products to the great 'Anon.' and insisting that personal creativity is at work (cf. Reid 1997, as Okely [1997] points out). For their pains such Romani artists are often typified by Gaje as 'unrepresentative' – as if the artist, in the very act of formalizing a representation as a cultural product, is not always carrying out an untypical, unrepresentative act.

To resolve such issues, we need a general theory of art and cultural representation that distinguishes different social functions of art in different contexts. While I wish to discard the notion of 'folk' music as part of nineteenth-century ideologies of class and race, we have to acknowledge distinctions such as that between domestic music-making and professional music-making. When we sing or play for ourselves at home, we consult only our own tastes and those of our immediate family, whereas when we do so professionally, the tastes of our customers are paramount. This is so in every culture that has ever existed, and cannot be the basis for any kind of distinction between 'folk' cultures and 'high' cultures, only between different social functions within cultures.

Domestic and professional music, however, influence one another. Whether we heard it on the radio, or from a strolling troubadour, we may then hum it to ourselves. But from the ballads of the Middle Ages to jazz, skiffle and punk in the more recent past, professional musicians have always sought to draw vigour from the vernacular, to co-opt the immediacy of domestic and street music to refresh the clichés of professional music. So, within any culture, professional and domestic music are engaged in a constant dialectical interaction.

It is not that the one is any more 'authentic' than the other. Hungarian Romologists were (and some still are) wont to contrast the authenticity of non-instrumental Lovari 'folk' music with the artificiality of the Café Gypsy music of Romungre or Bashalde Rom musicians. This is simply a category mistake, as these two musical idioms are not the corresponding domestic and professional idioms of the same culture. Hungarian Lovari domestic music is an immigrant idiom that relates to a professional musical culture of the Balkans and Eastern Mediterranean to which a variety of Orthodox Christian and Muslim cultures, including both Christian and Muslim Roma professional musicians, contribute. Bashaldo music comes from a northern European Romani tradition that diverged in its social context from Balkan music some 500 years ago at least, and in fact has its domestic music counterparts in northern Romani households across Europe, not least in the Gypsy themes that were brought into the new Gypsy Jazz of the 1930s and 1940s by Django Reinhardt, who brilliantly exemplifies the role of the professional musician who drew on 'folk' roots to construct supremely saleable works of art (Delaunay 1961: 24–30; Cruickshank 1994). But the story does not end there, for every Sinte or Manouche teenage boy who can pick up a guitar has for the last fifty years been picking out tunes in the style of Django, who thus becomes the patriarch founder of a style of domestic Romani music as surely as Jimmy Berry was the patriarch founder of contemporary Romanichal wagon decoration (cf. Smith 1997). Smith's essay shows that we can extend arguments of the type made above about music to pictorial art. Daroczi's (1989) collection of short biographies shows how even in Hungary, where there is the greatest concentration of Romani painters selling their work, they have internalized labels for their style such as 'naive' and 'auto-didactic'.

In this dialectic between domestic and professional cultural production, there is a third factor, a wild card, which is religion. The way in which I typified East Mediterranean music as Muslim or Orthodox above was a response to my perception that different religious styles not only permeate culture, but also act as a conduit of motifs between cultures.

Among Pentecostal Romani musicians we see a third kind of motivation which makes a difference to performance: when one is playing primarily not for oneself, nor for one's customers or audience, but above all for God. In Europe today this has released an extraordinary creativity among Romani musicians, and some remarkable syntheses that draw upon Gypsy Jazz, Vlach Romani singing, Bashaldo orchestral music, flamenco and American gospel and country music. What you hear in the great evangelical rallies is striking enough; but what you will hear if you sneak around the caravans of the musicians after the evening services will blow your mind.

Is this one of those inspired moments of creativity that will make a lasting contribution to world music? And if so will it do anything to reshape general representations of Gypsies in general international culture? To answer such questions we would need to have a theory of why some moments in cultural production seem to transcend their place in history and catch on to become 'classics', overleaping boundaries of time, place and culture. Why, when we speak of 'classical music' in everyday language, are we referring to a corpus that was composed in German-speaking lands or in imitation of German styles between 1750 and 1850? Why then? Why there? Why do some other moments of cultural production – medieval plainsong, Josquin des Prés, early jazz, Fela Kuti – seem to speak to us across distances of time and space even though a contemporary European listener can have but the sketchiest understanding of the social context of these artists?

The answer appears to be 'because they have meaning for us'. If we 'read' artistic productions as systems of interconnected meaningful symbols, then we give the motifs of the work a symbolism that is useful for us in our current social context. In this way poststructuralism can offer a general dissolution of the problem of connection between representation and reality: our systems of meaning, the ways in which we read texts, are things that we, the readers and listeners and viewers, visit upon texts and other cultural productions. Poststructuralism suggests that we have no way of knowing whether our reading is anything like the original meaning of the artist, which is not relevant to anything anyway. Then, however, we have landed ourselves with all the problems of relativism again. For this reason I would argue that any critical analysis of representations must take into account the historical development of their symbolic systems as well as the social context of their current uses. But we still have a problem of relativism, because our critical analysis does not exist outside history.

The device that poststructuralists can use to produce an illusion of standing outside history is to reify the historically produced recent past as a thing in itself called 'modernity' (a fairly old trick that modernists have used to discount the past in most literate cultures[1]) – and then to assert that we have transcended it – hence the self-ascription 'postmodernist' (which of course remains a variety of philosophical modernism in the same way that 'death of God' theory remains a variety of theology).

One of the more influential and acceptable postmodernist texts is Zygmunt Bauman's *Modernity and the Holocaust* (1989). This is unusual in modern social science scholarship in that, although it is a general work of sociology, it neither ignores the role of Roma in historical events, nor treats them as a mere footnote, but integrates them fully and relatively accurately into the broader story. It has, however, been relatively little cited within specialist Romani Studies, because it doesn't tell us experts much about Gypsies that we didn't know already. The overall uses of a theory of modernity, however, emerge much more clearly in a book that presents a general theory of the way the world is going than they do in writings that treat of Romani society in particular, and which tend to treat the wider world and modernity as given external constraints.

Bauman (1989) sets out to examine how we should understand the genocidal Nazi regime. He presents a historical account that treads well-worn paths in showing how technological changes in and after the Industrial Revolution led to economic changes which led to more highly

---

[1] For a discussion of the logical fallacies of using 'modernity' and other chronologically essentialist concepts as forms of social explanation see Acton 1974: 24–33.

populated and highly organized, disciplined societies. These in turn, when loaded into the dynamics of the nation-state monarchies established after the delegitimation of feudalism, produced authoritarian regimes which employed increasingly violent high-technology force against their perceived internal and external enemies. For modernists and postmodernists, however, these phenomena associated with industrialization and urbanization are more than the sum of their parts; or rather, they are not just ways of describing social reality, but are characteristics of some overarching thing called modernity. A non-modernist such as myself may have difficulty in seeing what 'modernity' actually adds to Bauman's explanations that is not accounted for by the other more concrete factors he adduces; but for Bauman, it is an independent causal factor. Modernity is seen as something brought about by industrialization, urbanization and changes in state formation, which in turn leads on to certain inhumane rationalizations that made us human beings capable of the Holocaust. This shapes and continues to shape representations of Gypsies and Jews. Once it is understood, we can perhaps transcend it, and return from the constraints of a mechanical rationality to a conscious humanity – or not, as the case may be, for once we abandon the notion of automatic progress, the importance and capriciousness of moral choice return, scaring us with the thought that the monsters might return at any time even if we avoid becoming monsters ourselves.

Once modernity is treated as a specific historical phenomenon in this way, lasting from, say, the middle of the eighteenth century to the middle of the twentieth century, then like the *Zeitgeist* of an earlier generation of idealist thinkers, it is available as a catch-all explanation of the social construction of representations of Gypsies. We shall examine the analyses of four young Dutch scholars, namely three historians, Leo Lucassen, Wim Willems and Annemarie Cottaar, and social anthropologist Mattijs Van de Port.

The three historians are members of the Dutch school of historical racism studies founded by Dik van Arkel, which, in parallel with, but without much reference to, similar Anglo-American projects, attempts to 'reveal the structure beneath the diverging manifestations of prejudices and social exclusions and thus to develop a general theory about the origins of racism' (Lucassen et al. 1998: vii). Within this school Lucassen has the greater reputation for scholarship, based on a number of works that earnestly analyse local authority and immigration records;[2] but Willems's (1997) attempt to reconstruct the entire western European understanding of and policy towards Gypsies over the past two centuries is the theoretical flagship of the enterprise.

---

[2] Although anyone who has spent much time assisting Roma facing immigration services (as I have) might be less inclined than Lucassen (1990) to take at face value immigration statistics on the origins of Romani immigrants.

Willems's book, based on his PhD thesis, suggests that contrary to accepted wisdom about Gypsies being of Indian origin, they were simply invented by Grellmann (1787, originally 1783). From the end of the Middle Ages Europe spawned a number of vagrant or Travelling groups, some of whom had picked up elements of Indian language. Traditionally these groups were seen as simply and wilfully deviant, and therefore to be repressed through criminal law. From the mid-eighteenth century, however, starting with Austria-Hungary, a new policy of enlightened assimilation began to be adopted, which required a new ideology. Grellmann, says Willems, supplied this through the application of another product of the Enlightenment, scientific racism. Based on the evidence (rather flimsy, in the view of these non-linguistic historians[3]) of words and phrases of Sanskritic origin, Grellmann racialized these disparate Travelling groups into a lost Indian race. The explanation of their social exclusion and the nomadism of some of them (now to be attributed to anyone who knows these Indian words) no longer needed to be their wickedness, but rather came to be their genetics. Policy towards them became not so much criminal as colonial – except that, of course, criminology itself, culminating in Lombroso, began to adopt geneticist explanations. And as the German polity moved from Enlightenment through eugenics towards the 'final solution', the 'noble savage' became the 'biological problem' and the discourse of scientific racism changed from one of respect for difference to one of extermination.

Willems attempts to trace this evolution of representations of Gypsies from Grellmann through nineteenth-century German-speaking admirers of George Borrow and the Gypsy Lore Society to the main ideologist of the Nazi genocide of Gypsies, Robert Ritter. The valuable section on Robert Ritter, drawing on previously unpublished evidence, shows that Ritter was not so much an enthusiast for the Nazi party as such, but was driven on by what he considered to be his own duty to science, which had to be put at the disposal of a government's policy on eugenics. This substantially undermines any notion that the Nazis were an aberration within European politics; rather, by utilizing well-established policy ideas, the Nazis merely took European racism to some of its logical conclusions. This is an important contribution to Holocaust studies.

Willems traces a line of racist ideas through continental Gypsylorists from Grellmann to Ritter – and which, as Kohn (1995) shows, can be extended on through Hermann Arnold and Josef Vekerdi to some contemporary Central and East European Romologists. All these colluded with the idea that Grellmann had made a great scientific advance in

---

[3] To look, as Cottaar (in Lucassen et al. 1998) does, at the ethnicity of a group such as the Woonwagenbewoner, but systematically to ignore their language, is absurd. Indeed, the resolute ignorance of, and ignoring of, linguistic scholarship is probably the Achilles heel of these Dutch historians.

'discovering' that the Rom come from India, thus enabling a 'racial' explanation of their otherness. What Willems clearly demonstrates, however, is that Grellmann took an idea that had been kicking around for some time and smoothed out its contradictions with prevailing policy ideas about Gypsies in the German-speaking world. But Willems takes his social contructionism to an extreme in suggesting that the Grellmann synthesis is the only reality of the phenomenon that it purports to describe, that Grellmann invented the Gypsies. For this position defines out of existence what must surely be – for scholars themselves Romani, at any rate – the most extraordinary problem about the European reaction to Gypsies: the denial for two centuries that Gypsies had a language of their own.

In fact for the first century of Romani migration into western Europe, the attitude to them was an open and enquiring one, very different from what it was to become. The 'Gypsies' had political leaders who could negotiate with kings and bishops; the king of Scotland even made one an earl. Local chroniclers did their best to describe these exotic dark-skinned visitors, and some even noted down bits of the Romani language (Fraser 1992). Between 1530 and 1550, however, this open attitude vanishes within a generation or so, as, across Europe, the nation-state began to define itself against foreigners and heretics, and agricultural capitalism defined itself against vagrants (Acton 1994). In fact vagrants were even more threatening than foreigners, and, as the early Romani word lists were forgotten, Gypsy claims to have a language of their own became treated as mere impudence.

If, for Europeans around 1600, 'Gypsies' were to be seen as just a social problem putting on exotic airs, it followed that they could not have a 'real' language of their own. When this conflicted with the clear evidence of their own ears, Europeans explained this away by saying that 'Gypsies' used secret, invented slang to make their ordinary speech unintelligible. Typical books of the seventeenth century give the story of *Gaje* (non-Gypsies) such as Bampfylde-Moore Carew (1750) in England, alleged to have organized vagrants into gangs of 'Gypsy' criminals – and give long lists of the slang (mostly not Romani) alleged to form 'the Gipsy tongue'. These lists were plagiarized from one book to another. Reprinted in dozens of editions, the Carew book encapsulates English understanding and representation of Gypsies immediately prior to the Grellmann revolution.

This wilful denial of the Romani language by Europeans could hardly have long survived the increasing trading and military incursions into India by Europeans in the eighteenth century, and indeed as soon as serious accounts of Indian languages began to be published in the West, the similarities with Romani began to be noticed. A 1776 report in a Vienna magazine claimed that a Hungarian pastor, Istvan Vali, had noticed the likeness as early as 1754. Eventually the connection was systematically tested by the German scholar Johann Rüdiger, who worked with a Romani woman – whose name he did not record – to translate a series of exercises specially designed to bring out the grammar and syntax of a language as well as its vocabulary. Rüdiger published their results in 1782, and the conclusions have never since been seriously challenged; indeed European scholars rushed to jump on the bandwaggon, claiming that this was what they had believed all along. In 1785, the Englishmen Jacob Bryant and William Marsden independently asserted the Indian origin on the basis of their earlier researches.

Most influential, however, was the young German named Heinrich Grellmann. In 1783 he published in German a synthesis that struck a chord with those who, since the 'reforms' of the Empress Maria Theresa, had been trying to assimilate Gypsies. In 1787 he rewrote it to make it even more politically correct and it was translated into most major European languages, often twice. Unfortunately, it was to become the definitive European textbook on Romani people for some forty years. Although Grellmann copied Rüdiger's most important conclusion, his understanding and methods were very different.

Rüdiger emphasized that the scholar's biggest asset was 'the living speech of the Gypsies' ('Man hatte ja überall die lebendige Sprache der Zigeuner' [Rüdiger 1782: 60]). Working with a Romani woman, even if he did not credit her by name, it was apparent to him that understanding the real linguistic history of the Roma also contradicted the racial hatred (*Volkshass* [1782: 49]) or nationalist hatred (*Nationalhass* [1782: 46]) of Europeans for Roma, which had prevented a proper understanding of their history. This astonishingly modern sociological analysis of the impact of racist ideology on both scientific and popular understanding had, however, little impact on the thinking of the time.[4]

European policy thinking, led by the Austro-Hungarian empire, saw 'Gypsies' as a marginal social group, whose wilful isolation (actually the separation enforced by earlier genocides) could no longer be tolerated. An analysis that presented them not as 'a-socials' but as a different people ('noble savages', in the idealistic discourse of the day) threatened these attempts at assimilation. Grellmann's genius was to accept that 'Gypsies' were 'a different race', and then to assert that their racial characteristics were the same as all the old social stereotypes had suggested, and thus justify official policy in the German-speaking lands. Unlike Rüdiger and his correspondents, who worked with actual Romani people, Grellmann worked primarily with books on Gypsies.

There are still Europeans who present Grellmann's recognition of the

---

[4] I am indebted to the late Sir Angus Fraser for guiding me to both these passsages of the text and these conclusions.

Indian origin of Romani as though it was a great scientific discovery by him, rather than a capitulation to what had become blindingly obvious. Where Rüdiger used science to confront racism, Grellmann used and misused the literature to accommodate the new scientific understanding to the old racism. To do this, he did not have to be consistent. Successive editions of his book contradicted earlier ones, and his translators added local racist anecdotes to make his work fit local circumstances. No matter! Racist ideology does not have to be consistent to be successful if it confirms the prejudices of the authorities.

Grellmann was rapidly promoted to a good university job, and Romani people were uneasily fitted into the new 'scientific racism' of nineteenth-century Europe – uneasily, because Romani people often did not live up to European fantasies about what a 'pure race' should be. Europeans justify their persecution of 'Gypsies' almost as often because they are allegedly not 'true Romanies' as they do on the basis of Romani 'racial characteristics'.

Willems takes at face value the self-representation of Grellmann and his successors as embodying the advanced thinking, the modernity of their day, without stopping to think about the ways in which that ideology was both inconsistent and contested. Willems has no difficulty in demonstrating that Grellmann was an opportunistic, intellectually dishonest, time-serving policy wonk of the type who would be right at home in a contemporary party-political thinktank or the Urban Migration Policy Unit of one of our redbrick universities; but Grellmann only produced his rationalizations in response to facts that had emerged to challenge the previous consensus. Willems is right to imply that there is no a priori reason to credit Grellmann as science; but equally there is no a priori reason to credit Bampfylde-Moore Carew, whose world-view Willems perversely seems to prefer to Rüdiger's; and there is no a priori reason to believe Willems either. In fact, the holy grail of a priori scientific authority is equally implausible whoever claims it; as Okely (1997) belatedly asserts, there are no methodological guarantees; nothing can relieve us of the responsibility of choosing, and choosing is not the same as copying. We have to examine evidence on its own merits; our methodology is part of the way we organize our appreciation of evidence, and its criteria are not external to the system of evidence.

The problem with adopting external theoretical criteria of truth – that is to say, an implicit metaphysics – is that it tends to make one cavalier with the evidence, to read texts in accordance with one's expectations. Willems (1997), for example, takes Borrow's fictions as straightforward autobiography, and takes their inconsistencies and contradictions as evidence of ideological misrepresentation, which 'provide the reader with a chance to distinguish shades of meaning in Borrow's text however far from his intentions the introduction of nuances might have been'

(Willems 1997: 122). Borrow is in fact one of the most ambiguous of English writers: a current of self-hatred underlies his narcissism; self-doubt punctuates his bombasticism, and contempt for pomposity his partisan evangelicalism. Any compliment he ever pays anyone is hedged about with sarcasm. He was the poet of the deliberate error planted to foil the plagiarist and the unwanted disciple. Anyone who can read Borrow's texts as unnuanced has simply failed to come to grips with them, and this is why, from the depths of racism, spleen and mock-cheerful desperation in Borrow, the critical reader still finds observations and insights that strike home not only on Gypsies and on nineteenth-century Britain, but on the human condition itself.

Superficial twentieth-century historians who take at face value Borrow's 'inspiration' of the Gypsy Lore Society, which became the main vehicle of scientific racism applied to Gypsies in the late nineteenth and the early twentieth century, fail to understand the importance of the mutual loathing of Borrow and the early Gypsylorists. Although Willems mentions some of the critical comments, he treats Borrow's casual and inconsistent racism as though it were the source of the systematic racism of the Gypsylorists. In fact he was their model of undisciplined auto-didacticism; they were as disdainful of him, and his pretence of being unaware of Grellmann, as the modern Romani Studies community is of Isabel Fonseca (1995).[5]

Willems and Lucassen seem unaware of the paradox involved in relying on the facts reported by the very writers, such as Gypsy Lore Society secretary Dora Yates, that they have discredited as a class, as I noted in my inaugural lecture (Acton 1998: 15). Piqued by that accusation, they responded with a critique (Willems and Lucassen 2000: 266–67) which presents that inaugural lecture as espousing Romani nationalism. That is perhaps a possible reading of it; but most English readers have seen it, as I intended, as a watershed self-critical renunciation of nationalist ideology.[6]

The historical method and theoretical ambition of these historians contrast sharply with Mattijs Van de Port's *Gypsies, Wars and Other Instances of the Wild* (1998), which stands in the tradition of social anthropology, even as it protests the inadequacy of the way this tradition has been observed. Van de Port, like Willems, Lucassen and Cottaar, focuses on the European psychological utilization of Gypsies as the 'other'. But whereas the historians assume the coherence of the actions of European states around a concept of Romani identity (or 'the true

---

[5] Critical reactions can be found in Hancock 1997: 185 and ní Shuinéar 1996.

[6] The Willems and Lucassen critique presents 'diaspora' as a biblical concept which leads to a danger of 'primordial notions creeping back [...] especially in the work of politically motivated scholars who identify with such victim groups as Gypsies, Jews, Armenians and former African Slaves' (Willems and Lucassen 2000: 206–207).

Gypsy') invented, according to them, by Grellmann, Van de Port assumes that there is a Romani reality behind Serbian misrepresentations of Gypsies, and deconstructs these to show the howling incoherence of Serbian self-conceptions. He completed in 1990 a more conventional PhD thesis about the role of Gypsy music in Serbia, and went back to Novi Sad in 1991 for a final postdoctoral bout of fieldwork to turn the thesis into a book. The real otherness of Serbia at war, however, turned the socially constructed otherness of the Gypsies into a dark farce of disintegration which challenges to the point of destruction not only the self-identities of the Serbs who are Van de Port's subjects, but also his own carefully constructed self-identity as a liberal, urbane, gay Dutch anthropologist interpreting a social world. At one level he has to recognize that the Dionysiac release of Serb intellectuals from everyday inhibitions in bars where Gypsy musicians play nationalistic music is as valid as any other empiricist search for knowledge. At another level it is shown to be as false and demeaning a relationship as that between southern aristocrats and nigger minstrels in the ante-bellum United States.

The enlisting of large Romani casts in the films of directors such as Emir Kusturica or Aleksander Petrovic may be seen as part of this relationship – the privileging of a fake Serbian largesse within a spurious Romani romanticism, especially in Kusturica's masterpiece, *Time of the Gypsies* (1988). Although the 'positive' stereotypes of these directors are to be preferred to the negative hostile stereotyping of the film *Guardian Angel* (1987), made at the same time, on the same theme of child-kidnapping, by Kusturica's Serbian contemporary Goran Paskaljevic (Gocić 2001: 101–02), a stereotype is still a stereotype. As the distinguished film critic Goran Gocić innocently explains:

> *Time of the Gypsies* is not a single film: it is all the films about Gypsies in one. Moreover, at least half a dozen quotes from well-known works can be identified in it. *Time of the Gypsies* might be the first work of fiction since *Carmen* to synthesise all the popular beliefs about Gypsies into a unique, all-embracing, eternal – and practically archetypal – narrative. It does so by mixing Eastern and Western worldviews and archetypes. It also shares some of *Carmen*'s ambition of being a treatise on Gypsy 'nature'. In the opening sequence, for example, a television set can be heard from the back of the room with an (English speaking) documentary mentioning genes and chromosomes, implying an essentialist explanation of the Gypsy ways displayed in the foreground.
>
> The approach of the script is balanced eclecticism: Gypsies are presented as thieves and con men but they are also musicians and dancers and constitute a proud, colourful culture. They are poor, ragged and vengeful, but also generous, compassionate and caring [...] This juggling with contradictions in *Time of the Gypsies* is done with apparent ease, assimilating all existing stereotypes and transcending them [...] Indeed the film represents a new chapter

in the Gypsy screen image, which comprises all existing stereotypes divided by different national cinemas. The most radical shift was made in respect of ethnic 'authenticity'. It is a film where traditional values are self-sufficient goals, without any 'higher' political or ideological purpose. While basically belonging to the same aesthetic school as his Serbian contemporaries, Kusturica moves a step further. He makes an extra effort to create a poetic level in his films (thus leaving raw 'naturalism' behind), establish a viable mythology (i.e. not remain fixed on politics) and secure stories with a strong and rich emotional content (i.e. not stick either to the futile despair of Eastern European 'engaged' cinema or the programmed optimism of Socialist Realism). In all these respects, *Time of the Gypsies* can be viewed as Kusturica's highest achievement. (Gocić 2001: 98)

In Kusturica's films, these representations are a transgressive embracing of the underworld; for the lone anthropologist Van de Port, sitting out the war in the Voivodina in northern Serbia, near to Hungary, this embracing of our humanity seems more like surrendering to inhumanity, an abandonment of the hope that understanding can bring forgiveness. With a shriek of pain, Van de Port (1998) repudiates the claim of the anthropologist to any special skill in interpretation; the cries of his subjects about all of us having the beast within make as much sense and provide as little excuse for human behaviour as any social scientist. Although this book was most immediately distressing for Serbian intellectuals and Romani musicians, the thrust of the book is that any of us would meet the same distress if our worlds were cut asunder in the same way. Serbian ethnocentrism is hardly unique. Indeed, to much critical acclaim, the French Gitano film-maker Tony Gatlif has bought his way into the eastern European Roma stereotypes in exactly the same way as Kusturica (Gocić 2001: 111).

One is driven back, with Van de Port, to the simple moralities of common sense, of judging oneself more harshly than others, of recognizing that 'intersubjectivity' is just a posh way of saying 'common sense', that empiricism may lead us not to confirmations, conjectures or refutations but simply into a wilderness, and that most of the energy of anthropologists is spent 'on ways of conferring academic respectability on fieldwork, an essentially non-academic form of collecting information', energy that 'would be better spent on trying to find different, better forms of expression for the knowledge acquired in the field' (Van de Port 1998: 225).

There is, however, one recent work on the social anthropology of Roma that shows us how we may begin to carry out fieldwork that will enable the scholar to put his or her own capacity to make representations in the same frame (to use film directors' jargon) as that of our Romani and Gajo subjects. Lemon's (2000) mould-breaking study of Roma in

Russia and of the Soviet paradigm of discourse about Roma combines real ethnography and real history. She moves beyond traditional social anthropology of Roma in linking the formations in Soviet and post-Soviet society to a clear account of the history and politics of Roma in Russia over the past 200 years.

Lemon reports on her extensive fieldwork on the kinship, weddings, funerals, food, dreams and daily lives of different Roma. But, perhaps because she has experience with Roma groups in America as well as Russia, she does not essentialize Romani culture, but deconstructs official, media and academic stereotypes of 'what Gypsies are like', and lets the truth emerge through highlighting differences between groups. Despite her refusal to generalize, however, anyone familiar with Roma society will experience the shock of recognition during the telling, both artful and insightful, of Lemon's stories.

Her mixture of anthropological and historical method allows her to document the ways in which, in both imperial and Soviet Russia, the dominant non-Gypsy discourses shaped and reshaped, sometimes directly, sometimes through provoking opposition, the self-understanding of Roma, whether poor and illiterate, or urban and intellectual. Through her ethnography she gives us the sense of how this continues to be true for individuals in post-Soviet Russia, and how it must be true generally that ethnicity depends on politics, despite our nationalist illusions that the opposite is true. She shows how fragile and changeable are our imaginations of 'imagined communities', especially through a detailed study of the chief focus of the public imagination of the Romani community in Soviet and post-Soviet Russia, the Moscow Romani Theatre. She shows the continuities between the public performance image of the Soviet era, and the pre-Soviet traditions. She also shows how immigrant Lovari Roma adapted the images established around the identities of Xaladitka and Russka Roma. The Theatre was an instrument of propaganda. Through it non-Rom directors often imposed stereotypes on Romani actors, and consultants from the Theatre often then imposed the same stereotypes on Roma in documentary and fictional films down to the present. At the same time, however, the Theatre and the large social circle associated with it was a kind of university for the nascent Romani intelligentsia. It linked the hidden strata of educated Roma in the armed forces, the civil services, and later the real universities with experimental Romani co-operatives, and the poor in their villages.

Looking at the inner workings of the production of performances, images and representations, 'making a frame', as one of her informants explained, Lemon begins to provide an answer to the infuriating paradox that some Rom intellectuals, such as Hancock (1991), have noted (as he contrasts the fantastic Hoskins with the more realistic Gatlif) about Romani cinema, that in many cases the more authentic the Roma involved in the performance, the more powerfully dangerous is the stereotyping, a stereotyping all the more persuasive and damaging because of the authenticity of the actors and the backgrounds, and the fact that Gypsies will be bowled over by the rare privilege of hearing Romani spoken on screen in any context at all.

This insight begins to enable us to put into context the mutual pathology of the relationship between Romani musicians and eastern European romantic nationalists in the excess of Voivodina's Gypsy bars, which shocked Van de Port into the anguished account that provoked cries of outrage from Serbs and Roma alike. Writing from within the fieldwork paradigm of ahistorical anthropology, Van de Port professes himself theoretically unable to do any more than describe the depths of human cognitive pain, to say that for a time the fearful abyss of the wild in his informants' understanding held more reality for him than the dream of societal structure.

Lemon's analysis of Romani performance, of Roma in cinema and, latterly, Romani cinema offers a historically based answer to Hancock's and Van de Port's questions about the artistic collusion of the oppressed with the oppressor, and, at the same time, the possibility of transcending it. Some may claim this as a postmodern analysis of the hybridity of culture. It parallels Van Peebles's (1995) analysis of the development of 'blaxploitation' movies as a dialectical opposition to, which yet could not escape, the stereotyping of Blacks in early American cinema. It seems to me, however, that the same Lemon who dares offer her own dreams as part of the grieving process at a Romani funeral feast also offers us the hope that old-fashioned scholarly rigour may help re-make the frame, and free us from our prisons of ignorance, ideology, stereotyping and partial knowledge.

For the developing Romani intelligentsia, this may suggest that the liberator they need may be not so much a Romani Martin Luther King as a Romani Melvin Van Peebles (who, after all, started his own career by taking the 'blaxploitation' movie to the point of self-destruction). If, as one leading Romani scholar-politician, Nicolae Gheorghe (1997: 157, 161), suggests, representation of Romani identity is a process of ethnogenesis which involves Roma self-consciously playing with their identities, then perhaps we must recognize that constructing (or prophesying, as Gheorghe has it) effective representations involves the artist as much as the scientist or politician.

But can such representations be accepted, or are they just an embracing of illusion and delusion? This is the question posed by Willems and Lucassen and their Dutch school. I propose to sidestep it to ask instead why the application of postmodernist deconstructionism to Romani Studies seems to be such a specialism of the Dutch. Any such profound questioning of the illusion of reality reinforces for us the necessity of a 'symptomatic' reading of postmodernist texts, one that 'listens atten-tively to their silences'. Such a reading is bound to bring into question the very identity of the Dutch themselves. Using the analytical methods of the authors, it is fairly easy to demonstrate that 'the Dutch', as Europeans have traditionally conceived them, are a disparate collection of groups whose supposed role in European politics is primarily deter-mined by the socio-political dynamics of the continental powers, who determined that some small 'nations' should exist in the space between France and Germany, and were able to seize on identities originally invented by the Habsburgs in their attempt to hang on to territory in the region. Traditionally, these 'Dutch' are supposed to have their own lan-guage (also called 'Dutch') which other Europeans do not understand, which could be held to explain the lack of European access to 'Dutch' self-conceptions. The 'Dutch' themselves – or at least all those who come into contact with other inhabitants of Europe – all speak other mainstream European languages and, in them, reflect back to other Europeans their preconceived ideas. Thus, in the texts of Willems, Lucassen and Cottaar, allegedly 'translated from the Dutch', the self-identification of the authors as 'Dutch' is presented initially as unprob-lematic; a close reading, however, requires us to question whether Dutch is indeed a separate language, or indeed a real language at all as opposed to a simple mispronunciation of the word 'Deutsch'. Close inspections of alleged specimens appear to differ from German only by the adoption of an odd orthography, and indeed a similar but slightly different orthog-raphy appears in another supposed language called Flemish in the neigh-bouring state of Belgium. How then can we see the Dutch as people in their own right as opposed to a mishmash of clog-wearing folk including Low Germans, Flemings and Walloons, who may have adapted elements of Germanic vocabulary during the course of a long march east across the Pas-de-Calais?

Such an experience might easily give rise to profound anxieties about their identity – not so much among ordinary folk, who are quite happy to call themselves 'Nederlanders', but among a more intellectual stratum who come into contact with other Europeans. 'There are only 14 million of us; how can we sustain high culture?' wailed a university professor, one of my informants during fieldwork in Leiden. One symptom of such anxieties might be to project them onto a more fortunate group, such as the Roma, whose identity is recognized transnationally and whose lan-guage is spoken all over the world. As so often when Gaje are talking about Roma, the longer one listens, the more one realizes that they are actually talking about themselves. Since Europe demands that its people be organized into nation-states, the 'Dutch' cannot acknowledge their deep fears about their own underlying non-existence. The conclusion is clear: the Dutch do not exist. They are a figment of our imagination, and that is why they so desperately seek to escape the paradoxes of their non-existence by projecting it on to the Roma.

References

Acton, Thomas. 1974. *Gypsy Politics and Social Change*. London: Routledge and Kegan Paul.

— 1994. 'Modernization, Moral Panics and the Gypsies', *Sociology Review*, 4.1: 24–28.

— 1998. *Authenticity, Expertise, Scholarship and Politics: Conflicting Goals in Romani Studies*. London: University of Greenwich Inaugural Lecture Series.

Acton, Thomas (ed.). 1997. *Gypsy Politics and Traveller Identity*. Hatfield: University of Hertfordshire Press

— 2000. *Scholarship and the Gypsy Struggle*. Hatfield: University of Hertfordshire Press

Acton, Thomas, and Mundy, Gary (eds). 1997. *Romani Culture and Gypsy Identity*. Hatfield: University of Hertfordshire Press.

Barany, Zoltan. 2000a. 'The Poverty of Gypsy Studies', *Newsnet: The Newsletter of the American Association for the Advancement of Slavic Studies*, 40.3: 1–4.

Bauman, Zygmunt. 1989. *Modernity and the Holocaust*. Cambridge: Polity Press.

— 2000b. 'In Defence of Disciplinary Scholarship', *Newsnet: The Newsletter of the American Association for the Advancement of Slavic Studies*, 40.5: 9–12.

Bryant, Jacob. 1785. 'Collections on the Zingara or Gipsey Language', *Archaeologia*, 7: 387–94.

Carew, Bampfylde-Moore. 1750. *An Apology for the Life of Bampfylde-Moore Carew*. London: R. Goadby and W. Owen.

Cruickshank, Ian. 1994. *Django's Gypsies: The Mystique of Django Reinhardt and his People*. Newcastle upon Tyne: Ashley Mark.

Daroczi, Agnes. 1989. *Autodidakta Cigány Képzömüvészek II. Országos Kiállítása*. Budapest: Ethnographic Museum.

Delaunay, Charles. 1961. *Django Reinhardt*. Trans. Michael James. London: Cassell.

Fonseca, Isabel. 1995. *Bury Me Standing: The Gypsies and their Journey*. London: Chatto and Windus.

Fraser, Sir Angus. 1992. *Gypsies*. Oxford: Blackwell.

Gheorghe, Nicolae. 1997. 'The Social Construction of Romani Identity', in Acton (ed.) 1997: 153–63.

Gocić, Goran. 2001. *The Cinema of Emir Kusturica: Notes from the Underground*. London: Wallflower Press.

Grellmann, Heinrich M.G. 1787. *Die Zigeuner: Ein historicher Versuch über die Lebensart und Verfassung, Sitten und Schicksale dieses Volks in Europa, nebst ihrem Ursprunge*. Göttingen: Johann Christian Dieterich, 2nd edn (1st edn Leipzig, 1783).

Hancock, Ian. 1991. Review of *The Raggedy Rawney* (dir. Bob Hoskins, 1990), *Traveller Education*, 26: 19–32.

—1997. 'Duty and Beauty, Possession and Truth: Lexical Impoverishment as Control', in Acton and Mundy (eds) 1997: 182–89.

Heuss, Herbert. 2000. 'Anti-Gypsyism Research: The Creation of a New Field of Study', in Acton (ed.) 2000: 52–67.

Kohn, Marek. 1995. *The Race Gallery: The Return of Racial Science*. London: Jonathan Cape.

Lemon, Alaina. 2000. *Between Two Fires: Gypsy Performance and Romani Memory from Pushkin to Postsocialism*. Durham, NC: Duke University Press.

Lucassen, Leo. 1990. *En men noemde hen zigeuners; De geschiednis van Kalderasch, Ursari, Lowara en Sinti in Nederland, 1750–1945*. Amsterdam and The Hague: Stichtung Breheer IISG and SDU.

Lucassen, Leo, Willems, Wim, and Cottaar, Annemarie. 1998. *Gypsies and Other Itinerant Groups – A Socio-Historical Study*. London: Macmillan.

Marsden, William. 1785. 'Observations on the Language of the People Commonly called Gypsies', *Archaeologia*, 7: 382–86.

ní Shuinéar, Sinéad. 1996. Review of Fonseca 1995, *JGLS*, Fifth Series, 6.2: 114–17.

Okely, Judith. 1983. *The Traveller: Gypsies*. Cambridge: Cambridge University Press.

—1997. 'Cultural Ingenuity and Travelling Autonomy: Not Copying, Just Choosing', in Acton and Mundy (eds) 1997: 190–205.

Reid, Willie. 1997. 'Scottish Gypsies/Travellers and the Folklorists', in Acton and Mundy (eds) 1997: 31–39.

Rüdiger, Johann C. C. 1782. 'Von der Sprache und Herkunft der Zigeuner aus Indien', in *Neuester Zuwachs der teutschen fremden und allgemeinen Sprachkunde in eigenen Aufsätzen, Bücherranzeigen und Nachrichten*, I: 37–84.

Smith, David. 1997. 'Gypsy Aesthetics, Identity and Creativity: The Painted Waggon', in Acton and Mundy (eds) 1997: 7–17.

Strawson, P.F. 1959. *Individuals: An Essay in Descriptive Metaphysics*. London: Methuen.

Van de Port, Mattijs. 1998. *Gypsies, Wars and Other Instances of the Wild*. Amsterdam: Amsterdam University Press.

Van Peebles, Melvin. 1995. *Panthers*. New York: Thunder's Mouth.

Willems, Wim. 1997. *In Search of the True Gypsy: From Enlightenment to Final Solution*. London: Frank Cass.

Willems, Wim, and Lucassen, Leo. 2000. 'Gypsies in the Diaspora? The Pitfalls of a Biblical Concept', *Histoire Sociale/Social History*, XXXIII(66): 251–69.

Part III

Orientalism and Gender Issues in Literature

Half a Gypsy: The Case of Ezra Jennings in Wilkie Collins's *The Moonstone* (1868)

Nicholas Saul

In this essay I shall investigate an aspect of the phenomenology of the Gypsies in European cultural history through an analysis of the European side of the encounter, in a novel by the nineteenth-century English writer Wilkie Collins, *The Moonstone: A Romance* (1868).[1] *The Moonstone*, as we shall see, is intimately concerned with the problem of Orientalism in British colonial India. I shall argue that Collins's novel also has something valuable to say in this context about the discourse on Gypsies.

First, some prefatory remarks on the novel's genre, cultural context and content. Collins, a longtime friend and colleague of Dickens, was one of the most widely read English novelists of the mid- to late nineteenth century. Probably his best-known book today is *The Woman in White* (1860). Like that work, *The Moonstone* is a frankly sensational detective novel. T.S. Eliot famously called it the 'the first and greatest of the English detective novels' (1950: 413). Sensation novels embody a separate sub-genre of the English tradition, and were all the rage in the third quarter of the nineteenth century. Generally speaking, they represented an aesthetic opposition to the sober realist or 'scientific' tradition of writing, and deliberately set out both to stimulate and to satisfy the appetite of the public for new, exciting, unprecedented, uncanny motifs, plots and arguments. Jenny Bourne Taylor argues that the sensation novel, characterized as it is by the obsession with the new and startling in endless variation, is a typical manifestation of the hunger for novelty characteristic of cultural modernity (Taylor 1988: 1–26, esp. 3ff.). The sensation novel, with its bold questioning of apparent certainties, was thus a medium eminently suited to expressing the widespread sense of cultural crisis and fear of decline in 1860s Britain.

The Moonstone is the tale of the sensational theft of the eponymous large and beautiful yellow diamond from the Yorkshire mansion of the

---

[1] I am not the first Professor of German at the University of Liverpool to 'transgress' disciplinary boundaries into Romany Studies. See Petsch 1911–12.

Verinder family in 1848, and of the attempts to recover the jewel – or at least to discover how it was stolen – in investigations by Sergeant Cuff, a mildly eccentric character with a razor-sharp analytical mind in the mould of Sherlock Holmes, and by other, unofficial detectives. One of the pleasures of this text lies in its cunning and often admired forensic narrative structure, in which the figures most involved in the action, rather like witnesses in a courtroom or under police interrogation, successively tell the tale from their individual perspectives. As narrative analysis of the case progresses, these individual perspectives increasingly overlap and qualify one another, error and truth crystallize out, and a single, authoritative narrative at last seems to emerge. The reader is compulsively engaged by this process of truth-finding. The basic, seemingly inscrutable facts of the tale are set out in the first, long narrative by the Verinder family's ancient and loyal retainer Gabriel Betteredge (pp. 17–195). Betteredge represents something like primeval Englishness. His favourite book, indeed quite literally his Bible (pp. 17ff.), is the archetypal colonial narrative, Defoe's *Robinson Crusoe* (1719). As he readily confesses (p. 19), having worn out six copies of this book, he is now on his seventh, which he allows complete authority over his interpretation of the world. Typically, as dissenters did with the real Bible, he will at moments of need turn to *Robinson Crusoe*, open it at random, and, as if this providential textual encounter were the necessary result of divine ordination, allow the first words he reads there (p. 404) to guide his opinions and actions. His report, indeed, begins with an authoritative citation from p. 129 in (his copy of) *Robinson Crusoe*, thus placing all he says squarely under this colonial hermeneutic perspective. Despite all the aid that *Robinson Crusoe* can provide, however, the theft of the Moonstone remains for Betteredge an utterly inexplicable event. Following a dinner party at which the current possessor of the Moonstone, Miss Rachel Verinder, her rival suitors, Franklin Blake (something of an adventurer) and Godfrey Ablewhite (as his name suggests, a prominent man in religious and charitable circles), Mr Murthwaite (a learned Orientalist specializing in Indian culture), and Dr Candy (the local medical practitioner) are present, the jewel disappears from Rachel's bedroom without trace. The house, we know, has been and remains securely locked, with no sign of entry, and the grounds too had been thoroughly searched by Betteredge with his bloodhound before retiring. Despite the best efforts even of Sergeant Cuff, who has been summoned by the leading male Franklin Blake, official investigations remain fruitless, and the major cognitive interest of the tale therefore follows the amateur sleuthing of Blake himself.

The significant feature of all this for our cognitive interest – as the prominence of *Robinson Crusoe* suggests – is what turns out to be the Oriental dimension of the theft. For suspicion is directed initially not at the guests, but at three interlopers into this securely English world,

Indian so-called jugglers, Brahmins in fact. The 'mahogany-coloured Indians' (p. 26), as Betteredge calls them, are repeatedly observed reconnoitring the house and grounds prior to Rachel's birthday dinner party. As exotic personages, they fascinate everyone, not least because they seem to possess occult knowledge: they use a small white boy under their control as a clairvoyant medium in pursuit of the object of their desire (pp. 27–28).[2] Despite the Orientalist Murthwaite's reservations, they are eventually granted entry to the house in order to perform their juggling act for the party. Despite the attested fact of their leaving and the observed presence of the diamond in the house afterwards, suspicion rests on them. This suspicion is not founded solely on the Indians' unnatural curiosity and otherwise motiveless appearance. It is further grounded in the characters' knowledge of the jewel's original Indian provenance, which takes us back through a long and intricate prehistory. For, as the reader is informed in a prefatory note (pp. 11–16), Rachel, strictly speaking, is not the legitimate possessor of the jewel. She has innocently received it as a gift from her uncle, Colonel Herncastle. However, he was not its legitimate owner. He participated in an imperialist crime, the sack of the Indian city of Seringapatam in 1799. During this, crazed with passion, he ruthlessly murdered the jewel's guardian and seized it for himself. There is a clear suggestion that he is crazed with passion to possess the jewel because he is the instrument and later victim of its curse. For Seringapatam is not the jewel's original provenance either. It is originally from the temple of Brahma in the holy city of Somnauth. Placed in the forehead of a statue of the four-armed god of the moon in the eleventh century (p. 12), it had been preserved from various depredations until finally desecrated and stolen by Muslim colonizers on its chequered path to Seringapatam. But it stands always under the special protection of Vishnu, preserver god, who has predicted 'certain disaster to the presumptuous mortal who laid hands on the sacred gem, and to all of his house and name who received it after him' (p. 12). Three specially delegated Brahmins watch for generation after generation over the Moonstone in its alienation. At the novel's conclusion, it is ascertained that the diamond does indeed end up in the keeping of the Indians. The suggestion is, then, that the theft from Rachel's possession is but one in a long series of fulfilments of the curse laid on the sacred object, executed through the agency of the three mysterious Indians as its Brahmin guardians. In this consists the novel's appeal as a sensation novel: the occult, Oriental power of the Indians confronts, and apparently conquers, the political and epistemological majesty of the Occident.

---

[2] Compare the closely parallel discussion of Indian jugglers, their mediums, and ink patterns in one of Collins's sources for the psychology of the novel, Elliotson 1835: 670.

It should be evident by now that *The Moonstone*, while undoubtedly sensational, is not merely a sensationalist detective novel. For this quintessentially English tale, constituted at one level (through Betteredge's eyes) in *Robinson Crusoe*'s colonial perspective, in fact begins and ends on another, pre- or postcolonial level in India. The jewel stolen in Yorkshire turns out originally to have been the centrepiece of an ancient and dignified Hindu cult, central organ of a strange but in itself legitimate value-system, which has been violently misappropriated and crassly degraded by an alien colonial power. As studies by John Reed and Sue Lonoff[3] have shown, the novel is therefore also to be seen as participating in the nineteenth-century discourse on Orientalism long since analysed by Edward Said – and participating critically in that discourse. What at first seemed a localized theft is finally disclosed to be the consequence of imperialist crime. The three disguised Hindu 'jugglers' who pursue the diamond to Yorkshire now appear less as sensationalized agents of the fateful curse than as heroes of their recognized community of faith. And the restoration of the jewel to its proper owners (and users), quite apart from the glamorous and sensationalist aura of the curse fulfilled, in fact finally reflects a (then hardly fashionable) negative authorial judgement on the constitutional and cultural legitimacy of the British colonial project. The authoritative Occidental narrative of the detective story thus acquires a parallel and subversive Oriental shadow.

All this brings us by way of Orientalism to this essay's interest in *The Moonstone*, which is to uncover a further dimension of the more recent Orientalist readings. The novel, it will be argued, not only criticizes the colonial project in India, but also participates in the nineteenth-century Orientalist discourse on 'Gypsies'. And this emerges as mediated through the novel's participation in another specialized discourse of the nineteenth century, that of psychology.[4] To turn to the text again, it becomes clear following the end of Betteredge's story that the forensic energy of the text is less directed to identifying the diamond thief than to explaining the extraordinary circumstances of the theft itself. The person who stole Miss Verinder's jewel from her boudoir (it is of course a transparent sexual metaphor) is soon revealed to be none other than her preferred lover Franklin Blake. This in itself is obviously another sensational motif. Like Œdipus, like Kleist's Judge Adam in *The Broken Jug* (1807), the amateur detective Blake discovers that the criminal he has been pursuing is in fact himself. But this identification was already fairly obvious, even without hindsight. The real interest lies not in his identification, but in how he came to steal the jewel without knowing or recalling having done the deed. Blake – and this is where the psycholog-

---

[3] See Reed 1973 and Lonoff 1982; also Thomas 1991, Roy 1993 and Duncan 1994.
[4] See Hutter 1998; Taylor 1988: 27–70, 174–206; and Heller 1998.

ical discourse comes in – is finally revealed to have removed the jewel from Miss Verinder's chamber in a somnambulist trance, that is to say in a state when his conscious mind was not active. The trance was occasioned by various factors, chiefly by an unwitting dose of opium after the dinner, which both stimulated him to the deed and effaced all traces from his conscious memory. He is thus – within the English perspective of the tale – both guilty and innocent, or neither. Oddly, neither the official detective Cuff nor his unofficial colleague Blake is the author of this insight into the method of the theft, but quite another character, whom I have not so far mentioned. It is of course the character named in the title, Ezra Jennings. Jennings is by profession a medical doctor, a kind of locum or deputy of Dr Candy. He is central to my interest by virtue of the fact that he is also half a Gypsy, so that not only the three Brahmin Hindus, but also a person in part of Gypsy provenance is placed at the heart of the novel's counter-Orientalist project.

Jennings is universally recognized as the most compelling character in the novel, and in Collins's extensive gallery of outsider types. As Blake's description (pp. 321–22) suggests, he is a dualistic figure, at once charismatic and repulsive, and in several ways. Jennings is, firstly, dualistic in terms of his appearance. His most striking, and obviously emblematic, feature is his bizarre black and white layered hair.[5] While 'thick' and 'closely-curling' all over, it is at the top 'deep black' (its 'natural colour'), but at the sides 'completely white' and 'without the slightest gradation of grey to break the force of the extraordinary contrast' (p. 321). His face is equally dualistic, both noble in spirit and repellent. The nose presents 'the fine shape and modelling so often found among the ancient people of the East, and so seldom visible among the newer races of the West' (p. 321) and the forehead rises 'high and straight from the brow' (p. 321). But the cheeks are 'fleshless' and 'fallen into deep hollows', the skin marked and comprehensively wrinkled, and the complexion 'of a gipsy darkness' (p. 321). This ancient face on a young body makes a deeply unfavourable impression, so that although Jennings is younger than Betteredge, he looks older than the ancient retainer. But if this repels most people, it compels Blake. Jennings's eyes, while 'of the softest brown […] dreamy and mournful, and deeply sunk in their orbits', are, says Blake, capable of taking 'your attention captive at their will' (p. 321). Secondly, as all this heavily symbolic physiognomic observation suggests, Jennings is dualistic in his ethnic provenance. Little is ever revealed of his past, but it does emerge that he 'was born, and partly brought up, in one of our colonies' (p. 366), the son of an 'Englishman' and a mother of whom he can bring

---

[5] In Collins's inspiration, Elliotson 1835, the physical appearance of mixed race is discussed in closely analogous terms (1096–97, 1108).

himself to say nothing (p. 366). Nothing more *is* said on this point. But the text suggests overwhelmingly that this woman was a Gypsy. For Jennings is not, like the Indians in the novel, merely described as being dark-skinned. The Indians are 'mahogany-coloured' (p. 26), have 'coffee-coloured face[s]' (p. 79) or are of 'swarthy complexion' (p. 278). Jennings's skin is equally dark, but not like mahogany or coffee. His skin is not qualified by reference to wood or drink, but (as Collins would say) in terms of *race*, and consistently so. It is, we have already heard, of 'gipsy darkness' (p. 321), and every other time it is mentioned it is always declared to be of 'gipsy complexion' (p. 322, Betteredge; pp. 364 and 373, Blake). Nor is this the only sense in which Jennings is dualistic. Describing Dr Candy's symptoms, he reveals at one point his own tears of distress: 'An hysterical relief, Mr Blake – nothing more', he explains, 'Physiology says, and says truly, that some men are born with female constitutions – and I am one of them!' (p. 369). Obviously, Jennings' male-female constitution[6] is an implicit reference to the well-known myth of androgyny as utopian human fulfilment. In a novel characterized by polar oppositions, then, Jennings, uniquely, is a joiner or a unifier. *The Moonstone* opposes in its symbolic order black and white, light and darkness, science and superstition, East and West, male and female. But Jennings, unlike the Indians, unlike all the English people, would appear to join in his own person Occident and Orient, *gadjo* and Gypsy, light and dark, male and female, old and young, and to represent in this sense a paradoxical wholeness.

It is this dualistic yet whole constitution that also uniquely qualifies him to solve the mystery of the jewel between East and West, Indian and English, man and woman. The riddle of the theft is that Blake has removed the jewel, but does not recall having done so. How is this possible? The key lies in Jennings's medical and in particular psychological knowledge. It emerges that Dr Candy, the family practitioner for whom Jennings works and who was present at the birthday dinner, urgently wishes to communicate something important about that night to Franklin Blake. Yet he proves quite incapable of doing so. For Candy, having returned home that night through a rainstorm, has contracted a fever which has irreparably damaged his memory (pp. 103, 153, 361–62). Try as he might, he can remember that he must reveal something to Blake, but not what. And this is where Jennings comes in. For not only did Jennings treat Candy during his illness, he also has a written record of Candy's incoherent utterances in his delirium, and a means to decode them. Jennings, in fact, is a regular scientist and scholar. In his isolation he has taken solace in science, and is writing 'a book on the intricate and delicate subject of the brain and the nervous system'

---

[6] Compare the gender discussion in Elliotson 1835: 707–14.

(p. 369). The existence of a general theory is clearly implied here, but we are only introduced to the relevant part of it, which suggests that in cases of delirium the loss of the speaking faculty does not necessarily imply the loss of the higher faculty of thinking. In short, Jennings has recorded the broken fragments of Candy's delirious discourse during the intensive phase of his illness and, on the basis of the theory, other studies of typical speech collocations, and his own creative intuition, has reconstructed the full intentional text of the statement (pp. 369–70, 381ff.). I am not the first to point out how strikingly analogous this procedure is to Freud's much later procedure for unravelling the latent text of dream discourse from the chaos of its manifest text. Be that as it may, Jennings's reconstruction suggests that Blake mocked the medical profession once too often during the night of the dinner. Having complained of sleeplessness yet sceptically rejected Candy's offer of treatment, he has in fact been treated by Candy against his will with an excessively large dose of laudanum (opium, that is) put in a glass when his attention was elsewhere, in order later, triumphantly, to demonstrate the power of scientific medicine (pp. 382–83). The opium, true to its established effect as both stimulant and sedative, would have stimulated his anxiety to preserve the jewel from theft, so that he was impelled in sleep to remove it from Miss Verinder's cabinet, but then, as the sedative effect set in, overpowered him and removed all trace of memory from his conscious mind (pp. 386–87). Later, even more sensationally, Jennings conducts an experiment on Blake to demonstrate the plausibility of this hypothesis: he reproduces as exactly as possible the internal and external circumstances of that night, administers the laudanum, and lo and behold, as the opium acts to revive the repressed memory traces, Franklin Blake repeats the sleepwalk one year after the fact in almost every detail.

Jennings, then, is a brilliant solver of the riddle. But not just this. It is in fact he, more than the three Brahmin seekers after the diamond, who emerges as the chief agent of the text's engagement with the Orientalist tradition. In him Collins evidently seeks under the figure of miscegenation to portray (perhaps in Bhabha's [1994] sense) a genuinely hybrid figure. Even his remarkable male-female androgynous constitution seems to be a part of this intended mediating role. In Orientalist discourse, we know, colonized cultures are portrayed stereotypically as feminine, sensual, childike, poetic (see for example Zantop 1997: 5, 50–51, 66), and colonizers conversely as masculine, intellectual, adult, scientific. *The Moonstone* itself cites the dominant metaphor of this discourse when the academic Orientalist Murthwaite announces his intention of returning to the scene of his Indian exploits and of 'penetrating into regions left still unexplored' (p. 282). There is certainly a tradition of emphasizing Gypsy femininity or androgyny in

Occidental discourse.[7] Jennings, evidently, unites in his remarkable person many of these stereotypical features – as we might say, the *dispositif* or discursive formation regulating the representation of Gypsies as Other in the West. In particular, as his brilliant resolution of the riddle of the theft suggests, Jennings incarnates both the Western tradition of analytical scientific knowledge and the Gypsy tradition of privileged intuition, ranging as it does from palmistry to soothsaying. Jennings, quite apart from his knowledge of mind-expanding drugs, is able both as Western scientist to formulate a theory of the relation between the various faculties of the mind, and as a Gypsy mind-reader to apply frankly poetic intuition, imagination or divination to the solution of the problem. The authorial suggestion is, no doubt, that *only* such a synthesis of powers is capable of resolving the cultural conflict originally occasioned by the imperialist crime. In this sense, then, the figure of Jennings cuts across the two competing Occidental and Oriental narratives of this text, and Jennings's person – the Gypsy who dwells in the West and (unlike the Indians) incorporates Western culture in his being – evidently represents a utopia or a redemptive figure. He unites East and West, man and woman, art and science, conscious and unconscious, and of course in this capacity reunites the lovers separated by imperialist crime.

This suggests where *The Moonstone* and in particular the figure of Jennings thus interpreted might fit into the history of Gypsy discourse in nineteenth-century English literature. Jennings is clearly a figure who transcends the stereotype of the Heathcliffe figure – the Gypsy from Liverpool who disrupts another Yorkshire idyll in Emily Brontë's *Wuthering Heights*. Is it too much to speculate that George Borrow, whom Willems (1997: 93–170, 171–96) sees as the founding father of disadvantaging discourse on the Gypsies, might be an implicit target as well? The mediating term here is *Robinson Crusoe*. We have seen to what extent that book figures in Collins's subversion of Orientalist discourse. It also features – centrally – in Borrow's *Lavengro* (1851), the foundational text of Gypsy discourse, and the use of the motif of this book provides a telling contrast with Collins. There is a striking scene in Borrow which relates the first encounter between the original scholar Gypsy as a boy and his very first Gypsies, Jasper Petulengro's family. *Robinson Crusoe*, the colonialist Bible, is, we learn, the book that has turned the narrator Borrow into a scholar. It is indeed

> a book which has exerted over the minds of Englishmen an influence certainly greater than any other of modern times, which has been in most people's

---

[7] See Saul 1998 and Breger 1998: 16–30 and passim; also, in the same volume, Otto Pankok's *Raklo im Frühling* (Plate 18).

hands, and with the contents of which even those who cannot read are to a certain extent acquainted; a book from which the most luxuriant and fertile of our modern prose writers have drunk inspiration; a book, moreover, to which, from the hardy deeds which it narrates, and the spirit of strange and romantic enterprise which it tends to awaken, England owes many of her astonishing discoveries both by sea and land, and no inconsiderable part of her naval glory [...] the wondrous volume was my only study and principal source of amusement [...] And it was in this manner that I first took to the paths of knowledge. (Borrow 1982 [1851]: 20)

In the episode in question Borrow has intimidated the initially aggressive Gypsies with the (in fact tame and toothless) viper in his bosom. But he then soothes their savage breast when, like Gabriel Betteredge, he takes out the great colonial narrative, opens it at random, and proceeds to read 'how a certain man [Crusoe], whilst wandering about a certain solitary island, entered a cave, the mouth of which was overgrown with brushwood, and how he was nearly frightened to death by something which he saw'.[8] The episode relates to the perennial theme of self-reliance. Crusoe sees two eyes glinting at him in the darkness and starts back, only to discover that they belong to a dying old he-goat – from which he draws the conclusion that fear lies in himself, not in the world. In *Lavengro* the Gypsies are mightily impressed with this, and praise the book as the best of prayers (p. 37). It is a prime example of the power of the colonial text, as the Robinsonian colonial scholar tames his objects of knowledge. *The Moonstone*'s Robinsonian counterpart, Betteredge, also confronts (at least half) a Gypsy with his secular Bible (pp. 403ff.). Betteredge is convinced that Gypsy-dark Jennings has designs on Miss Verinder's virtue, and resists the planned opium experiment with all the power at his command. This of course includes *Robinson Crusoe*. He too cites a random passage from *Crusoe* (this time p. 178), to the effect that they should heed the warning voice of an inner moral dictate, and abandon the experiment. Expecting Jennings to crumble at this awful warning from the ultimate textual authority, Betteredge is bitterly disappointed. Jennings of course sees nothing in this but 'coincidence' (p. 404) from a children's book, and the Englishman retires crushed. The utopian figure is proof against *Crusoe*'s discursive power, and conducts his experiment, we know, successfully. Read thus, *The Moonstone* is a subtle attack on Orientalist Gypsy discourse.

Yet utopias were never meant to be realized, and Jennings is of course consistently presented by Collins as a doomed, if not tragic figure. Jennings is an outcast wanderer – yet another basic feature of the Gypsy stereotype. Despite his 'inscrutable appeal' to Blake's sympathy (p. 364),

---

[8] Borrow 1982 [1851]: 36–37; compare Defoe 1979 [1719]: 183–84.

Jennings always makes 'an unfavourable impression' (p. 364) and is 'unpopular everywhere' (p. 364). Quite apart from the fact that his mere appearance inspires instant social exclusion, he has from the outset of his professional career in England also been dogged by an unexplained slander and the resultant scandal. Forced to leave one post after another and to abandon the woman he loves (p. 374), always the accusation that is 'death to his character' (p. 374) follows him and finds him out, so that he only ever finds repose with Candy, the man with no memory. His love of wild flowers is obviously derived from this nomadic existence (pp. 366, 374, 410). Even his hybrid physical constitution seems to be fundamentally suspect, and he is of course fatally ill (p. 375). All this, then, has perverted his ideal humanity into outward misanthropy. While he brings the cultures together, then, in his person and in his work, Jennings also represents a doomed Romantic synthesis. And this ambivalence is also typified by the symbol of opium. The drug of Eastern provenance both causes and cures Blake's problem.

One of the major motifs of the novel, the silencing of forbidden voices, perhaps best symbolizes Jennings's status as doomed utopian hybrid. Strikingly, the male detective's solution of the riddle of the jewel is more often than not won as a victory over woman's silence. The most notable of these silences is that of Rachel Verinder herself. She intervenes in the action of the novel most significantly by remaining silent. For she has all along been the sole witness of the actual theft, known the identity of the thief and, in an attempt to protect her beloved, remained silent. When she does speak, she is compelled to do so through the forceful interrogation by the male investigator Blake. Even then her information is invalidated by the repressive diagnosis of hysteria (pp. 341–42, 349–50). Only when Jennings provides his explanation is the woman's voice validated, and even then only by a figure who transcends the gender divide. The same is true of Rosanna Spearman, the disfigured servant girl who transgressively loves Blake too. In possession of damning evidence of Blake's guilt (a paint-stained nightgown), she buries the evidence and a long explanatory letter in the 'broad brown face' (p. 35) of the quivering quicksand known as the Shivering Sands, in which she also perishes. From this emblematic image of female sexuality her evidence is extracted with considerable fear and disgust by Blake. The male-female, Gypsy-*gadjo* Jennings also preserves a silence. He has of course written his book and kept an extensive diary of his life and thoughts. Yet he too insists that his only happiness lies in the hope of 'complete oblivion of the past' (p. 366), and determines: 'My story will die with me' (p. 373). Both the book and his diary are lowered into his unmarked grave (pp. 455–56). Unlike the knowledge contained in *Robinson Crusoe* or indeed the never-fading writing of the Indian curse, and indeed unlike the truth locked up in the language of Rachel and

Rosanna Spearman, the privileged and redemptive body of knowledge stored in Jennings's book on the brain and the nervous system will perhaps never be retrieved, especially since only Dr Candy, the man who cannot speak his memory, knows where the grave is. The only part of Jennings' writings that ever reaches the public is the extract from his diary which he specifically sends to Blake and which is incorporated in the novel *The Moonstone* (pp. 392–425). In this willed burial of cultural self-expression, Jennings's function as emblem of the Romany fate is perhaps most poignantly expressed. Read thus, *The Moonstone* is Collins's monument to the lost transgressive discourse[9] that might mediate between Gypsy and *gadjo*, and in this it also circumscribes the limits of European self-understanding (see Breger 1988: 7–8).

References

Bhabha, Homi. 1994. *The Location of Culture*. London and New York: Routledge.

Borrow, George. 1982 [1851]. *Lavengro: The Scholar – the Gypsy – the Priest*. Oxford and New York: Oxford University Press.

Breger, Claudia. 1998. *Ortlosigkeit des Fremden: 'Zigeunerinnen' und 'Zigeuner' in der deutschsprachigen Literatur um 1800*. Cologne: Böhlau.

Collins, Wilkie. 1994 [1868]. *The Moonstone*. Harmondsworth: Penguin.

Defoe, Daniel. 1979 [1719]. *The Life and Adventures of Robinson Crusoe*. Ed. Angus Ross. Harmondsworth: Penguin.

Duncan, Ian. 1994. '*The Moonstone*, the Victorian Novel, and Imperialist Panic', *Modern Language Quarterly*, 55: 297–319.

Eliot, T.S. 1950. 'Wilkie Collins and Dickens', in *T.S. Eliot: Selected Essays*. New York: Harcourt, Brace, 2nd edn (1st edn 1927).

Elliotson, John R. 1835. *Human Physiology*. London: Longman, Rees.

Heller, Tamar. 1998. 'Blank Spaces: Ideological Fictions and the Detective Work of *The Moonstone*', in Pykett (ed.) 1998: 244–70.

Hutter, A.D. 1998. 'Dreams, Transformations and Literature: The Implications of Detective Fiction', in Pykett (ed.) 1998: 175–96.

Lonoff, Sue. 1982. *Wilkie Collins and his Victorian Readers: A Study in the Rhetoric of Authorship*. New York: AMS.

Petsch, Robert. 1911–12. 'Fifty Welsh Gypsy Riddles. Edited with Notes and Introduction (from the Text of Dr. John Sampson)', *JGLS*, New Series, 5: 241–55.

Pykett, Lyn (ed.). 1998. *Wilkie Collins*. New York: St Martin's Press.

Reed, John R. 1973. 'English Imperialism and the Unacknowledged Crime of *The Moonstone*', *Clio*, 2: 281–90.

---

[9] 'Lavengro' of course means 'word master' in Romany (see Borrow 1982 [1851]: 115).

Roy, Ashish. 1993. 'The Fabulous Imperialist Semiotic of Wilkie Collins's *The Moonstone*', *New Literary History*, 24: 657–81.

Saul, Nicholas. 1998. 'Leiche und Humor: Clemens Brentanos Schauspielfragment *Zigeunerin* und der Patriotismus um 1813', *Jahrbuch des Freien Deutschen Hochstifts*: 111–66.

Taylor, Jenny Bourne. 1988. *In the Secret Theatre of Home: Wilkie Collins, Sensation Narrative, and Nineteenth-Century Psychology*. London and New York. Routledge.

Thomas, Ronald R. 1991. 'Minding the Body Politic: The Romance of Science and the Revision of History in Victorian Detective Fiction', *Victorian Literature and Culture*, 19: 233–35.

Willems, Wim. 1997. *In Search of the True Gypsy: From Enlightenment to Final Solution*. London: Frank Cass.

Zantop, Susanne. 1997. *Colonial Fantasies: Conquest, Family and Nation in Precolonial Germany, 1770–1870*. Durham, NC: Duke University Press.

Understanding the 'Other'?
Communication, History and Narration in Margriet de Moor's *Hertog van Egypte* (1996)

Claudia Breger

The representation of so-called 'Gypsies' (the term used to refer to Roma, the German Sinti and different travelling groups) in modern European literatures and cultures reads as a somewhat monolithic story: even more than in the case of other 'minority' groups, a hegemonic discourse seems to persist almost unchallenged by alternative voices or historical changes throughout the centuries. The exclusion of Roma and Sinti from the dominant culture's institutions of education has prevented the emergence of an extensive body of self-representations, and the enormous quantity of 'Gypsy' texts by non-'Gypsy' authors attests not least to the degree to which racial stereotypes are unaffected by differences in genre, political stance or historical change. This does not mean that the representation of 'Gypsies' is ahistorical: in the decades before and after 1800, the dominant early modern approach to 'Gypsies' – based on the ascription of social deviance – was replaced by an anthropological *dispositif* (Foucault), i.e. a set of discourses, policies and institutions gathered around the idea of ethnic and, eventually, racial identity. This modern perception, however, was informed by traditional anti-'Gypsy' discourse: the putative 'anti-social' vagabonds turned into a 'nomad race unfit for civilization'.[1] It was in this guise that the imaginary figure of the 'Gypsy' was handed down through the twentieth century. In Germany, the racist concept of the 'uncivilized', 'anti-social' nomadic people (on which Nazi ideology drew) resurfaced in the anti-foreigner campaigns of the 1990s focused on the icon of the Gypsy as the quintessential stranger.[2]

Even contemporary literature that attempts to treat the history of persecution and genocide critically seems to be overpowered by the force of this hegemonic discourse: thus, in her book *Der weibliche Name des*

---

[1] For a more in-depth account of the genealogy of this modern perception, see Breger 1998.
[2] For example, the Roma are described as that group of immigrants that is most difficult to integrate – because of a mode of behaviour that 'seems partially archaic' (from an article in *Der Spiegel*, 37 [1992]: 31).

Widerstands: Sieben Berichte (Woman's Face of Resistance: Seven Reports) (1980), Marie-Thérèse Kerschbaumer treats 'the Gypsy woman' differently from all other (individualized) protagonists, having the narrator reflect on her inability to get over her own prejudice and her stereotypical view of 'the Gypsy woman'. Struggling with the 'given' traits of the represented 'Gypsy', these texts show the force of the dominant anthropological discourse which constructs 'the Gypsy' as an eternal other to civilization and modernity. This discursive frame of 'essential otherness' is not necessarily challenged by good intentions or personal experience: from George Borrow's nineteenth-century writings to Isabel Fonseca's *Bury Me Standing* (1996), ethnographic literature claiming to sympathize with and 'understand' the 'Gypsies' has reiterated dominant tropes and concepts.

While the discourse on 'Gypsies' constitutes a particularly striking case in point, the problem of representing 'otherness' is, of course, a more general one. For several decades now, it has been the subject of critical debates within anthropology (see Berg and Fuchs [eds] 1993). With the growing awareness of the social contingency of knowledge, the anthropologist's claim to 'understand the Other' has begun to be challenged in many ways. Even more recently, highly sophisticated hermeneutic approaches such as Clifford Geertz's concept of 'thick description' (Geertz 1993) have been criticized for perpetuating the dominant asymmetrical structures of representation.[3] With this questioning of the claim to understand and speak for 'the other', anthropologists seem to be facing two methodological alternatives. On the one hand, the conceptualization of dialogic models (see Berg and Fuchs [eds] 1993: 23, 77–82) reflects the attempt to acknowledge the agency of the represented 'other' and, more generally, the demand for the self-representation of subaltern and marginalized subjects. On the other hand, the 'postmodern' answer to the problematic of representation radicalizes the analysis of discourse and rhetoric by abandoning the search for 'realities behind the words' altogether.

On closer investigation, however, these two competing approaches turn out to be deficient without each other. While self-representation is obviously of crucial political importance as both a prerequisite and a

---

[3] With his notion of 'culture as text' Clifford Geertz not only replaces the problematic foundation of hermeneutics in 'empathy' by a process of interpreting sign systems, but also reflects the problematic of representation. While Geertz stresses the constructed, always 'fictional' (i.e. fabricated) character of ethnographic literature, however, he also reinstates the anthropological claim to look from the perspective of 'the other'. His methodological image according to which the anthropologist looks over the shoulder of the 'native' reveals the asymmetrical relationship that underlies this revised hermeneutical concept, once more objectifying the 'other' rather than allowing him or her to speak as a subject (see Berg and Fuchs [eds] 1993: 43–69).

medium for political, social and symbolic change, self-representation does not constitute a way out of the problem of representation. Recent theoretical discussions, especially within the fields of postcolonial and gender studies, have challenged the idea of authenticity in minority discourse, analysed its rhetorical constitution, and conceptualized the complex implications of hegemonic and marginal discourse (see e.g. Bhabha 1994, Butler 1997). To conclude, however, that positionality – i.e. the 'set of specific social and discursive relations' in which the embodied agency of the subject is constituted at a given moment (Adelson 1993: 64) – does not make a difference, or that biographical experience is simply 'fictional' in the world of discourse, is obviously unacceptable in political terms – and uncouth on the level of theory. Discourse shapes realities, and in this process of shaping, 'performative' and 'referential' modes of speech overlap in complex, often inseparable ways. Nonetheless, we need to engage in the work of evaluating individual texts in terms of their strategies of engaging with discourse and experience, making political, and theoretical, distinctions in the process of reading.

The challenge of re-reading – and rewriting – the dominant discourse on 'Gypsies' consists, I believe, in the methodological effort to negotiate questions of positionality and rhetoricity. In order to displace the hegemonic forms of representation, we might have to read stories about 'Gypsies' – by both *'gadjos'* and Roma or Sinti – in terms of their discursive constitution as well as with regard to the (fictional and/or historical) lives of their protagonists, narrators and authors.

Margriet de Moor's novel *Hertog van Egypte* (first published in 1996) is a fascinating attempt to intervene critically in the process of representing 'Gypsies' by negotiating questions of history and textuality. The novel tells the stories – and histories – of a Dutch horse-dealer whose father is a Rom and mother a Sintizza (2001: 176). The (hi)stories revolve around his love for a red-haired Dutch peasant, his family and his people in the twentieth and earlier centuries. In her writing, de Moor (herself a Dutch 'non-Gypsy' born in 1941) engages stereotypical ethnographic tropes of writing about Roma and other people called 'Gypsies' or *Zigeuner*, but she does so with what could be called a 'critical difference'. I am deliberately phrasing this with some grammatical reservation, since I shall argue that de Moor's attempt to rewrite ethnographic discourse fails to a qualified extent: judging from the reviews of her book in Germany, *Hertog van Egypte* is not unlikely to be read as reiterating stereotypes in hurtful and dangerous ways (see e.g. Schneider 1997, Anon. 1997). And what is the meaning of 'critical difference' if it should turn out to signify 'difference perceived by a critic informed by postcolonial theory'? While, however, the actual political impact of de Moor's novel may be (at least) ambivalent, I do believe that her literary

experiment deserves a closer look. If the project of challenging hegemonic discourse requires that we explore strategies of rewriting – and
also re-reading – stereotypes, it does make sense to look at the subtle
differences engendered by de Moor's narrative, and narratological,
negotiation of histories.

One day in September 1963, Joseph Plato stops at Lucie's stud-farm
because his car has broken down, and starts talking to the woman about
a sick mare that is causing her concern. They fall in love with each other,
get married and have children. Every spring, Joseph leaves in order to
travel during the summer, but he always returns in September to stay for
the winter, bringing home stories for the winter nights. Lucie accepts
this arrangement until, one year, when on his way back home, Joseph is
seduced by a blonde neighbour, Christina Cruyse. Christina, a long-
standing enemy of Lucie since their childhood, lures Joseph to her house
by asking him for advice about her sick Appaloosa mare. The next
morning, Christina calls Lucie (who has yearned to find such a mare for
a long time) and offers to let her see the horse – thus ensuring that she
finds her husband asleep in Christina's bed. Now, things have got out of
order (de Moor 2001: 42). The following summer, Joseph stays at home
(for unknown reasons), and, somewhat paradoxically, Gerard, Lucie's
father, begins to develop anti-'Gypsy' feelings against his hitherto well-
liked son-in-law – who is finally behaving 'like a model husband' (p. 32).
Joseph falls ill, is diagnosed as suffering from cancer, and dies in the
course of the following winter.

Rather than being linked by causal connections or other explicit
explanatory devices, the events and images in de Moor's novel are associated by way of narrative contiguity – and they are thus associated in
rather disturbing ways. Through its emplotment, the story of love is
encoded as a story of race and miscegenation. The sick mare is a cross
between a heavy, warm-blooded Gelderland mare and an Anglo-Arab
thoroughbred (p. 70), and the Appaloosa that Christina exploits in order
to disillusion Lucie belongs to a racy breed descended from 'Spanish
ancestors with Moorish blood' (p. 38). How are we to read the rhetoric
of race that associates these 'hybrids' both with the intercultural sexual
relationship and with the object of the women's desire, Joseph himself?[4]

In his study *Colonial Desire* Robert Young has analysed the crucial
function of metaphors and concepts of hybridity in nineteenth- and
twentieth-century racist discourse. By engaging the imagery of horse-
breeding, de Moor takes up this discourse. Contrary to the dominant
negative treatment of hybridity within racial theories, but in accordance

---

[4] While the narrator *parallels* the two objects – or 'mysteries' – when focalizing Lucie (p. 172),
the 'Gypsy' and the Appaloosa mare start to merge into each other from Christina's point of
view (p. 192).

with a less common argumentation in favour of 'racial amalgamation' (see Young 1995: 142ff.), de Moor's narrator comments on the probable positive effects of miscegenation (p. 187). This, however, clearly refers to horses, not to humans. Repeatedly, the text problematizes the metonymic displacement of the metaphors of race that it evokes. For example, the narrator uses the word 'species' for 'Gypsies' as a cynical comment on the disciplinary measures of the Dutch government, thus exposing the use of the word as inadequate (p. 42). In the scene preceding this commentary, the narrator supplements her description of the 'Gypsy' (p. 41) by having him say 'Crossbreeding will always need new blood', and afterwards qualifies this statement by explaining that he has just returned from a discussion of the association of the Dutch royal warm-blooded horse (p. 41). With its alternating connection and separation of humans and animals in the discourse of race, the text can be read as criticizing the rhetoric it evokes, commenting on its presence in racist discourse. When Lucie is presented with a Gitane, i.e. a cigarette named after 'exotic' Spanish 'Gypsies', in the corner of her mouth, and filled with nothing but 'inexpressible longing' for, as it seems, an Appaloosa horse (p. 170), we may imagine the narrator blinking her eyes, ironically exposing other people's stereotypes by this recourse to their commercial reproductions. We might, however, also suspect the narrator of uncritically *sharing* the stereotypical associations she evokes – particularly when we consider that not just the discourse of and on the characters, but also the plot of our love story, is constructed from the analogy of 'racy' 'Gypsies' and horses.

At this point we can briefly introduce the narrator, who, as one irritated critic complained (see Schneider 1997), lacks clear contours. Almost constantly reminding us of her presence, this narrator intrigues the reader by keeping in suspense both her relationship with the characters, especially Lucie, and her mode of existence. While she introduces herself as someone of Lucie's age who was born in the same village and sat on the same school bench, she (my gender assignment results from this proximity to the female protagonist) stresses her intellectual superiority to the rather slower Lucie, who had trouble keeping up at school (pp. 40, 4). Sometimes the narrator is apparently a different person (p. 104), but in other situations (pp. 24, 225–26) we are tempted to interpret her as a part of Lucie herself, as the voice of reflection and intellect – almost like the Freudian ego as compared to the id. And while she often establishes her physical presence by commenting on her spatial self-positioning as it conditions her perception of the narrated events (pp. 18, 116), she does not always seem to be subject to the conventional rules of human embodiment and perception (see e.g. p. 23). With her 'reproducing eyes' (p. 45) and her alternating distance from or proximity to the protagonists, the narrator sometimes functions like a camera (p. 220).

As an agent of perception and speech, this narrator functions, in any case, as the medium of both an obsessive thematization of narrative perspective and extensive experimentation with this perspective. Thus, her constant renegotiation of positionality enables her to expose – and comment on – the workings of 'Gypsy'-discourse. Sometimes, she mimics dominant anti-'Gypsy' rhetoric and ironically displaces it through its recontextualization (pp. 42, 91). She also comments on the genealogy of the notion of *Zigeuner* – a term that she avoids using most of the time – in the context of racist speech and persecution (pp. 16, 91). At the same time, this narrator is not completely flexible, but rather acts from a specific point of view: whatever her exact relationship with Lucie may be, she is definitely as 'Gadjo' as this character (see e.g. p. 24). More than once, she comments on the limits of her ability to understand 'those', i.e. Joseph's 'people' (p. 22; see also pp. 5, 11, 21), who seem from her perspective to inhabit a realm of otherness. Since she constantly reminds us that this perspective is 'personal' (p. 86), and conditioned not least by her ethnic positionality, readers who are familiar with the issues surrounding the representation of Roma and Sinti will feel invited to show some reservation with regard to her account of the histories she relates.

The narrator's staging of Joseph is also somewhat suspicious. First of all, in the tradition of ethnographic othering, he seems to function as a representative, a metonym of his entire people. The title of the book pre-emptively suggests this link. After his death, Joseph returns as some kind of spectre, talking to Lucie and telling her another of his many stories. At the very end of the book, he assumes the title role of the *Hertog van Egypte*, a duke whose name is Joseph Andrías, and who is the leader of a group of so-called Egyptians who arrived in the Netherlands in 1422 (at a time when, as the reader may know, the chronicles of many European cities report the first appearance of these travellers). Joseph's ghost tells this story in the first person, and thus the novel ends with a fiction of ethnic identity: an image of inter-generational continuity in the name and figure of Joseph, the Egyptian. Of course, this figure of 'Joseph the Egyptian' functions only ambivalently as an image of 'Gypsy' identity: intertextually, it is primarily associated with Jewish identity,[5] and, furthermore, with stories of ethnic mimicry (see e.g. Thomas Mann's Joseph novels) and cross-ethnic movement (e.g. with Sigmund Freud[6]) rather than clear-cut ethnic identity. Furthermore, the reader knows that this identity is just a fiction, an effect of a spectre's narration (see pp.

---

[5] The history of the discursive association – and dissociation – of 'Gypsies' and Jews is not yet written. In Breger 1998 I comment on some nineteenth-century configurations.

[6] In his *Moses and Monotheism* Freud of course postulates that Moses, the founder of the Jewish nation, was originally an Egyptian.

235–36). Nonetheless, its performative enactment can produce the effect of verisimilitude: the reader may perceive Joseph's narration as proof of his belonging to an ethnic group that has remained fundamentally the same for the last 500 years. As suggested above, the reviews of de Moor's novel suggest that at least some of its recipients have, indeed, read the text as confirming their projections about Gypsy identity rather than questioning this identity's genealogy. Keeping these effects in mind, we will have to look more closely at the narrator's staging of Joseph. How does she constitute his identity? What haunts him, and how does he haunt us in de Moor's narration?

With his eyes of a 'drifter', his golden watch, his 'expansive' gestures (pp. 3–4), his habit of talking noisily on the telephone (p. 10), and his 'special', theatrical way of telling stories (p. 8), Joseph is constructed by the narrator as an image of visible difference – seemingly lacking the moderate mentality constitutive of the self-presentation of modern, civilized, 'Aryan' Europeans. Or at least this is a conclusion that anthropologists have offered from similar descriptions. While de Moor's narrator, however, evokes stereotypical topoi familiar from ethnographic literature in her presentation of Joseph and his people,[7] she displaces the 'grand narratives' that accompany them in the dominant discourse. Although her 'Egyptians' are clearly ethnically different from all other Dutch, they are no 'Oriental strangers', but Europeans. Ending with the story of their arrival in the Netherlands, the novel limits its historical excursions into the 'Gypsy' past to their European travel routes, which turn out to function as the 'foundations' of their identity: Joseph's people are 'Europe' itself (p. 52), constituted by the 'co-ordinates of the whole of Europe', which 'run right through them' (p. 11) as a result of their travelling.

This spatial description of identity – or rather of *non*-identity – seems to draw on postmodern notions of difference from hegemonic forms of identification. As sketched by de Moor's narrator, 'Gypsies' are no stable, homogeneous ethnic entity, but rather 'nomadic subjects', as described by Rosi Braidotti: 'The nomad's identity is a map of where s/he has already been.' (1994: 14). While Braidotti develops her concept of the nomad as a 'theoretical figuration for contemporary subjectivity' (1994: 1) in general, she also associates her nomadic subjects with 'Gypsies', whose 'nomad identity' she does not question in terms of its discursive constitution (see 1994: 27). With this metaphoric reiteration of hegemonic images of otherness, her postmodern discourse risks affirming rather than analysing stereotypes. The same can be said for de Moor's novel: it is the so-called Egyptians – and not the Dutch 'gadjo'

---

[7] Stereotypical traits ascribed to de Moor's 'Gypsies' in accordance with ethnographic literature also include their 'bare feet' (p. 11), their boundless love of children (p. 105) and the description of their rituals of death and funerals (p. 22). For the standard ethnographical account of these issues see Grellmann 1783.

farmers – whose identity is described as being constituted through nomadic movement. 'Those people' – as de Moor's narrator calls the 'Egyptians', both exposing and repeating the operation of othering an anonymous (albeit seemingly familiar) entity (de Moor 2001: 22) – 'those people' who represent Europe 'in a moving form' (p. 52) seem to function as a reservoir of difference in an emphatic sense.[8] Informed by postmodern concepts of difference, de Moor's 'nomadic subjects' thus revitalize topoi familiar from the representation of 'Gypsies' in modern European literature – outside, however, their modern emplotment into theories of racial essence.

The narrator's reluctance to name the group[9] also seems to point to her knowledge about the heterogeneity and historicity of their 'identity', which is homogenized only by those who call them 'Gypsies'. When asked for his origin, Joseph, in the role of his ancestor, the Duke of Egypt, replies: 'What is a people, a race? Our descent is manifold; to mention a single country of origin is misleading' (p. 238), and begins to enumerate some of the stories that have been told with regard to the origin of the 'Gypsies' – among them the theory of their Indian descent, which was to become the scientific solution of their so-called 'mystery' in modernity. 'Origin' is a collection of stories – the retroactively installed, fluid and heterogeneous effect of intertextual negotiations.

This textualization of ethnic identity, however, does not imply that Gypsy history might be unreal – or 'merely' literary – in de Moor's novel. As stated above, her text combines strategies of deconstructive intervention into hegemonic discourse with the attempt to account for historical experience and positionality. The stories told in the novel recount histories, and histories are transformed into stories which serve as roadmarkings (p. 5). 'These people' are not 'afraid of space', but unlike the 'uncivilized races' described by anthropologists, they are familiar with 'time' – and thus history – as well (p. 53). 'Nomad identity', with de Moor, is also an effect of historical experience: the narrator ascribes Joseph's restlessness to his memories of expulsion, his being 'dumped across the border immediately after [...] birth, [...] in 1936' (p. 5). The space of identity is historical space,[10] a site of the accumulation, conflict, and negotiation of histories – histories of Joseph's life

---

[8] Thus, they do not fix their (hi)stories in the linear shape of the written text (22, 53, 167). In this context it is also significant that Joseph is feminized through the images associated with him (the mare, and also Scheherezade, who tells stories at the court of the Sultan, i.e. Lucie [p. 104]). This metaphor is one of the few clearly Orientalist images of the novel.

[9] They are not only described as 'those people', but also characterized by descriptions such as 'types with droopy moustaches and romantic eyes' (de Moor 2001: 11–12).

[10] See also de Moor 2001: 53–54. From Lucie's perspective, however, Joseph's wandering during the summer is also associated with 'tradition' (p. 46): historicizing and culturalist arguments coexist in the novel.

and the lives of his family, his ancestors and relatives, their friends and enemies. These are histories of harassment and forced integration, criminalization (see e.g. p. 29), persecution – and genocide: lifetimes of being troubled by 'people in various uniforms for papers, for passport photographs, for fingerprints, for stamps and numbers, including that one searing number that had been stamped on his arm forever' (p. 15). This refers to a cousin of Joseph's father. Joseph was not in Auschwitz; he was saved because an absent-minded police officer nodded when his cousin Paulko asked to leave the train with the child in order to 'buy some cigarettes' (pp. 57–58). De Moor's novel stages both the inescapability of persecution and the improbable spaces of survival, both the lasting persecution of 'Gypsies' throughout the centuries, and the Nazi terror and genocide during the Second World War – making it visible as just another history of persecution yet also, simultaneously, as something completely different: the other of history, emptiness (p. 54).

These histories can only be told as a narrative. Not all experience, however, can be rendered as a story. 'At the edge of the wood' – at the site, in other words, where the literary cliché locates the 'Gypsies' and where de Moor's novel applies its historicizing moves – 'there are a number of men and women who have no words for certain images. Decades ago they went in through their eyes […]. Such things leave gaps in a story, empty spaces that on the contrary in the reality of the time, began with such unambiguous place names: Bialá Podlaska, Częstochowa, Warsaw, Łodz, Belgrade, Hamburg, Munich, The Hague' (p. 54). Traumatic experience is characterized by feelings of rupture and disconnection, emptiness, and the loss of narration (see Laub and Podell 1998). For the survivors, their experiences in the concentration camps are not part of but rather the 'other' of their biographies (see de Moor 2001: 179). De Moor's novel engages with this problem of representation. Suggesting on the one hand that, if this experience can be captured at all, it might only be possible in the interstices of narrative (see Laub and Podell 1998 for a similar argument), the novel on the other hand also attempts to 'give voice' to experiences of persecution and genocide. Exploring different narrative strategies and artifices, de Moor strives to construct testimony, to remember the biographies of the survivors who struggle with the narration of their experiences, as well as of those who died or who, like Joseph's father, simply disappeared – but probably died too.

This attempt to 'give voice' to the silenced, however (*prosopopoeia* in the language of rhetoric), takes place in the field of representation. In his *Writing and Rewriting the Holocaust* (1998) James E. Young insists on the rhetorical constitution of Holocaust testimonies in general – analysing, in particular, the political functions of the rhetoric of authenticity (1998: 91ff.). As Young points out, the 'authentic voice' is always enacted; its

discourse is necessarily mediated by metaphoric, metonymic displacements, and its actuality cannot be located in an immediate relationship
to historical reality. One of de Moor's strategies for representing the
experience of genocide is her recourse to the memoir of Jaap Hemelrijk,
a survivor of Buchenwald. She has been criticized for not explicitly
marking the citations from his manuscript. Leaving aside the issue of
plagiarism,[11] this rejection of authorization could be read as a rejection
of the rhetoric of historical authenticity criticized by Young: de Moor's
novel does not claim the authority of the witness, but rather reflects the
necessarily re-presented character of testimony.

A narrative tool to mark this mediation – the rhetorical foundation of
the narrator's attempt to remember the histories of those who were
silenced and killed – is the use of the spectre. As Derrida has argued in
Marx' Gespenster (Spectres of Marx) (1996), the thinking of this figure
between absence and presence or death and life creates logical space for
a politics of memory which takes responsibility for those murdered and
forgotten (1996: 11). Joseph appears as a spectre even before his death
and his return as/with the voice of his ancestor: when Gerard, Lucie's
father, first meets him, he confuses his daughter's lover with the memory
of an old friend (de Moor 2001: 74). Just as in the scene discussed above,
this spectral appearance is threatened by incorporation into the (racist)
logic of identity: 'That lot are easily mixed up, aren't they?' (p. 88), the
narrator comments somewhat cynically. Collecting circumstantial evidence in the course of the novel, however, the reader finds a different
explanation for Gerard's confusion: his old friend was Joseph's father. By
making this connection, we can use Gerard's memory to supplement the
missing testimony of the disappeared Romanies, and thus, at least ten-
tatively, fill one of the gaps in Joseph's family history: both men were part
of a cell of resistance that was eventually destroyed by betrayal. On the
night of their deportation, Gerard and his Rom friend were in the same
situation (p. 30). Gerard, however, returned, but Jannosch Franz never
came back.

It is this difference that haunts Gerard (pp. 88–89) – and will eventually condition his turning against Joseph. When first meeting him,
though, he engages in a conversation with the spectre he sees, asking it
to tell its story. In this way, he compensates for the missing testimony
with his own fantasy. With some intertextual support from Jaap
Hemelrijk, the fictional survivor imagines his – probably dead – friend
as the impossible author of his own testimony from Sachsenhausen. The
impossibility of this 'ghostly agency' – and thus the merely substitute
function of the given representation – is staged in the narrator's split

---

[11] In an article in the *Algemene Dagblad*, de Moor was accused of plagiarism. She argued that
Hemelrijk's son gave the memoir to her, and allowed her to use it (see W.S. 1998).

position: 'I didn't even notice myself that I began shuffling about and talking in a whine [...] Damn it, Gerard, I died' (pp. 82–83). Thus reminded of its representative status, we can question the account: Gerard's fantasy is too conciliatory to be credible. He imagines his friend tragically to have died after the liberation of the camp, listening to the music of trumpets. Gerard's attempt to remember his dead friend is insufficient; it is governed by the guilt that the survivor feels. His 'dialogue' with the fantasized spectre is no dialogue between equal partners: when Gerard starts complaining about how hard it is to survive, the ghost unsuccessfully tries to stop him, hardly able even to suggest that not surviving is much harder (p. 78).

De Moor's staging of this scenario of recollection points out not only that testimony is necessarily rhetorical, but also that within this horizon of representation, positionality is of crucial importance. Gerard – and Jaap Hemelrijk – cannot ('authentically') speak for Jannosch Franz – just as the narrator cannot ('authentically') speak for the minority called 'Gypsies' (as de Moor, at least according to one review, tries to do in *Hertog van Egypte*; Klein 1998: 26). The narrator tries to account for this impossibility by stressing issues of rhetoricity and positionality. As mentioned earlier, she knows that her 'gadjo' identity limits her flexibility and conditions her unwilling complicity with the perpetrators, rather than the closeness to Joseph she is seeking (pp. 24, 60). Nonetheless, she keeps trying. Exploring different narrative voices, focalizations and modes of speech in the course of the novel, she eventually even dares to speak from Joseph's perspective without, as hitherto, 'properly' embedding this change of perspective in the plot (pp. 173ff.).[12] How ought we to understand the narrator's act of 'usurping his voice'? Does it not constitute the collapse of her attempt to account carefully for positionality?

The text clearly runs the risk of appropriating the authority of the 'other' here. At the same time, however, this exploration of Joseph's perspective can be regarded as a consistent pursuit of the novel's project – imaginatively – to change the conditions of dominant 'Gypsy' discourse: staging dialogues (albeit fictional ones) not only between different characters, but also in the larger frame of the novel's extra-diegetic narrative voice, the text breaks up the homogeneity of the dominant discourse,

---

[12] Earlier in the novel, Joseph's life story is told in the third person, and, although this narration is mostly focalized through him, the narrator's voice here is marked as the voice of the non-'gadjo' other by, for example, its occasional choice of distanced vocabulary (see pp. 54ff.). Then the narrator creates the fiction of Joseph telling stories, which she also reports in the third person (pp. 109ff.), before she makes him speak himself (p. 129; this change of perspective is introduced through Lucie's memory of his narration). Another strategy is the narrator's staging of fictive dialogues with her character(s). Directly addressing the 'Gypsy' as 'you', the narrator endows him with subjectivity and agency, but also declares her intimacy with this 'other' (pp. 14, 93, 162) and, occasionally, her authority over his history by forcing him to listen rather than to speak himself (p. 94).

and allows space for the telling of different stories. But what qualifies as 'difference' here? Does de Moor's text, with its merely imaginary dialogue, not rather appropriate for her exoticist fictions about romantic foreign dukes the promise of difference connected to the 'Gypsy's' voice? As argued earlier, the novel can be read in this way. With its ongoing reflection on textuality and narrative voice, however, the text also invites a different reading of the splendidly regal appearance of the 'Duke of Egypt' in its last chapter: rather than a realistic image of ethnic difference, the narrative evocation of this figure (who elicits respect in the officials of the Dutch city) might present an allegory of the dignity belonging to the 'other' Europeans. For, as stated above, the narrator persistently deconstructs images of ethnic difference. One of her means of displacing the asymmetrical binary oppositions of received anthropological discourse is her reflection on the difficulty not only of 'understanding' Joseph's people, but also of 'understanding' Lucie, her 'other self' and/or 'sister' (pp. 225–26). Knowing that the 'self' is haunted by otherness, and that the stories about the 'other' are also stories about ourselves (see p. 23), the narrator engages in a process of renegotiating positionality. In the course of telling her story (as well as in the course of the story she tells), she imagines the transformation of positions as a process of gradual understanding – a process mediated by the telling, listening to and rewriting of stories which constitute the relationship between Joseph and Lucie (see pp. 110–11, 122, 188) and also that between Joseph and the narrator.

To sum up, the novel's project is twofold. It seeks to combine deconstructive interventions into dominant discourse with the reconstruction of a polyphony of 'different' fictions (see Berg and Fuchs [eds] 1993: 87). Also, while taking positionality into account and staging the lasting force of stereotypes, de Moor's writing explores strategies of change, of displacing the dominant representation of 'the Gypsy' as the 'other'. This double project is obviously a risky undertaking: the novel's negotiation of histories in a fictive, openly textual dialogue does imply an appropriation of other voices, and it effects the reiteration of stereotypical concepts and figures. De Moor's narration turns out in many ways to be at least as deficient and problematic as Gerard's recounting of Jannosch's history.

It is necessary to keep insisting on this deficiency – on the problematic inherent in the gesture of representation enacted by de Moor's book, on the difficulties associated with challenging the hurtful significations attached to images of 'Gypsy' difference, and on the need for dialogues not just between fictive 'gadjo' and 'non-gadjo' voices, but also between 'gadjo' and Romany authors, activists and scholars. Nonetheless, I would like to suggest that we consider de Moor's novel as a contribution to this dialogue, and that we encourage the continuation of the text's twofold project, as part of the urgent task to rewrite both the stories about and the histories of the Roma, Sinti and other so-called 'Gypsies' in European literature.

References

Adelson, Leslie. 1993. *Making Bodies, Making History: Feminism and German Identity.* Lincoln, NE, and London: University of Nebraska Press.

Anon. 1997. 'Trauriges Zigeunerlied', *Der Spiegel,* 51 (15 December): 201.

Berg, Eberhard, and Fuchs, Martin (eds). 1993. *Kultur, soziale Praxis, Text: Die Krise der ethnographischen Repräsentation.* Frankfurt: Suhrkamp.

Bhabha, Homi K. 1994. *The Location of Culture.* New York: Routledge.

Braidotti, Rosi. 1994. *Nomadic Subjects: Embodiment and Sexual Difference in Contemporary Feminist Theory.* New York: Columbia University Press.

Breger, Claudia. 1998. *Ortlosigkeit des Fremden: 'Zigeunerinnen' und 'Zigeuner' in der deutschsprachigen Literatur um 1800.* Cologne: Böhlau.

Butler, Judith. 1997. *Excitable Speech: A Politics of the Performative.* New York: Routledge.

de Moor, Margriet. 2001. *Duke of Egypt.* Trans. Paul Vincent. London: Picador. (Original *Hertog van Egypte.* Amsterdam: Querido, 1996.)

Deggerich, Georg. 1997–98. 'Pferdegeflüster', *Am Erker: Zeitschrift für Literatur,* 34 (Winter): 102–03.

Derrida, Jacques. 1996: *Marx' Gespenster: Der Staat der Schuld, die Trauerarbeit und die neue Internationale.* Frankfurt: Fischer.

Fonseca, Isabel. 1996. *Bury Me Standing: The Gypsies and their Journey.* New York: Random House/Vintage Books.

Freud, Sigmund. 1975 (1st edn 1939). *Der Mann Moses und die monotheistische Religion: Schriften über die Religion.* Frankfurt: Fischer.

Geertz, Clifford. 1993. 'Thick Description: Toward an Interpretative Theory of Culture', in *idem, The Interpretation of Culture: Selected Essays.* London: Fontana. (1st edn, New York: Basic, 1973.)

Grellmann, Heinrich Moritz Gottlieb. 1783. *Die Zigeuner: Ein historischer Versuch über die Lebensart und Verfassung, Sitten und Schicksale dieses Volkes in Europa, nebst ihrem Ursprunge.* Leipzig: n.p.

Kerschbaumer, Marie-Thérèse. 1980. *Der weibliche Name des Widerstands: Sieben Berichte.* Olten: Walter (Eng. trans. *Woman's Face of Resistance: Seven Reports.* Riverside, CA: Ariadne, 1996)

Klein, Erdmute. 1998. 'Ein anderes Leben – ganz in der Nähe. Im Gespräch: Margriet de Moor', *Rheinischer Merkur,* 12 (20 March): 25–26.

Laub, Dori, and Podell, Daniel. 1998. 'Kunst und Trauma', in Cathy Gelbin, Eva Lezzi, Geoffrey H. Hartman and Julius H. Schoeps (eds), *Archiv der Erinnerung: Interviews mit Überlebenden der Shoah. I: Videographierte Lebenserzählungen und ihre Interpretationen.* Potsdam: Verlag für Berlin-

Brandenburg/Moses Mendelssohn Zentrum für europäisch-jüdische Studien: 65–92.

Mann, Thomas. 1986. *Joseph in Ägypten. Joseph der Ernährer (Joseph und seine Brüder*, II). Frankfurt: Fischer.

Schneider, Wolfgang. 1997. 'Komm auf meine graue Pferdedecke. Von der Empfänglichkeit der Einfaltspinsel: Margriet de Moors neue Liebes geschichte', *Frankfurter Allgemeine Zeitung*, 238 (14 October): 10.

W.S. 1998. 'Ein Plagiat: Margriet de Moor hat abgeschrieben', *Süddeutsche Zeitung*, 232 (9 October): 14.

Young, James E. 1997. *Beschreiben des Holocaust: Darstellung und Folgen der Interpretation*. Trans. Christa Scheunke. Frankfurt: Suhrkamp.

Young, Robert. 1995. *Colonial Desire: Hybridity in Theory, Culture, and Race*. London and New York: Routledge.

From Survival to Subversion: Strategies of Self-Representation in Selected Works by Mariella Mehr

Carmel Finnan

Until recently very little was known about the Yenish people who have lived in Switzerland for over 300 years.[1] As a result of media revelations in the early 1970s which exposed a brutal, state-run assimilation programme directed against the Yenish for over half a century, Swiss society was confronted with one of the darkest chapters of its recent history. Since then the Yenish writer Mariella Mehr has ensured that the plight of this minority ethnic group does not vanish from Swiss public consciousness. Along with other Yenish voices,[2] Mehr's texts have enabled the silenced Yenish people to participate in the public discourse on their own history, which until recently has been written exclusively by non-Yenish bureaucrats, many of whom were actively involved in various coercive assimilation programmes directed against the Yenish. Her texts explore the experience of oppression, focusing on the individual consequences for the victim of the state-endorsed settlement programmes. Mehr's literary œuvre is concerned with finding suitable discursive forms that express these hitherto unarticulated experiences of oppression. The act of writing for Mehr is consequently an act of resistance, challenging the linguistic structures of the dominant discourse, structures that are analogous to those responsible for perpetrating, justifying and subsequently concealing this oppression.

---

[1] The Yenish people live mainly in Switzerland, but are also found in the neighbouring countries of Austria, Germany and France. Today, approximately 35,000 Yenish live in Switzerland, about 5000 of whom still lead nomadic or semi-nomadic lives. Their unusual fair skin and blue eyes have given rise to some contentious theories about their origins, such as that they are of Celtic origin, or that they are the descendants of dispossessed non-Gypsy settlers in Switzerland. Other theories claim that they are part of a migration of Gypsies from India, belonging to a fair-skinned group. In German-speaking areas the Yenish language is loosely based on the structures of German grammar and has incorporated many words from Hebrew, Yiddish, German and Rotwelsch. See, in this context, Huonker and Radgenossenschaft der Landstrasse 1987: 16–19; Meyer 1988.

[2] Other published Yenish writers include Hansjörg Roth (1996).

Before elaborating on the specifically subversive potential of Mehr's writings, I want to give a brief summary of the state-run settlement programmes directed against the Yenish by the Swiss authorities. These programmes were carried out with the approval and financial assistance of Swiss federal, cantonal and community organizations from the early nineteenth century until they were officially ended in 1973. During the 1920s these programmes were informed by the race and eugenics theories that enjoyed popular support in many quarters during the early decades of the twentieth century. As members of a group officially categorized as 'racially degenerate', the Yenish were systematically abused as wards of the Swiss authorities in prisons, reform institutions, orphanages, foster homes and psychiatric clinics and prisons. These assimilation projects included 'curative' medical treatments for their 'genetic deformity', such as frequent EST, insulin therapy and compulsory sterilization.[3] One of these assimilation programmes involved the removal of Yenish children from their biological families and their forcible assimilation into a Swiss-gadjo culture, the ultimate aim of which was the gradual erasure of the nomadic Yenish culture in Switzerland. The abduction of Yenish children was run by a number of highly respected organizations, the most famous of which is Pro Juventute. Between the years 1926 and 1973 Pro Juventute officially 'adopted' over 600 Yenish children as part of a programme ironically titled 'Relief Work for Children of the Road' (Hilfswerk für Kinder der Landstrasse).[4]

The long history of this practice and the brutality with which it was carried out expose one of the enduring myths of Switzerland as a harmonious multicultural and multilingual society. The political and social ideologies underpinning the coercive settlement programme were closely linked to National-Socialist racial politics.[5] The writings and case studies of the programme's first coordinator, Alfred Siegfried, demonstrate the strong influence of the Nazi psychiatrist and race theorist

---

[3] For a detailed account of the abusive activities of these programmes see Leimgruber et al. 1998.

[4] The authorized abduction of Gypsy children has a long history, stretching right across Europe. It is also woven into the numerous myths associated with European Gypsies, one of which accuses them of child abduction. However, the origin of this myth reveals an insidious falsification of historical events, reversing the true origins and instigators of the crime. The children who were kidnapped were actually Gypsy children, abducted from their families and isolated as early as possible from their community and culture. The so-called 'kidnappings' carried out by the Gypsies were subsequent attempts by the biological families to rescue their own children from foster families and institutions. In eighteenth- and nineteenth-century Europe various authorized assimilation programmes were run by the police and the judicial system. In the twentieth century, however, medical and social institutions became willing participants in this practice, which was coordinated by the state in conjunction with various private bodies.

[5] The collaboration between Nazi racial 'experts' and the Swiss authorities running this programme is highlighted in Leimgruber et al. 1998.

Robert Ritter on his work.[6] In describing the difficulties his organization encountered in the course of their settlement project with the Yenish, Siegfried's choice of metaphor illustrates the blatantly racist politics that pervaded the programme: 'One has to say that sometimes the wood was simply too rotten and a lot is achieved when these people do not start a family, when they no longer continue to reproduce in an unrestrained manner, giving birth to future generations of depraved and abnormal children.'[7] Nonetheless, the obvious racial and political bias that defines the writings of Siegfried and those he admired did not deter Swiss bureaucrats and academics in the succeeding decades from basing their own studies on these theories, revealing the degree to which Nazi racial politics continued to inform this programme in Switzerland long after 1945.[8]

The programme was officially terminated in 1973, following public outcry arising from a series of articles published a year previously in the Swiss magazine *Der schweizerische Beobachter* about the abusive activities of this organization.[9] Despite official studies which have admitted the discriminatory activities of 'Relief Work for Children of the Road', the Swiss authorities have been slow to acknowledge officially the systematic abuse committed against the Yenish people by a state-run organization. The first official apology by a Swiss authority to the Yenish people followed in 1986, fourteen years after the publication of the magazine articles. Despite the findings of a historical investigation, published in 1998, and the response of the serving Swiss president, Ruth Dreyfuss, to the report's highly critical conclusions, financial compensation for the victims and unrestricted access to their files have been fraught with legal problems. Thomas Huonker describes the neglect and indifference that continue to define the treatment of Yenish victims by the Swiss authorities:

> Foreign observers of Switzerland are baffled by the lateness of the official protests against the ideology and actions of the 'Relief Work for Children of the

---

[6] Robert Ritter later became a leading figure in coordinating Nazi eugenics policies during the 1930s. These policies defined racially inferior groups, i.e. those described as 'asocial' and 'morally degenerate' according to the Nuremberg Laws of 1935.

[7] Siegfried 1990: 13–14. All translations into English are my own.

[8] In her examination of academic case studies on Yenish patients, Mehr (1998: 74–86) points out the blatant medical negligence and the accompanying racist attitude that characterize these studies. In one doctoral thesis, submitted to the University of Berne in 1968, the theories of famous Nazi racial 'experts' and their admirers, such as Robert Ritter and Hermann Arnold, are uncritically applied to Yenish case studies.

[9] One of the numerous scandals revealed in the articles was directly related to the programme's first coordinator, Alfred Siegfried. He had been found guilty of sexually abusing children in his care in 1924, the same year in which he became coordinator of the programme.

Road' as well as by the fact that the state has never instituted a legal investigation into the serious accusations levelled against the actions of the 'Relief Work' revealed in 1972, despite the fact that some victims had repeatedly taken legal action and on occasion were even able to avert the implementation of certain measures.[10]

The life and writings of Mariella Mehr are closely bound up with Pro Juventute's adoption programme. Mehr was born in Zürich in 1947 and shortly after her birth was forcibly removed from her biological mother. She spent the next years in 16 orphanages, three reform institutions, four psychiatric institutions and a women's prison.[11] Her son, also adopted by compulsory order by Pro Juventute after her release from prison, suffered the same fate as his mother and previous generations of his people. Mehr's mother was diagnosed as schizophrenic and spent most of her later life in a psychiatric clinic. Among the 600 children adopted under the 'Relief Work' programme, at least 80 belonged to the clan referred to as 'Xenos'. This code name, meaning 'strange' or 'foreign', was given to certain interrelated Yenish families, to which Mehr's family belongs.[12] Mehr's adult life has been devoted to fighting the injustices suffered by her own ethnic group and other disadvantaged minorities through her involvement in various civic pressure-groups such as *Radgenossenschaft der Landstrasse*, as well as through her journalistic and literary writings.

The central theme of Mehr's literary work is defined by her experiences of displacement, brutality and alienation as a member of a persecuted ethnic minority and a victim of Pro Juventute's assimilation programme.[13] In her exploration of these themes she focuses specifically on the multifaceted nature of violence and its long-term effects on the individual.

A brief summary of Mehr's literary œuvre reflects her major concerns

[10] Huonker and Radgenossenschaft der Landstrasse 1987: 110. For the findings of the historical investigation see Leimgruber et al. 1998. Since 1987 all files concerning the activities of the 'Relief Work' have been relocated from the various cantonal archives to the federal archives in Berne. The many difficulties encountered by the Yenish in their battle with cantonal and federal authorities in Switzerland are outlined in Huonker 1998: 110–15. See also in this context Jourdan 2000: 60–62.

[11] After becoming pregnant, Mehr was sentenced to prison as a means of deterring her from marrying the Yenish father of her child (Mehr 1998: 182–83).

[12] The term 'Xenos' is used to refer to this interrelated group in the various legal, medical, psychological, social and anthropological studies undertaken in the context of the 'Relief Work' programme. The tribe 'Xenos' is the 'rotten wood' referred to by Siegfried in the assimilation programme he coordinated, i.e. those whom he considered to be so genetically inferior that they were beyond 're-education'.

[13] Mehr writes, 'My central themes were always concerned with the socially disadvantaged, women, children and Yenish, prisoners and the victims of psychiatric treatment. But I also wanted to write about what I had endured as a member of the Yenish people' (1998: 176–77).

and their distinctive poetic articulation. In her prose works, including her first book, *steinzeit* ('stone age') (1981) and *Daskind* ('The child') (1995), Mehr gives literary expression to the unarticulated suffering of victims, describing events, emotions, impressions from the perspective of those persecuted.[14] Her characters in these early works are children – society's most muted, most vulnerable and least visible victims. Other novels written during this period include *Das Licht der Frau* ('The Light of Woman') (1984), in which Mehr examines ritualized violence, using the bullfighting arena for her exploration of the impulses that drive a woman to become a matador. Her novel *Zeus oder der Zwillingston* ('Zeus or the Twin Tone') from 1994 probes the link between the creative and the destructive process. A distinctive change in her literary intentions is visible in her novel *Brandzauber* ('Inflammatory Magic'), published in 1998. While Mehr retains many of the characters from her earlier texts, she focuses here on the pernicious consequences of victimhood, specifically the process through which some victims of violence become the perpetrators of violence and abuse. Mehr herself states that the question of guilt, central to this shift from victim to perpetrator, is a fundamental theme of her most recent work.[15]

Mehr examines this theme primarily through her use of language, experimenting with various narrative strategies, such as fractured narrative perspectives, shifting levels of consciousness, conspicuous gaps and caesura that produce ruptured rhythms in syntax and diverse literary styles. She employs these narrative devices as a means of probing the invidious permutations of violence. The stylistic distinctiveness of each of her texts testifies to her continuous search for an appropriate language to communicate this central theme. Stylistically, Mehr's texts are characterized by their apparent break with the norms of standard German grammar. Her subversive literary strategies are a means of representing an ethnic minority self in the master discourse, a marginalized other that is defined by its experiences of oppression and injustice. Because these experiences generate their own specific rhythms and syntax, finding an appropriate literary form in which to articulate them invariably becomes a transgressive act against the discursive norms of standard language. Writing, in this context, is a means of opposing the structures of German grammar, structures that are metonymic of the oppression and discrimination exercised by state authorities over the Yenish people.[16]

[14] Mehr has also written a number of plays dealing with this topic, including *Kinder der Landstrasse* (1987) and two unpublished plays, *Silvia Z* (1986) and *Anni B* (1989). A collection of essays written between 1976 and 1990 is published in *RückBlitze* (1990).
[15] Mehr summarizes the thematic development in her later works in the interview, 'Die Lust an der Selbstpreisgabe' (1997: 35).
[16] Julia Kristeva (1984) elaborates on the subversive potential of writing practices such as Mehr's that challenge the linguistic norms.

The intrinsic relationship between content and form in Mehr's writing is apparent in all of her texts. In order to demonstrate this relationship and its subversive potential, I shall examine two of her works: her first novel, *steinzeit*, and a more recently published novel, *Brandzauber*. *steinzeit* is based on diary excerpts written while Mehr was undergoing therapy, which, as Mehr claims, actually saved her life (1981: 187). The text is written as a series of fragments, each of which represents a defining event in Mehr's life as a ward of Pro Juventute. The experiences narrated throughout are defined by the sense of abandonment, the indifference and the brutality endured at the hands of her state guardians. These events are articulated via fictionalized characters, Silvia, Silvano and Silvana, who are the splintered perspectives of the main character, giving voice to different experiences and their attendant emotional states. This splitting of the narrative perspective is a rhetorical device that facilitates the necessary emotional and temporal distance from the traumas being remembered, while simultaneously allowing the remembered experiences to be articulated. These events include continuous physical and emotional violation via beatings, EST and sexual abuse. Other literary features that illustrate the fragmented nature of this narrative and its non-compliance with grammatical norms include the use of lower case letters throughout, the replacement of normative syntax with elliptical sentences, and the linking of scenes by spatial association rather than by logical temporal sequence.

This highly fragmented textual form is, however, an appropriate representation of the life depicted. It translates the series of physical and emotion mutilations inflicted by state-run institutions and their representatives into a literary form, thus breaking the subsequent silence of the traumatized victim and simultaneously challenging the power structures responsible. In finding an appropriate literary form that gives expression to hitherto silenced experiences, Mehr creates a narrative style that undermines existing linguistic and literary norms, automatically expanding existing discursive possibilities.

Mehr's narrative transgressions in *steinzeit* are employed to illuminate certain experiences that would otherwise remain outside the existing discursive space. The following example illustrates how, by juxtaposing different perspectives on the use of EST, Mehr captures the viewpoint of the helpless patient who receives it and that of those who administer it. In the scene being described from the point of view of the patient, the text becomes particularly ruptured and disjointed. Sentences are suddenly interrupted. Single words become autonomous: sometimes they appear in isolation, or are repeated, and on some occasions related words are attached to form a long sequence (pp. 105–11). In the scene directly following, the scientific, medical and sociological history of EST is presented in a factual, precise language in the present tense, using the first-person perspective (pp. 112–13). The stark stylistic contrast between these two scenes highlights the divergent experiences of this 'curative' treatment and the disparate social positions they represent: the pain inflicted on the muted victim and the structures that implemented and justified it. However, the positions of persecutor and victim do not remain mutually exclusive. A fatal bond ensues between persecutor and victim. In trying to understand the pain inflicted, the victim can only comprehend it as a punishment, which creates feelings of guilt. Pain and suffering for the victim thus become inextricably linked to feelings of guilt and self-blame (p. 110). A vicious circle is generated, in which the victim inadvertently becomes an accomplice in her own suffering.

The question of guilt and its disastrous consequences is central to the novel *Brandzauber*. It depicts two girls from marginalized, persecuted ethnic groups, a Gypsy and a Jew, who meet in an orphanage. The commonality of their abandonment and suffering forms the basis of a friendship that develops between these two girls. However, their friendship slowly evolves into a sado-masochistic relationship, in which Anna (the Gypsy girl) takes on the role of the sadist and Franziska (the Jewish girl) that of the masochist. The history of their friendship is recalled by Anna, who now works in a private clinic. At the very beginning of the novel we glean the extent of the emotional abyss lurking underneath the thin veneer of normality that Anna has meticulously constructed. In the introductory scene we are presented with Anna, sitting in her greenhouse with a stopwatch in her hand, observing the struggle to the death between her carnivorous plants and the insects she has just fed them (1998: 7–9). Anna's fascination with death and killing, we learn later on, also has other outlets. She catches birds and kills them slowly, watching their struggle to the end and later observing the marks the killing process has left on their corpses (pp. 52–53).

The introductory scene, initially narrated by an external observer, shifts quickly to the first-person perspective. Anna introduces herself briefly: 'I am Anna. Anna Priska Kreuz. Death' (p. 10). Her terse self-introduction continues, revealing further details of her fascination with the process of death and the pleasure she experiences from watching her plants devour the prey, as well as the possible origin of this pleasure:

> Even though I'm on good terms with death, I am not unnecessarily cruel. I am interested in the process that leads to death, not in the pain of beetles, wasps, flies and mosquitoes that disappear into the gullet of my flowers. It is so to speak a clinical interest, which has nothing to do with my own memories of death. However, sometimes I cannot avoid comparison. There are delicate moments and I have to remind myself each time that I am only observing, not active as on previous occasions. (p. 13)

Brandzauber is written in a clear, simple, almost conversational style with no apparent attempt made to reflect stylistically on the events depicted. However, the casual narrative style employed here has a more subtly subversive quality than Mehr's earlier texts. It communicates the beguiling and corrupting nature of violence in an easily accessible language, without playing down the seriousness of events depicted, or rendering violence in a more pleasing form than in Mehr's earlier texts. Violence and the accompanying sense of guilt are depicted as familiar aspects of everyday life that are nonetheless also inherently cruel and destructive.

The narrative shift in the text between the first and the third person depicts the violent actions from a double perspective. From the detached, external point of view they are rendered gruesome. From the interior perspective of the perpetrator, Anna, we are given access to emotions that drive her to participate in violent acts, without minimizing their brutality. This impulse, we learn, is generated by the sense of security she derives from inflicting pain (p. 13), which in turn is closely bound up with Anna's lifelong familiarity with violence. The impulse towards violence is above all connected with her memory of pain, which at times becomes autonomous and threatens to overwhelm her (p. 41). Anna struggles between the memory of the pain she endured and the emotions these memories evoke – hate, vengeance, helplessness and guilt, which also threaten to destroy her. The sadistic acts provide Anna with momentary release from the potentially self-destructive emotions she cannot otherwise control. They also offer the fractured and tormented Anna a fleeting sense of unity and peace: 'Guilt and pleasure, pain and enjoyment became one' (p. 101).

That the once persecuted Anna should now commit the most brutal and heinous of crimes, including murder, is both shocking and challenging. Mehr confronts the reader here with the long-term, destructive consequences of oppression. It becomes a self-perpetuating activity, not, as one wishes to believe, a purifying and redemptive experience for the victim. In this context one can apply the contention expressed by Joan Ringelheim with reference to Shoah testimonies, regarding the destructive permutations of persecution on victims: 'Oppression does not make people better. Oppression makes people oppressed' (1993: 404).

Both novels examined here demonstrate how Mehr succeeds in translating personal experiences into universal studies of the complex and abstruse dynamics of oppression. Her texts reveal how oppression can become a self-perpetuating vicious circle, reproducing fatal patterns of interaction between persecutor and victim. Mehr's almost exclusive use of female literary characters, including the violent Anna, is closely related to her own experiences and subsequent exploration in textual form of the sinister nature of oppression. She does not accept the argument put forward by some feminists that women are less inclined to commit violent acts than are men. Instead of embracing the assertion that women are biologically or socially immune to participating in violent acts, Mehr argues that violence is all-pervasive and self-perpetuating (1998: 179–81). Her texts do not provide quick 'solutions', via cathartic experiences, to the question of violence, but are studies of its long-term effects and are therefore critically pessimistic.

Gender and its role in victimhood plays an important role in Mehr's work. Her texts question the tendency still prevalent in various studies to use ethnicity as the sole category of analysis in examining the institutional persecution of minority groups, such as Yenish victims. Mehr argues that there are important differences between male and female victims. Yenish women, she claims, suffered a more de-individualizing and degrading form of persecution than did men. For example, women outnumbered men as victims of compulsory sterilization measures. More women were put into institutional care, either in prisons or as patients in psychiatric clinics, as a means of preventing them from intermarrying. As Mehr points out, the bureaucratic case studies demonstrate that the institutional discourse was also gender-specific. While an obviously racist and condescending language is used to describe both sexes, Yenish women are also defined in moral and biological terms as sexually depraved and congenitally tainted. Even though both men and women were persecuted as members of an ethnic minority, women, as the carriers and primary carers of future generations, were targeted and persecuted specifically as women.[17] Their experiences have been excluded from Yenish history by the definition of the Yenish experience exclusively in terms of ethnic persecution. For Yenish women ethnicity and gender are primary categories that define their experiences (Mehr 1990: 183–84). As Mehr points out, even within the Yenish community, the intersection between ethnicity and gender in the experiences of oppression is largely ignored.[18] Mehr's texts demonstrate that including gender as a factor in representing and interpreting the Yenish experience is a powerful act of resistance to the attempts to silence and depersonalize Yenish history and subjectivity.

---

[17] A report on the activities of the 'Relief Work' from 1964 by Siegfried highlights the gender-based discrimination inherent in the programme's policy: 'Nomadism, like certain dangerous diseases, is primarily transmitted by women' (see Jourdan 2000: 62).

[18] For example, despite the fact that various women were instrumental in bringing the activities of Pro Juventute into the public arena in the early 1970s, women's voices have been gradually silenced from the Yenish history-making process and women are still very under-represented on the decision-making forum for Yenish affairs.

It is the fun I have writing and of course that includes creating new languages. For the past 30 years I have focused exclusively on the topic of violence because it was the central theme of my youth; violence suffered and violence inflicted on others. But violence is so extraordinary and incomprehensible that even at the age of 200 I would still not have grasped it and would still have to create new languages and reach new levels of consciousness just to advance one step along the road in understanding violence. (Mehr 1997: 35)

Mariella Mehr's literary project exposes the state-endorsed injustices suffered by her people at an individual level. It also transforms these experiences into universal studies of the darker side of the human condition. Through this project Mehr creates new textual strategies that inscribe the muted Yenish voice in public discourse, challenging these discursive norms as well as the power structures they represent.

References

Huonker, Thomas, and Radgenossenschaft der Landstrasse. 1987. *Fahrendes Volk – verfolgt und verfemt. Jenische Lebensläufe.* Zürich: Limmat Verlag Genossenschaft.

Jourdan, Laurence. 2000. 'Gypsy Hunt in Switzerland: Long Pursuit of Racial Purity', *Roma Rights*, 4.

Kristeva, Julia. 1984. *Revolution in Poetic Language.* New York: Columbia University Press.

Leimgruber, Walter, Meier, Thomas, and Sablonier, Roger. 1998. *Das Hilfswerk für Kinder der Landstrasse: Historische Studie aufgrund der Akten der Stiftung Pro Juventute im Schweizerischen Bundesarchiv.* Berne: Bundesarchiv Dossier 9.

Mehr, Mariella. 1981. *steinzeit.* Berne: Zytglogge Verlag.

— 1987. *Kinder der Landstrasse.* Berne: Zytglogge Verlag.

— 1990. *RückBlitze.* Berne: Zytglogge Verlag.

— 1995. *Daskind.* Zürich and Frauenfeld: Nagel & Kimche.

— 1997. 'Die Lust an der Selbstpreisgabe: Mariella Mehr im Werkstattgespräch', *Neue Züricher Zeitung*, 25 November.

— 1998. *Brandzauber.* Zürich and Frauenfeld: Nagel & Kimche.

Meyer, Clo. 1988. *'Unkraut der Landstrasse': Industriegesellschaft und Nichtsesshaftigkeit am Beispiel der Wandersippen und der schweizerischen Politik an den Bündner Jenischen vom Ende des 18. Jahrhunderts bis zum ersten Weltkrieg.* Disentis: Desertina Verlag.

Ringelheim, Joan. 1993. 'Women and the Holocaust: A Reconsideration of Research', in Carol Ritter and John Roth (eds), *Different Voices: Women and the Holocaust.* New York: Paragon House: 374–404.

Roth, Hansjörg. 1996. *Allein auf dieser verdammten Welt: Das andere Leben des Josef Knöpflein*. Basle and Frankfurt: Helbing and Lichtenhahn.
Siegfried, Albert. 1990. 'Zwanzig Jahre Fürsorgearbeit für die Kinder der Landstraße', in Mehr 1990: 13–14.

Part IV

Memory, Records and the Romany Experience

Disproportional Representation: Romanies and European Art[1]

Susan Tebbutt

Figure 1. Karl Stojka, 'We Sinti are in the gas chambers of Auschwitz'.

No ordinary caption. The words are paradoxical, the combination of the first-person pronoun ('we'), the present tense ('are') and the adverbial phrase ('in the gas chambers') shocking. The letters themselves, upper

[1] My title intentionally connotes an association with the electoral system of proportional representation. It thus interweaves the themes of political justice and iconography. I would like to thank the Austrian Institute, which provided the financial support for Ceija Stojka's visit to the University of Liverpool, where she spoke about her experiences of the National Socialist period and exhibited and talked about a selection of her paintings. I would also like to record my gratitude to the staff at the Research Center at the National Gallery of Art in Washington, DC for all their help and for enabling me to access their archives.

case, spiky, thrown graphically across the entire width of the foreground, look striking, confrontational. In the middle ground we see two trees, their branches bare of leaves, a wagon, a lamp-post. Far away in the distance the tiny spire of a church and the roofs of buildings are silhouetted against the horizon. No ordinary painting.

'We Sinti are in the gas chambers of Auschwitz',[2] painted by Austrian Romany Auschwitz-survivor Karl Stojka (1931–2003), encapsulates the two sides of the inherently disproportional representation of Romanies in European art. On the one hand, images of Romanies in European art are few and far between, their totality disproportional to the presence of Romanies in Europe.[3] The group is marginalized or conjured up for the viewer by means of stereotypical images. On the other hand, the lack of proportion in the depiction of Romanies may be a deliberate, perhaps alienating, device on the part of the artist, a method of attracting attention in order to emphasize the individuality and ethnicity of the Romanies. Although the first category is linked more to works by non-Romanies, there are works by Romanies that reproduce stereotypical images; equally, there are works by non-Romanies that fall into the second category.[4]

At first glance Stojka's painting is an example of the first type of disproportional representation. There is a traditional wagon, perhaps the most familiar of all stereotypical images, and there are no Romanies actually in sight. Yet the Romanies are absent because they have been gassed in Auschwitz. Stojka's artistic attempt to depict the fate of the Romanies is symptomatic of the huge task he has set himself. He is not depicting the actual historical reality, but using the absence of the Gypsies to (re-)instate them in public memory.[5] Their absence is thus in inverse proportion to the importance that Stojka attaches to them.

---

[2] Karl Stojka's painting is reproduced in the catalogue *Gas* (1996). There are no 'official' titles for the paintings. Stojka added his own, sometimes lengthy, descriptions. No sizes are given. The pages are not numbered. The paintings are reproduced here by kind permission of Karl Stojka's estate.

[3] Historiographers also note a paucity of attention paid to the Romanies in works about local, regional and European history. Of the few available studies Fraser 1995 gives the best overview of the history of the Romanies in Europe, and Guy (ed.) 2001 provides the most comprehensive analysis of the situation in central and eastern Europe following the ending of Communist rule.

[4] This study is not intended to cover all images of Gypsies in European art. Ficowsky's study of Polish Gypsies, for example, contains over two dozen colour and black-and-white reproductions of drawings, engravings and oil paintings depicting Gypsies. My aim is to provide an analytical model that could be applied to other works.

[5] This technique has much in common with Jewish American artist Shimon Attie's series of European installations between 1991 and 1996. Attie projected what Young calls a ' necessarily mediated memory of a now-lost Jewish past onto otherwise forgetful sites' (2000: 64). See Young (2000: 62–89) for a fascinating exploration of the role of the spectator in the 'gaping space between a site and its past, between its history and our memory of it' (2000: 89).

Jostling for attention with memories of the unforgettable, unforgivable and unimaginable fate of the Gypsies under Nazi rule are interlocking discursive scenarios relating to the depiction of Romanies in European art, scenarios that originate in the images of Gypsies produced by *gadjos* (non-Romanies) over the last five centuries, and culminate in images produced by those who have so frequently been the object of misrepresentation in the past, the Romanies themselves.

In order to understand why artists select or resort to the technique of disproportional representation, it is necessary to appreciate the cumulative impact that distortion, demonization, romanticization and even Orientalization have had on public perceptions of Europe's most marginalized ethnic group.[6] The ubiquitous emphasis on otherness, the exotic, and often the erotic, serves to conceptualize the Romanies as a metaphor for the artist's own longings or an *ex negativo* image of himself or herself.

Sixteenth- to Nineteenth-Century Images of Fortune-Tellers and Rogues

The failure to represent the Romanies appropriately is due in no small degree to the fact that while the Romanies are, and always have been, perceived as a minority group, this perception itself helps to perpetuate discrimination. It is important to move away from the coarse polarization and hierarchy of power and importance so frequently associated with the distinction between the 'majority' and the 'minority'. Ceija Stojka (1933–), sister of Karl and herself also a survivor of Auschwitz, who has recorded her experiences in memoirs and art,[7] highlights the inadequacy of the distinction: 'What does the word "minority" mean? It has to do with inferiority, and I don't think that's right. I am a person and not a minority, and people ought to treat me as a person and not as a minority, and they should get out of the habit and stop labelling people a "minority".'[8]

Unfortunately, the Romany minority in Europe is still viewed as part of society's underbelly or underclass, its alleged criminal propensities rarely far from the surface, and this erroneous perception is reflected in

---

[6] See Tebbutt 2000b for an examination of the links between anti-Semitism, anti-Gypsyism and Orientalism.

[7] See Ceija Stojka's memoirs *Wir leben im Verborgenen* (1988) and *Reisende auf dieser Welt* (1992), and Tebbutt 1998 for an analysis of the effects of marginalization on Ceija Stojka, and the ways in which she counteracts this.

[8] From a private interview that I recorded with Ceija Stojka in Vienna on 9 September 1998. All translations from the German are my own.

images of Romanies in art.[9] Just as pop bands today mix and remix versions of songs, so the artists from the sixteenth, seventeenth and eighteenth centuries entered into artistic dialogues with one another, relaying, reinterpreting and reconfiguring variations on a theme.

French artist Georges de la Tour's oil painting *The Fortune-Teller* (c. 1630–34)[10] is a fascinating example of the intersection of reality and its various cultural representations. Although typical in the disproportionate attention accorded to the imputed dishonesty of the Gypsies, all is not what it seems. Of the five people in the tableau one young girl is picking a pocket, while another cuts the chain from which hangs a gold medal. Yet as Feigenbaum points out:

> The porcelain-skinned maiden is not quite what she first seems either, a member of a Gypsy clan. Her creamy complexion and hazel eyes contrast with the black eyes and dark skin of her companions. There can be little doubt that she is Preciosa, a well-born baby kidnapped and reared by a Gypsy who declared her to be her own granddaughter. Preciosa, the heroine of Cervantes' novella *La Gitanilla*, grew up to be the most beautiful, gracious, and accomplished of all the Gypsy maidens. (1997: 176).

Thus a painting apparently portraying a real group of people in fact depicts fictional characters. The first impression, namely that two 'Gypsies' are thieves, is incorrect, since one of them is not of Gypsy origin. Yet the deconstruction of one stereotype does not preclude the reproduction of another. The knowledgeable viewer may register (indirectly, through familiarity with a literary work) the representation of child-snatching, another crime often associated with Gypsies.

Georges de la Tour was not the only artist to depict a grasping Gypsy hand reaching into an unwitting victim's pocket. Simon Vouet and Bartolemeo Manfredi are but two of many.[11] Right through to the twentieth century the presence of a Gypsy in a work of art is often connected with what is effectively the reconstruction of the scene of a crime. Gypsies are depicted not as named individuals but as participants in nefarious encounters or confrontation with law-enforcers. Yet, despite the existence of such images, it is surprising that European art historians have ignored them so systematically.

---

[9] When people were asked to place ethnic groups in order, with those they would most like to have as neighbours first, the results were similar across the whole of Europe, with the Romanies right at the bottom (Tebbutt 1998: ix–x). German author Luise Rinser (1985) argues persuasively that criminality is by no means the prerogative of the Romanies.

[10] Reproduced in Conisbee (ed.) 1997 with details of dating, provenance, where exhibited and selected literature (1997: 268), and discussed in detail by Feigenbaum (1997). Oil on canvas 102 × 103 cm. The Metropolitan Museum of Art, New York, acquired 1960 with Rogers Fund.

[11] See Feigenbaum 1997 for a discussion of images of gamblers, cheats and fortune-tellers in the work of Georges de la Tour and his contemporaries.

The one exception is Marilyn Brown, whose volume entitled *Gypsies and Other Bohemians: The Artist in Nineteenth-Century France* (1985) confronts the conflation of the ethnic Gypsy and the pseudo-Gypsy or bohemian. She points out that images of Gypsies, a rich seam of metaphors for artists themselves, 'became distanced from the historical, political and social conditions of the actual vagabonds they purported to depict' (1985: 2).

Ironically, these disproportional images, part of a mythical system, pervade Brown's own argumentation, particularly when she argues that '[i]mages of gypsies and other related "bohemians" – including *saltimbanques* (vagabond circus performers), the *commedia dell'arte*, beggars, vagrants, street people, tramps, brigands, *chiffonniers* (ragpickers), ambulant musicians, charlatans, wandering provincials, the Wandering Jew, and urban *flâneurs* – all became interwoven in the process' (1985: 3). In interweaving these images and failing to distinguish between the dozen different types she lists above, Brown polarizes society into the bohemian and the bourgeois, not only oversimplifying the case, but effectively removing the Gypsies from the equation. While admitting that by the end of the nineteenth century the bohemian myth had lost its potency and had become 'canonized, controlled and embalmed' (1985: 5), Brown perhaps unwittingly positions herself among the 'embalmers'.

Brown concludes:

> The artistic bohemian is or may become bourgeois, but never the gypsy: his mobility is geographic rather than social. Gypsies rarely have the notion of changing society, despite their dissidence from it, even hatred for it: they live in spite of it, by hoodwinking it. Theirs is a nonconformity which can only superficially challenge the dominant social order. According to the myth, they never change, but with their proverbial vision of the future, are the immutable oracle of change. (1985: 17)

Evocations of the Rural Idyll in the *Gadjo* Art of the Nineteenth and Twentieth Centuries

From the late nineteenth century onwards the Gypsy is no longer portrayed primarily as the oracle of change, the fortune-teller, but as the symbol of continuity and stability within a bucolic landscape, firmly rooted in a world that, if truth be told, is rapidly vanishing. Once again, the 'real' Gypsy is of lesser interest.[12] The utility value lies in colourfulness rather than individuality. The choice of Gypsy as subject matter

---

[12] Arguably the artists, like Wim Willems (1997), who looks for the 'true Gypsy' through the lens of the Gypsiologist, are not looking in the right direction.

forms part of a general reaction against the impact of the Industrial Revolution on the countryside, work and the individual. It is relatively uncommon in nineteenth-century art to find works depicting the smoke-belching factories, mills, railways and houses, uncommon to find images of the harsh reality of industrial work, but easy to locate images of the unspoilt countryside, agricultural workers, and the beauties of nature. It is therefore not surprising that a group of people who are generally associated with a more primitive, 'natural' way of life, who often lived under the stars,[13] should exert a magnetic pull on artists.

The magnetism does not always extend to an interest in those individuals who choose to reject life in the city. Within the landscape of Van Gogh's impressionist painting of a Gypsy camp in the south of France (1888) the Gypsies are represented by smudgy blobs of colour near their horses, indistinct, amorphous.[14] The style of English artist Alfred Munnings (1878–1959), who painted many scenes of Gypsy life in England, is far removed from Van Gogh's impressionistic, bold brush-strokes. Munnings paints both landscape and figures in more detail, yet although he appears to be more interested in portraying individuals than Van Gogh, it is the costume rather than the wearer that catches Munnings' eye. With reference to his two thematically linked paintings *Gypsy Life: The Hop-Pickers* (1913)[15] and *The Departure of the Hop-Pickers* (1913),[16] he writes:

> The families that I got to know had picturesque children, dogs and horses. The women had, somewhere in the back of each caravan, great black hats with ostrich feathers, laid away for gala days, or to be worn when selling baskets or brushes on the road. Nobody could beat their style of dress, with black silk apron over a full-pleated skirt, a pink or mauve blouse showing off a tough, lithe figure; strings of red beads, and wonderful earrings glinting under blue-black hair, came into their make-up, and sure enough, if I needed it, the large black hat – complete with ostrich feathers – was produced and worn.[17]

---

[13] There is a time lag in the portrayal of the changing lifestyle of the Romanies, just as there was a general reluctance to record in art the move from the country to the city. Even as early as the end of the nineteenth century a sizeable number of Romanies were not leading a nomadic life.

[14] Brown sees the work as 'a vision of an isolated and archaic remnant of the notion of community by one who remained separated from it' (1985: 97).

[15] Reproduced in Booth 1978: 99, oil on canvas, 24½ × 29½, in the collection of Mr and Mrs Paul Mellon.

[16] Reproduced in Booth 1978: 101. Painted in 1913 at Binsted near Alton, Hampshire, oil on canvas, 36″ × 40″, in the National Gallery of Victoria, Melbourne, Australia.

[17] Munnings, quoted in Booth 1978: 98. In the commentary on a oil painting of a Gypsy boy on horseback, *Shrimp on White Welsh Pony* (1911), a work of dramatic contrasts in colours, reproduced in Booth 1978: 93, Munnings expresses his fondness for the boy. As well as appreciating his models as aesthetically pleasing, he respects them as people.

To overstate the case, the source of fascination is not the ethnic Gypsy but the colourful clothes-horse. But should this be considered 'misrepresentation'? In terms of authenticity the phenomenon of staging reality is more suspect. Munnings is portraying actual Romanies with their own 'props', but for some artists the borderline between the real and the staged is more fluid. Choosing to depict Gypsies as a foil to the bourgeois, some artists, such as French Impressionist Jean Baptiste Camille Corot (1796–1875)[18] and the Spaniard Ignacio Zuloaga (1870–1945),[19] use their own models dressed as Gypsies. These pseudo-Gypsies then function as the 'mythic archetype of the other bohemian subcategories', with studio props providing the stimulus for flights of exotic artistic fantasy,[20] the ethnographic documentation of social history subordinated to an escapist, manufactured vision.

Authenticity and Other Values

Authenticity or the lack of it is not the sole criterion for value in a work of art. A work of art may have many values, historical, sentimental, or therapeutic. In addition, a work of art may have one value for the artist, one for the owner and one for the viewer of the work. It may have different resonances for people of different ethnic groups. The black feminist critic bell hooks argues persuasively in *Black Looks* (1992) that it is essential that we move away from merely seeing the discussion of race and representation in terms of good and bad imagery. She argues that 'we are always in the process of both remembering the past even as we create new ways to imagine and make the future' (1992: 5). In light of this, in remembering the past, with its deep-rooted images of Gypsies who are misrepresented by *gadjos*, it is important not to fall into the trap of automatically judging all *gadjo* images of Romanies to be inadequate, disproportionate.

The German Expressionist artist Otto Mueller, who was on the fringes of *Die Brücke* (The Bridge) group of artists based in Dresden in the 1910s, has been called the *Zigeunermaler* (Gypsy painter).[21] The

[18] Corot's oil on canvas *Gypsy Girl with Mandolin* (c. 1870), 25″ × 20″, was a gift of Count Cecil Pecci-Blunt to the National Gallery of Art, Washington, DC.
[19] For *The Family of the Bullfighter*, oil on canvas, 210 × 205 cm, New York, The Hispanic Society of America, reproduced in Fundación MAPFRE 1998: 87, Zuloaga used professional models from Madrid.
[20] See Brown 1985: 36–50. Another variation of the inauthenticity of the representation of the Romany is to be found in the elongated features of *Gypsy Woman with Baby* (1919) by Amedeo Modigliani (1884–1920), oil on canvas, 1.159 × 0.730 m, Chester Dale Collection, National Gallery of Art, Washington, DC, which bear witness more to Modigliani's own ideal of beauty than to the actual features of the woman.
[21] See Tebbutt 2000b for an analysis of the role of skin-colour in the images of Gypsies produced by Otto Mueller and Otto Pankok.

term refers not to his origins but to the fact that he produced many works depicting Gypsies. Allegedly from Gypsy stock on his mother's side, Otto Mueller spent several weeks with Gypsies in Hungary, spending some time in Szolnok near Budapest in a Gypsy village. He also painted Gypsies in Yugoslavia, Bulgaria, Rumania and Slovakia. In 1937 the infamous *Entartete Kunst* (Degenerate Art) exhibition, organized to purge galleries and museums of works that did not conform to the Nazi concepts of aesthetics, resulted in the removal of some 357 works by Mueller from public ownership, including images of Gypsies.

Mueller's *Zigeunermappe* (Gypsy Portfolio), completed in 1927 and exhibited by Karl Nierendorf in his gallery, comprised nine colour lithographs, in an edition of 100 copies, to which Mueller himself added watercolours or chalks.[22] There is a Romantic tendency in the works to idealize the pre-industrial world in which people were in harmony with nature,[23] and Mueller's interest in the primitive and 'primitive peoples'[24] is reflected in the angular facial features, reminiscent of African art, that characterize his semi-naked Gypsy woman, the *Zigeunerin mit Kind vor dem Planwagen* (1926–27).[25] Yet does this romanticized, exoticized, sensual, erotic image, which for Mueller had sentimental and aesthetic value, have the same resonance for the Gypsies? In an interview Austrian Romany artist Ceija Stojka says:

> You can only imagine a Gypsy woman in a clichéd way, as something which has never existed, which is a lie with its bright flowers and white blouse and brightly-coloured skirt. Yes she does wear a blouse but she will never show her bosom. She, that is the Romany woman, unlike the way she is always shown in pictures, will never show her knees when she is dancing. The Romany woman is really a retiring mother, who gets on with life because she has children, because she has grandchildren and always has to be a role-model, for her children and for her brothers. She would never show her bosom in front of her brothers and sisters.[26]

Bearing in mind such reservations about the portrayal of the naked body, Mueller's paintings would thus not necessarily have the same appeal for Romanies as they might have for Gadjo viewers.

---

[22] See Galerie Nierendorf 1990: 16 for reproductions of other images of Gypsies.

[23] Mueller, like fellow artists Ernst Ludwig Kirchner, Erich Heckel and Karl Schmidt-Rottluff, sought this harmony through nudist bathing and painting naked models on the Baltic coast and in the Mecklenburg lakes.

[24] Cf. the work of artists such as Pablo Picasso and Paul Gauguin.

[25] Reproduced in colour in Moeller (ed.) 1996: Ill. 33e, 69.7 × 50 cm, from the *Zigeuner* portfolio of 9 coloured lithographs, Breslau, 1927, acquired 1969 by the Brücke-Museum in Berlin as a gift from artist Erich Heckel.

[26] Private interview recorded with Ceija Stojka in Vienna on 9 September 1998.

Historical and Political Value

A number of twentieth-century works of art representing the Romanies have a particular historical and political value because of their connection with the genocide of the Gypsies. One of the key reasons why their historical and political value would appear to out-weigh their artistic value is that there are so few images specifically and visibly of Gypsies, whereas there are large numbers of works in which Jews are depicted.

Yet such a conclusion would not do justice to the works in question. During the Nazi period German Expressionist artist Otto Pankok (1893–1966) was one of a very small number of artists to be sympathetic towards the cause of the Gypsies.[27] Like Otto Mueller, Pankok had his work banned by the Nazis as degenerate and was forbidden in 1937 from exercising his skills as an artist. Yet, whereas Mueller only spent a few weeks at a time with Gypsies,[28] Pankok lived with the inhabitants of the sprawling Heinefeld estate in Düsseldorf for many years. His numerous woodcuts, charcoal drawings and lithographs of Gypsies, and in partic-ular his Gypsy 'Passion' cycle,[29] first exhibited in Essen in 1935,[30] are important historically as documents of a way of life soon to disappear. In *Die Zigeuner* (1947) there are over 130 images of Gypsies and their way of life, their music-making, their superstitions. Pankok's deep affection for the Romanies pervades the work. There is not one standard image but a multitude of different aspects, moods and customs captured here for posterity. *Ringela mit dem Brüderchen*[31] (Ringela with her Little Brother), a portrait of two Gypsies, is unusual in that there is a large crucifix around the boy's neck. This highlights the Catholic faith of most western European Gypsies (in eastern Europe most are Muslim), who are so often inadvertently or deliberately portrayed as associated with the devil.[32] A charcoal drawing (1948) of the Gypsy Wilhelmine Lafontaine, one of only two Gypsies from the Heinefeld estate to survive Auschwitz,

---

[27] Pankok first encountered Gypsies in the south of France at Saintes-Maries-de-la-Mer, the place where Romanies from all over Europe gather each year to worship their patron saint, Saint Sara. See Plorutti 1990 for a dramatic collection of black and white photographs recording Romanies celebrating the festival.

[28] Like Mueller, Dame Laura Knight also spent periods of time with Gypsies. For Mueller and Knight the option to return to their bourgeois homes was always present, and to some extent they were enjoying a 'time-out' phase, playing at being 'Gypsies'.

[29] There are echoes of the Spanish artist El Greco here, with whose work Pankok became familiar during a visit to Spain.

[30] They were taken down immediately. The pictures were shown again in 1937, but it was only after the end of the war that Pankok was allowed to exhibit his work again.

[31] Reproduced in Pankok 1947: Plate 89.

[32] See Solms 1998 for a study of the link between devil-figures and Gypsies in fairy tales, even those supposedly passed on orally by Gypsy storytellers.

illustrates the historical value of art, as a kind of memorial, a homage to those who had not returned.[33] Pankok writes:

> They were taken away to the death camps and the eastern slaughter-houses. We heard the children screaming and the mothers sobbing under the whips of the brown executioners. We saw how people hit out with their fists in the street at the poor faces of dying people, and that the Gypsies cleaned the pavements with their last dying strength for the scoundrels in uniform. Murder stood over us like a black colossus and took up the whole space of the sky over the world. (1947: 10, my translation)

Pankok was not the only *gadjo* to portray the world of the Gypsies prior to deportation, but his works are the most significant in aesthetic terms. In Berlin one of his friends, Jewish artist and art teacher Julo Levin (1901–1943), who taught in Jewish schools in Düsseldorf and Berlin (see Milton 1989), was arrested in 1943. He was listed among those on a transport to Auschwitz on 17 May 1943. There are a small number of paintings by him and by the children he taught that depict Gypsies, images created by members of one persecuted group depicting another.

Works by Jewish artists depicting Gypsies were, however, also painted at the Nazis' behest. Czech Jewish artist Dinah Gottliebova (1923–) was deported in 1943 from Theresienstadt to Auschwitz, where she was assigned to the camp hospital and ordered by Mengele to make drawings and watercolour portraits of Gypsy prisoners.[34] Her work belongs to the category of 'Holocaust art' in that it was produced during the Nazi period and depicts aspects of the processes leading to the attempted genocide.

After the war some artists chose to reflect or recall experiences of the Holocaust, and such works can also be classified as 'Holocaust art'. Two of the few *gadjo* artists to depict the fate of the Romanies are the Austrian

---

[33] In a letter to Otto Pankok dated 29 December 1963 East German dramatist Heiner Müller expresses his admiration for Pankok's paintings of the Gypsies: 'It is a sad and painful image, as if the two of them already knew what fate would befall them. It touches me deeply [...] Yet in "Gypsies in Front of Gathering Clouds", one of my favourites among your woodcuts, you show me that life is fundamentally indestructible.' Letter from the Otto-Pankok-Archive, reprinted in Otto Pankok Gesellschaft et al. (eds) 1993: 65.

[34] See Costanza 1982: 44–45 and 148) for reproductions of *German Gypsy Auschwitz Camp* (1944), watercolour, 8″ × 10″, *Polish Gypsy Auschwitz Camp* (1944), watercolour, 7″ × 9″, *Portrait of a Gypsy, Auschwitz Camp* (1944), watercolour, 8″ × 6″, and *French Gypsy, Auschwitz Camp* (1944), watercolour, 15″ × 12″, all in the Auschwitz Memorial Museum. See also Milton 1990: 148 on the five broad categories of surviving art of the Holocaust. Milton divides works into portraits (25 per cent of the total of surviving works), drawings of inanimate objects (nearly 20 per cent), evidentiary art (about 20 per cent), caricatures (20 per cent) and abstracts (15 per cent). It is not coincidence that women artists painted a larger proportion of children's portraits, since the women and children were usually kept together in the camps and their infirmaries.

Auschwitz survivor Adolf Frankl (1903–1983), born in Pressburg (Bratislava), then part of the Austro-Hungarian Empire, and the Hungarian secular Jewish artist György Kádár (1912–).[35] Frankl, tortured by nightmares and insomnia, began to paint his visions of the 'inferno' through which he had lived. Professor Walter Huder from the Akademie der Künste in Berlin described his works as 'telegrams to the future [...] "historical paintings" [...] both expressive and impressionist in style' (quoted in Frankl n.d.: 11); they were intended as a warning to future generations, and thus foreground images of the Gypsy camp in Auschwitz-Birkenau.[36] Like Frankl, Kádár had personally witnessed the liquidation of the Gypsy camp in August 1944. Born in Budapest, he fled to France in 1937, but was repatriated to Hungary in late 1938, drafted into the Hungarian labour service in 1941 and taken in mid-1944 to Auschwitz, then to Sachsenhausen, Oranienburg and Ohrdruf, a satellite of Buchenwald, where he was finally liberated. In the eight months after liberation he produced a cycle of 57 drawings in ink, charcoal and pittcrayon, among them being images of the Gypsy camp.

Despite the fact that they are offering insights via their art into the lives of real Romanies, and their anthropological commitment to showing the Gypsy experience, Pankok, Levin, Gottliebova and Kádár are not in the metaphorical sense from the 'Gypsy camp', but are *gadjos*, outsiders looking in. How, then, do Romanies depict their own lives?

Romanies Record their Presence

Romanies, so often perceived as outsiders, may themselves begin to move 'inside' when they create works of art, but their success is dependent on the vagaries of the art-consuming world. In his survey of *Outsider Art* (2000) Rhodes points out that the 'success of artists from diasporic backgrounds must be viewed against an institutional arts policy', and (writing with reference to the situation in Great Britain) notes the need for the recognition of hybridity: 'at the moment many groups might be legitimately (and productively, in a political sense) described as outsiders, but their trajectory, even as they assert their difference to the machine of dominant culture, is towards the inside, where that inside holds the possibility of true multiculturalism' (Rhodes 2000: 216–17). Like other artists from diasporic backgrounds, the

[35] Kádár uses art as a mnemonic device and presents what is effectively an eyewitness account of his experiences of the 'Gypsy camp' in Auschwitz-Birkenau.
[36] *Die Zigeuner*, oil on canvas, 90 × 101 cm, reproduced in Frankl n.d.: 12, shows a tightly packed mass of faces, the whites of the eyes larger than normal in expressions of extreme pain and anguish, the Nazi with cap having large black spaces where the eyes should be.

Romanies are beginning to be recognized in a Europe in which many cultures are increasingly threatened by globalization. Rather like the artist-ethnographers described by Hal Foster in *The Return of the Real* (1996: 170–203), the Romanies' new impetus is to bring art and politics closer together, to record elements of the identity of an ethnic group, of a particular community, or *ethnie*, through the medium of art, and to avoid the dissemination of time-worn clichés, transparent in their tenuous link to reality.

Paradoxically, one of the ways in which clichés can be circumvented is by producing images that do not attempt to reproduce reality, but force the viewer to think. Unreality is thus a type of alienation technique, intended to promote greater awareness of the ethnic group. The art of a group of Slovakian schoolchildren and of Karl and Ceija Stojka provides evidence of this type of disproportional representation.

In the far eastern corner of Slovakia, in Jarovnice, near the border with the Ukraine, a town in which some 2200 out of 3550 inhabitants are Romanies, and in which unemployment is extremely high among Romanies, art has a therapeutic and psychological value in one particular school. Following a 30-minute catastrophic flood on 20 July 1998 which destroyed much of their village and swept away 50 people, including ten schoolchildren and seven pre-school children, some of the surviving children have created works of art which have won many international prizes in Japan, Hungary, India, Germany, the USA, the Czech Republic, Macedonia, Bulgaria and Finland, and have been used for the cover of a cassette, for the International Roma calendar and for a work on the anthropology of Gypsies published in the Czech Republic. As teacher Jan Sajko says: 'The openness, freedom and impulsiveness of the Romany children touches us, without words, without boundaries. They show their longings and dreams, paint with the heart. Without preconceptions. Deep inside they perhaps sense that their themes touch everybody, including you too.'[37] Under the guidance of Sajko the pupils have found a channel for their emotions. Whether the topic is their homes, their friends or their everyday lives, the children paint with a tangible enthusiasm and dynamism. Their self-confidence and self-worth are heightened through the act of depicting part of their own story, and for the viewer the works thus have historical and social interest as documents of a tragedy in the lives of a Romany community.

Yet these are not documentary works in the strictest sense. There is a disproportionate use of vivid, primary colours, used without regard for

---

[37] Quoted in a press release with information about the children's work sent by Jan Sajko. I am extremely grateful to Jan for sending me the photographs of the school and the work of the children and information about the disaster in the village.

perspective. The brightness of the colours belies the seriousness of the subject matter. In one painting five musicians are sitting symbolically in a cart marked 'Roma', while horses pull the cart. The wheel, the international symbol of the Romany movement, has a prominent place in this painting. In another painting portraying the first female Gypsy violinist, Cinka Panna, the exuberance of the colours has echoes of eastern European folk art. Against the raspberry-red background the birds, butterflies and creatures of nature, themselves key elements in the oral culture of Romany songs and stories, float around her.

This two-dimensional technique is typical of modernism. Like the children from Jarovnice, Karl Stojka and his sister Ceija use a technique common in medieval times, the highlighting of elements of symbolic importance. Here the technique forms part of a socially critical message. Both Karl and Ceija started to paint their odyssey through a series of concentration camps some decades after the liberation of the camps. For them the therapeutic value of art was uppermost. Both still suffer from recurring nightmares, and evoke memories of the past in order that future generations of Romanies may have some insight into their experiences, while recognizing how impossible it is to capture this adequately in any form of cultural representation.

I would like to look first at two paintings by Karl Stojka.[38] In the 'Group Portrait' of his brothers and sisters (Fig. 2) it is the barbed wire that is disproportionately large in scale, larger than it would have been in real life. It represents the oppression of the Nazi regime that constrains the family. The children are regimented, all sitting in the same pose, the tattooed Z (for *Zigeuner*, Gypsy) and concentration camp numbers clearly visible on their left arms. This is not only the pose of a group to be photographed or captured for posterity, but a group representing thousands who were later murdered by the Nazis. The geometric lines of the barbed wire not only echo the forms of the carpets that Stojka once sold, but also show the regimentation under which the Romanies suffered.[39] In the title image of the catalogue *Gas* (1996) (Fig. 3), Stojka is attempting the impossible, the depiction of the mass gassing of over 2000 Romanies in Auschwitz-Birkenau in one night. Here it is the grotesque size of the showerheads that attracts our attention, hovering as they do over the masses of tiny bodies, closely packed together. The naked bodies are at the mercy of the Cyclon B gas, which is about to pour from the ceiling. Here, as in the family portrait, there is a sense of pattern and rhythms, which against all the odds create an impression almost of beauty, even though the subject matter is a world that has lost

---

[38] See Tebbutt 2000a for an assessment of Karl Stojka's political art.
[39] Although it is extremely unlikely that Karl Stojka was familiar with it, the work has clear echoes of Pankok's woodcut *Gypsy Children behind Barbed Wire*, 1937, 55.5. × 76.7 cm.

Figure 2. Karl Stojka, 'My brother and sisters and me. They deprived us of our names and we were nothing but numbers.'

all sense of reason, one in which pseudo-scientific racist policies have led to cataclysmic horror, to genocide. The catalogue text that Stojka has chosen to place under the painting reads, 'That's how they deceived the people'. The words peel away the thin veneer of civilization with which the Nazis seduced the victims into what was supposedly a shower-room. The artist uses distortion of the literal reality not to deceive but to unmask the true dimensions of depravity.

Distortion and disproportional representation are a key technique in the art of Ceija Stojka.[40] Ceija was a mere child when she was incarcerated in the concentration camps, and her paintings are reconstructed from her memories of events almost half a century previously. In an interview she pointed out: 'I have the number here on my arm. Look. You can see it. Well, I didn't paint it on my arm myself. And I don't need to feel ashamed about it. Those who should be ashamed are the people who did it to me and my Mama and my brothers and sisters.'[41] This accusing tone

[40] The cover painting is in Ceija Stojka's own private collection. I am extremely grateful to her for her hospitality, her friendship and her willingness to talk about her experiences with me. She is an inspiration.

[41] Private interview recorded with Ceija Stojka in Vienna on 9 September 1998.

Figure 3. Karl Stojka, 'That's how they deceived the people.'

is evident in her image of four disproportionately large, black, shiny, empty boots[42] (are there perhaps echoes here of the fairy-tale world of giants with their supernatural powers and seven-league boots?) pointing menacingly from left to right, about to crush all in their path. To the right the gentle beauty of nature is about to be rendered irrelevant.

According to Freud a traumatic event may be repeated over and over again in order to integrate it into a symbolic order[43] and master the trauma. For Ceija Stojka and her brother Karl, the act of recollection

[42] Reproduced on the cover of this book. The boots are a recurring motif in a number of Ceija Stojka's paintings. See also *Mächtige Stiefel*, 1993, 50 × 65 cm, in the catalogue *Ceija Stojka: Bilder und Texte 1989–1995* (Meier-Rogan [ed.] 1995), pages not numbered. The boots and shoes piled high in display cases in the US Holocaust Memorial Museum and the Imperial War Museum Holocaust exhibition also make a strong visual impact, the footwear representing metonymically those who perished.

[43] See Foster 1996: 130–44 for a discussion of traumatic realism and traumatic illusionism within the context of modern art.

may relate to attempts to overcome trauma. In their adaptation of the strategy of disproportionate representation, with its eloquent, haunting primitivism, they implicitly criticize *gadjo* strategies of remembrance and crystallize the concentration camp experience of the Romanies.

Conclusion

Over the centuries the Romanies have been misrepresented and marginalized in art, just as they have been in European society. Paintings such as Georges de la Tour's *The Fortune-Teller* are of historical interest, and in their depiction of criminality and otherness at first glance reflect widespread prejudices and antipathy to the Romanies. Yet these works also contain a critical approach to these all-too-pervasive prejudices. Furthermore, the romanticized view of the Gypsy as a nature-loving person on the fringes of society, rarely encountered in an urban environment, highlights the differentiation made between the Gypsies and the 'civilized' world. Just such a distinction was part and parcel of the motivation behind moves to assimilate and control the Gypsies.

The love of the exotic and the primitive, which the Gypsies were considered to exemplify, peaked at the end of the nineteenth century and the beginning of the twentieth. Works such as those by Otto Mueller give disproportionate emphasis to the naked body, and are, in truth, out of line with Romanies' own views on the desirability of displaying naked flesh publicly. This Orientalist approach, the projection of the artist's own occidental ideals onto another person, has severe limitations.

For *gadjo* artists such as Pankok, Levin, Gottliebova and Kádár, the wish to record experiences of the attempted genocide of the Gypsies provides important insights into the fate of the Gypsies, although, in the case of Gottliebova, the fact that the work was commissioned by Nazis means that all elements of suffering or maltreatment are carefully filtered out.

In the late twentieth century Romanies themselves employ disproportional representation: not to misrepresent, but to highlight the essence of the situation. Although these works might arguably be seen as unrealistic, perhaps symbolic, their iconographic impact is in fact strong, particularly in the dramatic images created by Karl and Ceija Stojka, who are brave enough to tackle the impossible, to attempt to convey the brutality, the horror, the oppression and the inhumanity of the concentration camp. They are Romanies, but they did not perish in the gas chambers of Auschwitz, and Karl Stojka's poignant painting 'We Sinti are in the gas chambers of Auschwitz' is but one of a hitherto neglected collection of paintings by Karl and Ceija[44] that use disproportional representation to put into proportion their own survival.

References

Booth, Stanley. 1978. *Sir Alfred Munnings 1878–1959: An Appreciation of the Artist and a Selection of his Paintings*. London: Sotheby Parke Bernet.

Brown, Marilyn R. 1985. *Gypsies and Other Bohemians: The Myth of the Artist in Nineteenth-Century France*. Ann Arbor, MI: UMI.

Buchheim, Lothar-Günther. 1968. *Otto Mueller*. Feldafing: Buchheim.

Conisbee, Philip (ed.). 1997. *Georges de la Tour and his World*. New Haven and London: Yale University Press.

Costanza, Mary S. 1982. *The Living Witness: Art in the Concentration Camps and Ghettos*. New York: Free Press.

Feigenbaum, Gail. 1997. 'Gamblers, Cheats and Fortune-Tellers', in Conisbee (ed.) 1997: 148–81.

Ficowski, Jerzy. n.d. *The Gypsies in Poland: History and Customs*. Trans. from Polish by Eileen Healey. Interpress.

Foster, Hal. 1996. *The Return of the Real: The Avant-Garde at the End of the Century*. Cambridge, MA, and London: MIT Press.

Fox, Caroline. 1998. *Dame Laura Knight*. Oxford: Phaidon.

Frankl, Thomas. n.d. 'Adolf Frankl', Collection Frankl.

Fraser, Angus. 1995. *The Gypsies*. Oxford: Blackwell. (1st edn 1992.)

Fundación MAPFRE. 1998. *Sorolla, Zuloaga: dos visions para un cambio de siglo, Madrid, 8 de abril–28 de junio de 1998*. Madrid: Fundación Cultural MAPFRE Vida.

Galerie Nierendorf. 1990. *Otto Mueller: Zum sechzigsten Todestag; Gemälde, Aquarelle, Zeichnungen, Graphiken: Ausstellung 9.4.–14.7.1990, Galerie Nierendorf, Berlin*. Berlin: Galerie Nierendorf.

Guy, Will (ed.). 2001. *Between Past and Future: The Roma of Central and Eastern Europe*. Hatfield: University of Hertfordshire Press.

hooks, bell. 1992. *Black Looks: Race and Representation*. London: Turnaround.

Lüttichau, Mario Andreas von. 1993. *Otto Mueller: Ein Romantiker unter den Expressionisten*. Cologne: Dumont.

Meier-Rogan, Patricia (ed.). 1995. *Ceija Stojka: Bilder und Texte 1989–1995*. Vienna.

Milton, Sybil. 1989. 'Julo Levin and his Düsseldorf Circle of Friends', in Sybil Milton (ed. and trans.), *Art of Jewish Children, Germany 1936–1941: Innocence and Persecution*. New York: Philosophical Library: 37–49 (=*Verjagt, ermordet: Zeichnungen jüdischer Schüler 1936–1941*. Ed. Landeshauptstadt Düsseldorf. Stadtmuseum, Düsseldorf: Claassen, 1988)

---

[44] Both artists are internationally acclaimed and have had exhibitions of their work in many countries but are still regularly excluded from the mainstream artistic canon.

— 1990. 'Art of the Holocaust: A Summary', in Randolph L. Braham (ed.), *Reflections of the Holocaust in Art and Literature*. New York: Columbia University Press: 147–52.

— 2000. 'Culture under Duress: Art and the Holocaust', in F.C. Decoste and Bernhard Schwartz (eds), *The Holocaust's Ghost: Writings on Art, Politics, Law and Education*. Edmonton, Alberta: University of Alberta Press: 84–96.

Moeller, Magdalena (ed.). 1996. *Otto Mueller: Gemälde, Aquarelle, Pastelle und Druckgraphik aus dem Brücke-Museum Berlin*. Munich: Hirmer.

Mueller, Otto. 1998. *Mädchenbilder und Zigeunerleben*. Afterword by Alfred Schmeller. Weyarn: Seehamer. (1st edn 1959.)

Otto Pankok Gesellschaft, Mensch, Bernhard, and Stempel, Karin (eds). 1993. *Otto Pankok, 1893–1966: Retrospektive zum 100. Geburtstag*. Oberhausen: Plitt.

Pankok, Otto. 1947. *Zigeuner*. With an introduction by Rudolf Schröder. Düsseldorf: Drei Eulen Verlag.

Plorutti, Giuliano. 1990. *Gitanes: Fotografie di Giuliano Plorutti*. Milan: Idea.

Rhodes, Colin. 2000. *Outsider Art: Spontaneous Alternatives*. London: Thames and Hudson.

Rinser, Luise. 1985. *Wer wirft den Stein? Zigeuner sein in Deutschland; Eine Anklage*. Stuttgart: Edition Weitbrecht.

Solms, Wilhelm. 1998. 'On the Demonising of Jews and Gypsies in Fairy Tales', in Tebbutt (ed.) 1998: 91–106.

Stojka, Ceija. 1988. *Wir leben im Verborgenen*. Ed. Karin Berger. Vienna: Picus.

— 1992. *Reisende auf dieser Welt*. Ed. Karin Berger. Vienna: Picus.

Stojka, Karl. 1995. *Ein Kind in Birkenau*. Vienna: Karl Stojka.

— 1996. *Gas*. Vienna: Karl Stojka.

Tebbutt, Susan. 1998. 'Marginalization and Memories: Ceija Stojka's Autobiographical Writing', in Allyson Fiddler (ed.), *'Other' Austrians*. Berne: Peter Lang: 141–51.

— 2000a. '"My Name in the Third Reich was Z:5742": The Political Art of the Austrian Rom, Karl Stojka', in Thomas Acton (ed.), *Scholarship and the Gypsy Struggle: Commitment in Romani Studies*. Hatfield: University of Hertfordshire Press: 69–80.

— 2000b. 'Sinti und Roma: Antiziganismus und Orientalismus', in Jim Jordan and Peter Barker (eds), *Migrants in German-Speaking Countries*. London: CILT: 156–82.

— 2002. 'Dark Strangers: The Role of Skin-Colour in Images of the Gypsy in Twentieth-Century Art', in Katrin Kohl and Ritchie Robertson (eds), *Words, Texts, Images*. Oxford and Berne: Peter Lang: 135–51.

Tebbutt, Susan (ed.). 1998. *Sinti and Roma: Gypsies in German-Speaking Society and Literature*. New York and Oxford: Berghahn.

Totten, Samuel, and Feinberg, Stephen (eds). 2001. *Teaching and Studying the Holocaust*. Boston, MA: Allyn and Bacon.

United States Holocaust Memorial Museum. 1992. *The Story of Karl Stojka: A*

Childhood in Birkenau. Washington, DC: United States Holocaust Memorial Museum.

Willems, Wim. 1997. *In Search of the True Gypsy: From Enlightenment to Final Solution*. Trans. Don Bloch. London: Frank Cass.

Woodall, Joanna (ed.). 1997. *Portraiture: Facing the Subject*. Manchester: Manchester University Press.

Young, James E. 2000. *At Memory's Edge: After-Images of the Holocaust in Contemporary Art and Architecture*. New Haven and London: Yale University Press.

A Photographer and his 'Victims' 1934–1964: Reconstructing a Shared Experience of the Romani Holocaust

Eve Rosenhaft

This chapter offers a sketch of a wider project, which attempts to reconstruct the Romani Holocaust as an experience shared by Romani and non-Romani Germans. The project is a regional case study, and the principal documents on which it rests are some 300 photographs, now in the holdings of the Liverpool University Library. The photographs were taken at locations in Central Germany during the 1930s by Hanns Weltzel, an amateur naturalist and freelance writer. Their subjects are Romanies, most of them members of a handful of Sinti families. Along with a small collection of manuscript papers, the photographs record a relationship between Weltzel and these families, carried on sometimes face to face, sometimes in letters, and sometimes at second hand or in the imaginations of the parties, which lasted into the 1960s. They also record the descent of German society into war, genocide and defeat. Most of Weltzel's subjects perished in concentration camps or in Auschwitz.[1] Weltzel himself was arrested and executed by the Soviet military authorities in 1952, and it was widely believed that his disappearance had something to do with his having betrayed 'his' Sinti to their Nazi persecutors. In addition to taking photographs, Weltzel had gathered genealogical information, and both the Sinti themselves and postwar Gypsiologists maintained that he had at least handed over his material to the race scientists and possibly even actively collaborated with the Nazi project of registration, selection and deportation. The documentary evidence for Weltzel's complicity is ambiguous at best.[2] But if he is a dubious candidate for the title of 'perpetrator behind the camera'

[1] The best general account of the Nazi persecution of the Romanies in English is Lewy 2000. Research for this article was funded by the University of Liverpool and by the Center for Advanced Holocaust Studies, United States Holocaust Memorial Museum, where I was a Charles Revson Fellow during 2001. It is dedicated to the memory of Reimar Gilsenbach (1925–2001), poet, activist and advocate, who knew some of its subjects.

[2] The surviving records of Robert Ritter's Racial Hygiene Institute in the German Federal Archives, for example, contain no material obviously originating with Weltzel, and the genealogical data on Sinti families of Weltzel's acquaintance recorded there differ in significant ways

(cf. Gilsenbach here), it is nonetheless clear that the Holocaust, in trans-
forming the lives of both photographer and subjects, exposed the ambivalence of their relationship.

As will become clear, Weltzel's photographs are not simply the artefact of that relationship, but were in an important way the medium
through which the relationship was constructed. Photography, of
course, has a central role in the history of Romani–*gadjo* relations. In his
memoirs, published in English translation in 1999 as *A Gypsy in
Auschwitz*, the Berlin Sinto Otto Rosenberg recounts a bizarre incident
from 1945. Like many Sinti and Roma transported back from Auschwitz
into Germany in the last months of the war, the 18-year-old Rosenberg
was in Bergen-Belsen when it was liberated by British troops. Mistrustful
of the liberators, he and his uncle and cousin set out with another man
to make their own way home. Coming to a bridge, they were halted by
a squad of British soldiers and ordered to line up on the bridge:

And then I thought:
'Dear God, now I have survived all this time, the tortures and all the depri-
vations, and you have got over all the hurdles – and now they come and shoot
you!'
But we let them line us up, the indifference was still with us. We did not
defend ourselves. None of us said no, or even asked why.
And then one of them unslung his machine pistol. The English had these little
things that looked like a tin toy.
I closed my eyes and waited for the bang, for the end. But nothing happened.
So I carefully peeped and then permitted myself to take a look.
Then he gives his machine pistol to the other one, reaches into his breast
pocket, takes out a little camera and takes our picture! (Rosenberg 1999: 112)

This account is paradigmatic in a number of respects. As a portrayal of
the act of photography, it seems to validate Susan Sontag's aphorism that
'the camera is a sublimation of the gun' (Sontag 1982: 14). In spite of its
comic outcome and the fact that the reader knows the soldiers to be liberators, the positioning of the photographic act as the moment of first
contact between armed conquerors and men who though nominally free
bear the marks of oppression (and will continue to do so in peacetime) is
also in keeping with the political implications of Sontag's metaphor.
Sontag argued in general terms that the photograph turns people into
objects that can be symbolically possessed. Later critics, and particularly
those tracing the linked histories of photography, anthropology and criminology, have seen the photograph as simultaneously artefact and instru-

from the data that Weltzel kept: Bundesarchiv Berlin (BAB), Zeitgeschichtliche Sammlung 142
and R165 Rassenhygienische und bevölkerungsbiologische Forschungsstelle im Reichs-
gesundheitsamt.

ment of class and colonial rule.[3] Through the eye of the camera, subaltern and colonial groups are subjected to the gaze which, while it purports only to be recording reality, always enacts power. It is in this sense that Allan Sekula characterized the photograph as 'a paradoxical yoking of a primitivist, Rousseauian dream, the dream of romantic naturalism, [to] a project of global domination' (Sekula 1984: 96). Photography is thus one of the more potent of the forms of visual representation that a specular culture employs to define and contain its 'others' – to generate stereotypes. If the first thing British soldiers think of when they see 'Gypsies' – even under the most extraordinary of circumstances – is to take a picture, what they are doing is acting out a social practice (a form of address) that is well established in the centuries-old, politically unequal relationship between Romanies and their fellow Europeans.

As a text, Rosenberg's account is also paradigmatic for the way we have come to read (and to write) the history of Romanies, of Roma and Sinti, in Germany. It presents a life in the form of a Holocaust memoir. Events before the onset of Nazi persecution are recounted in the light of the persecution. This is not surprising, since like most survivors who began to tell their stories only in the 1980s and 1990s, Rosenberg was a child when Hitler came to power and the years of persecution were his formative years. But in the case of Romani survivors, the Holocaust narrative itself is at least a product, to some degree a retrospective inscription or rationalization of post-1945 discrimination; the relatively late recovery and recording of Holocaust memory is part of a political project of identity construction which developed in dialectic with campaigns for civil rights in post-Holocaust Europe. Those campaigns themselves often crystallized around the official discrimination that Romanies suffered in the process of identifying and compensating Holocaust victims. In Rosenberg's story, the central character – the memoirist – is pre-eminently a victim, the fact of survival and any success in the post-war period more grudgingly than triumphantly recorded, since the story is conceived as an indictment. And the individual stands for the whole community. Rosenberg's text shares these qualities with many of the Romani Holocaust memoirs that have appeared in the last fifteen years, among which might be included much of the secondary literature, based as it is on interviews.[4] Like those texts,

[3] See for example Tagg 1988, Regener 1999. On the role of photography in the Nazi persecution of the Romanies, see Hägele 1998.

[4] Recent Romani Holocaust memoirs include Reinhardt 1999, Mettbach and Behringer 1999, Winter 1999, and Franz 1992. The memoirs of Ceija Stojka (1988 and 1992) and Karl Stojka (1994) are exceptional in their coverage of life after the war, Karl Stojka's being unique in foregrounding the present and evoking the Holocaust experience through 'flashbacks'. Secondary literature based on interviews includes Krausnick (ed.) 1983 and Eiber 1993, which has a brief but useful section on everyday life before 1933.

too, Rosenberg's memoirs take the form of a transcript of the subject's oral account, and readers are invited (by a preface which is neither Rosenberg's nor that of the transcriber-editor, Ulrich Enzensberger, and still more explicitly by a publisher's note in the English edition) to see in this text the naive – and thus authentic – voice of an unlettered 'natural'.[5]

But naivety is a problematic subject position. Public awareness of the Nazi persecution of Roma and Sinti has increased, and non-Romani academics have devoted increasing amounts of time and space to investigating the social and historical context of the persecution. Predictably, perhaps, what has resulted has been a mass of studies that, while written from a position of sympathy with the Romanies, have as their subject the majority (non-Romani) population – and a select portion of that population at that. Focusing on official policy and publicly recorded ideology, these trace not the history of a relationship, still less the history of the situation of the Romanies, but a history of persecution and discrimination. Nearly all historical studies of Roma and Sinti in Germany are in fact histories of anti-Gypsyism.[6] The proposition that the 'Gypsies' are a people without history is often cited critically as a component of the ideological construction, at worst anti-Gypsy and at best orientalist, that denies them subjectivity.[7] But the counter-construction of them as victims in perpetuity is simply the mirror image of that same proposition. Even if all we want to do is to understand the moment of persecution – how it arose, how effective it was, what role popular collaboration played in relation to official policy – we need to see how events emerged out of local circumstances and day-to-day relationships among all the historical actors, in a society that was itself subject to complex historical dynamics.

This is not easy. The difficulty of placing Romanies in history is in part a reflection of the state of the historical evidence. The most accessible written sources for Romani life in Germany before the mid-twentieth century are the records of outsiders: police authorities whose concern was at least to control, at worst to banish the Roma and Sinti,

---

[5] Rosenberg 1999: 4, 8. Rosenberg only completed two years of formal schooling, but by the time he dictated his memoirs he was a respected political activist. The knowledge and authority that qualified him for community leadership are suppressed in the memoir, which consistently maintains the unique perspective of the (at the time juvenile) victim. The authoritative voice remains that of the editor, heard in lengthy endnotes which explain historical events and policies that Rosenberg only experiences.

[6] In addition to the now extensive literature on the roots and manifestations of anti-Gypsy sentiment and the treatment of Romanies by bureaucracy and police, it may suffice to cite the work of Katrin Reemtsma (1996), one of the more conscientious efforts to counter stereotypes with an empirically grounded account of Romani history and culture in Germany; even this book treats developments up to the 1960s entirely in terms of *gadje* attitudes and police measures.

[7] See for example Trumpener 1992. On Orientalism, see Lee 2000.

and ethnographers for whom their subjects were of interest only in so far as they stood outside everyday life. Those few who claimed to speak *as* Romanies were of dubious authenticity and could only make themselves heard through the patronage of the ethnographers and Gypsiologists with whom they thereby became complicit.[8] In the absence of memoir literature, and in a situation in which the oral tradition has been interrupted by the experience of Holocaust (and is being recovered, if at all, largely in relation to the Holocaust events), it is difficult to reconstruct how Sinti and Roma lived their lives in the stretches of normality between major persecutions and policy initiatives. Similarly, it is difficult to access the forms and structures of interaction between non-Romanies and Romanies, although we know that these must have been sustained and complex, particularly in the case of the Sinti, who had been part of the German population for some 500 years before Hitler came to power.

None of this absolves scholars of the duty to read what sources there are carefully and imaginatively. Whatever its intended object, the police eye routinely records a range of information which can be used to reconstruct aspects of social life: occupation, education, geographical movements, means of transport, place of residence. The fact that in the early to mid-1930s the initiative for separation and incarceration of Sinti and Roma in 'Gypsy camps' (*Zigeunerlager*) came from municipalities should direct our attention to the possibilities of documentation at the local level, and some local studies that have taken the Holocaust as their starting point have begun to provide insights into the nature of daily life in German communities with a significant Sinti population before 1933.[9] This is a reminder of the inherent ambivalence of all documentary records. Any record to which two actors are party, however unequal their subject positions may be, documents an encounter and a negotiation; both subjects are present, though one may be claiming to speak for both.

This is an observation that, to return to the theme with which this essay opened, critics have made with increasing force about photographs. In an article of 1992 on 'the parallel histories of anthropology and photography', Christopher Pinney proposes a reading that emphasizes the indeterminacy of photographic images. Tellingly, for my purposes, he takes as his example the photograph of a Jewish boy alighting from a train at Auschwitz, which (he argues) can be read either as a certification of Nazi power or as an injunction to prevent genocide, and concludes in the light of this that 'the study of anthropology and the

---

[8] The most notorious example of this is the career of Engelbert Wittich; see Wittich 1911, Willems 1997: 189–91.

[9] On the setting up of *Zigeunerlager*, see Lewy 2000: 20–23. For studies of two localities with long-settled Sinti populations, see Kiderlen 1997 and Opfermann 1999 and 2001.

camera [should be] a study of the determination [...] of that "what is" [...] which lies in the photograph, through a study of the significatory frameworks whereby these images are endowed and closed with meaning' (Pinney 1992: 90). This is not only a warning about the fragility of ethnographic (and photographic) 'truth' but also an invitation to consider that there may be more than one significatory framework in play – that the photograph, whatever its provenance, is not an unproblematic record of the photographer's disciplinary intent, but the product of an interaction between observer and observed. Subsequent work on photography in colonial, postcolonial and neo-colonial settings has tended to look for the fissures and inconsistencies in the image that mark it as the product of a social process and allow access to the subjectivity of the sitters.[10] At the same time, historians of photography have foregrounded evidence for colonial subjects actively intervening in the process, to shape the image or to take control of the camera itself.[11] It is to these elements of interaction, process and negotiation that I want to be attentive in the case study that the rest of this essay will sketch out.

The Story

This is the story of a relationship between two 'families', on the one hand the Sinti, and on the other Weltzel and his household and, through him, an international community of *gadje* interested in the Sinti for academic, charitable or missionary reasons. In the interests of concision, I shall focus on the two men at its centre, both born in 1902. The one we know the most about is Johannes Otto Luis (Hanns) Weltzel, the son of a commercial employee. He was born in Breslau, but his family moved to Leipzig in 1910, and after his father's death (probably during the First World War) he and his mother settled with his maternal grandmother in Rosslau, an industrial suburb of Dessau. After finishing secondary school there, Weltzel went on to train for work in the lumber business. He worked for various firms in Rosslau in the 1920s, suffered unemployment in the Depression, and developed his literary and scientific interests into a small-scale journalistic career. By his own account, he began publishing in the *Anhalter Anzeiger* (Dessau) in 1932, and throughout the late 1930s he regularly published vignettes of Rosslau life and history in its daily pages and full-page features in the weekend supplement. He also published occasional pieces of literary criticism, but the principal emphasis of his journalism alongside local history was natural history, and particularly the study of snakes. From 1934 onwards, he regularly

---

[10] See the review of recent publications in Spyer 2001.
[11] See for example Pinney 1997, Maxwell 1999, Ginsburg 1995.

gave radio talks on natural science, and his first book (Weltzel 1934) was a popular study of the qualities and habits of snakes published in the same year. Two further volumes followed, *Erk Alburger* (Weltzel 1936), a family saga set in and around Rosslau, and *Der Vormittagsreiter* (Weltzel 1941), an essayistic study of equestrianism. In November 1935 Weltzel married Klara Czychowski, four years his junior, whose family owned a men's outfitting shop in Rosslau; the marriage was childless.[12]

The second man at the centre of this story is Lamperli, a Sinto born in Waldow, south of Berlin.[13] While Hanns Weltzel's family was settling in Leipzig, Lamperli was on the road with his father, Max, his mother and four brothers and a sister. By 1936, Max would be the authoritative elder (*puru*) of a group of interconnected families who could trace their ancestry to the Friedrichslohra Sinti, objects of a notorious early-nineteenth-century experiment in sedentarization. Since before the First World War they had travelled regularly in a circuit that took them from Berlin and its environs through what is now Sachsen-Anhalt and Thuringia, sometimes as far south as Leipzig. They had regular stopping places in the principal cities, Magdeburg, Halle and Dessau, as well as in smaller towns. Their itinerary was determined to some extent by the calendar of provincial fairs and markets, which provided them with opportunities to earn, mainly by horse-trading, peddling and performing. Their visits to the provinces were accordingly seasonal, concentrated in the spring and autumn, when Rosslau drew them to its livestock market and the neighbouring town, Zerbst, to its horse fair. A local churchyard was also known to be the site of the grave of a 'Gypsy baron'; local residents thought that this explained the area's appeal for the Sinti, but it was at the very least testimony to a long-standing Sinti presence in the district. In Kochstedt, just south of Dessau, there was a wheelwright who specialized in building and repairing caravans. In Rosslau, Lamperli's family tended to camp on the Weinberg, a wooded spot overlooking the main road and the place where the livestock market was held.[14] Winter usually found them in the cities. The registered address of many members of the family before the First World War was Berlin.

[12] Biographical details provided by Weltzel's file in the Reichskulturkammer, National Archives and Records Administration (NARA), RG242 Foreign Records Seized Collection, Reichskulturkammer, Series A3339-RKK, Reel B229, Frames 2018–2048; communication from Archiwum państwowe we Wrocławiu (Wrocław city archives), 21 August 2001.

[13] Individual Sinti are identified here only by their Sinti names, both in order to protect their anonymity and because these were the names by which they were known to their friends and families. The 'German' names by which they were identified to agents of the state were variable and contested. Except where otherwise indicated, biographical details on Lamperli and other individual Sinti are from files kept by the Magdeburg police, Landeshauptarchiv Sachsen-Anhalt/Magdeburg (LHAM), Rep. C29 Polizeipräsidium Magdeburg Anh. II.

[14] For the movements of these families, see the reports of the Halberstadt police for 27 April and 5 June 1912, LHAM, Rep. C28IV Regierung Magdeburg–Bezirksausschuß.

In cities, Sinti set up their caravans on rented pitches in special sites or private yards and gardens, or rejoined relatives who had rented dwellings of their own. The children attended school while the adults carried on their trades.[15]

Weltzel and Lamperli may have met as early as 1932; Weltzel's earliest dated photograph of a Romani subject dates from that year. It is not clear how they met, or what prompted Weltzel to start paying attention to the Sinti, who had always been part of the Rosslau scene. It is possible that Weltzel's interest was sparked by the increased visibility of Sinti that resulted from the economic depression. An incident that took place south of Dessau in late 1930 suggests such a development, and also illustrates the complex interaction between Romani travellers and the *gadje*. A group of Sinti signed a contract with the landlord of a village tavern permitting them to rent space in his yard to pitch their caravans over the winter. When the police insisted that they move on, it emerged that they had already sold their horses, and so had no means of shifting. Moreover, the innkeeper himself objected, protesting that the police were ruining his business, and he went so far as to apply to the local authorities for permission to 'keep' his Gypsies, citing extenuating personal circumstances on their behalf. In the end, the police paid local teamsters to tow the caravans away, but the tug of war between this particular innkeeper and the police over his right to do business with the Romanies was still going on in 1935.[16]

Weltzel was something of a linguist, with an interest in philology and dialectology as well as local history, and the relationship on his side took an academic form: he learned and recorded the language of the Sinti and observed their way of life. By 1936 he had gathered sufficient data to be invited to submit an article to the *Journal of the Gypsy Lore Society*. In the course of their meetings, Lamperli became the man on whom Weltzel relied for information about Sinti culture. As his subsequent publications show, Weltzel increasingly saw his role as that of an ethnographer; while he shared the philological interest of successive generations of

---

Gewerbepolizei: Zigeunerangelegenheiten, no. 646: 46 and 50; Landjägeramt Jeßnitz to Kreisdirektion Dessau, 22 July 1927, Landesarchiv Oranienbaum (LAO), Kreisdirektion Dessau-Köthen, no. 593: 19. See also Hanns Weltzel, 'Kleine Liebe zu den Zigeunern', clipping from periodical publication, source unidentified, c. 1936?, Weltzel files from the private papers of Georg Althaus, Liverpool University Gypsy Collections, donation of Mrs Dorothée Althaus-Pultke (SJL/WA).

[15] Eyewitness accounts of the lives of Berlin Sinti before 1933 include Rosenberg 1999, Adler 1960 and Zeller-Plinzner 1934. See also Block 1936: 48 (specifying 13 'Gypsy' colonies [*Siedlungen*] in Berlin comprising some 1600 individuals), 205–08, and photographs; Wittich 1911.

[16] Report (source unclear), Mosigkau, to Kreisdirektion Dessau, 25 December 1930, LAO, Kreisdirektion Dessau-Köthen, no. 593: 66; Amtsvorsteher Mosigkau to Kreisamt Köthen, 6 July 1935, ibid.: 73.

Gypsiologists – perhaps because nearly all the existing literature on Romanies focused on language – he argued that an informed understanding of their culture was necessary in order to comprehend fully their linguistic practice. The photographs he took were intended to reinforce the ethnographic record by 'fixing' the personalities of his interlocutors (Weltzel 1938: 9–11). In ethnographic terms, Lamperli was Weltzel's informant. But Lamperli and his family clearly also exercised a degree of attraction for Weltzel which made him seek intimacy with them, hanging around their camps and conversing (as far as he could) in Romanes; cosmopolitan and unconventional in the context of his provincial home town, Weltzel liked and admired the Sinti. In this sense, he regarded Lamperli as his friend, and they always addressed each other as such.

The relationship between ethnographer and informant is often characterized by ambivalence, an echo of the inherently ambivalent character of the ethnographic project of 'participant observation' (Clifford 1988). But the mid-1930s were a particularly difficult time for a Sinto and a *gadjo* to carry on a friendship. The Nazi takeover in 1933 brought a change in atmosphere, which set in at local level even before national politics took notice of the Sinti. The summer of 1935 witnessed a wave of complaints from residents of the villages around Dessau and from the offices of the official farmers' organization (*Reichsbauernschaft*). In their wording and in the anxieties they express about thieving and arson on the part of Sinti travellers, these complaints echo those being made in other rural areas so closely as to suggest a concerted campaign. In some of their details they do seem to reflect changing circumstances: Sinti travelling in larger groups than ever (one report cited a train of 34 caravans and 147 horses), and noticeably short of cash. At the same time, increased – and increasingly hostile – scrutiny by police and villagers (who themselves had little surplus to spare) tightened the constraints on the ability of the Sinti to support themselves.[17]

In the winter of 1935, Max and his wife and Lamperli were still travelling. By the spring of 1937, Max was living in Rosslau. At some point in the intervening months, intensified harassment had effectively made travelling and horse-trading impossible, and the family had sold their horses and settled down. They rented space for their caravans at inflated rates at two addresses on the edge of town. The older women continued to try peddling lace and other textile goods in town, though without much success, while the younger men took up work in local factories.[18]

[17] Correspondence from summer and autumn 1935 in LAO, Kreisdirektion Dessau-Köthen, no. 593. For comparable developments in north-western Germany (Oldenburg), see Hesse and Schreiber 1999: 222–24.

[18] Letter to Kiter (Lamperli's brother-in-law) from his father, Erfurt, 16 March 1937, SJL/WA; Geheime Staatspolizei, Staatspolizeistelle Dessau to Staatsministerium Dessau, 3 January 1938, LAO, Kreisdirektion Bernburg II, no. 941: 67–68.

Lamperli was sometimes one of their number, but his official place of residence was Magdeburg. During this same period a *Zigeunerlager* was set up on the outskirts of the city, and this was Lamperli's address at the end of 1937. While in the camp he, like other Sinti, was subject to registration measures which involved extensive documentation and interviews with himself and his mother. One result was the requirement that he take on his mother's maiden name on the grounds that he was formally illegitimate.[19] In January 1938, 54 Sinti, most of them members of the families headed by Max, were formally ordered to leave Rosslau and the state of Anhalt. In view of the recent construction of a barracks and training unit there, their presence constituted 'an immediate threat to public order and security'.[20]

In December 1939, the local authorities declared that there were no Gypsies left in the district around Rosslau.[21] Most of the individuals expelled from Rosslau the previous year had been escorted by the police to the camp in Magdeburg, from which the men were sent to Buchenwald in June of 1938.[22] Those still in the camp in March 1943 were sent to Auschwitz, among the first to be affected by Himmler's order that all 'Gypsy mongrels' (*Mischlinge*) be deported. Some of the Rosslau families either avoided the Magdeburg camp completely or made their way from there back to Berlin, where the deportation of April 1943 found them living in the notorious Marzahn *Zigeunerlager* or in slum apartments.[23] Lamperli's brother-in-law, Kiter, spent some time working in Erfurt during 1938, and wrote to Weltzel to report that 'evil times' had befallen the Sinti and to ask him to intervene with the local authorities on behalf of the Magdeburg families; at some point he apparently returned to Magdeburg and was deported with the others.[24]

[19] It has not been possible to determine the precise date and circumstances of the erection of the Magdeburg *Zigeunerlager* (or, indeed, its exact location): letters to the author from Stadtarchiv Magdeburg (12 July 2001) and Katasteramt Magdeburg (21 August 2001); compare Gilsenbach 2000: 109–13. Lamperli continued to sign letters using this 'imposed' name into the post-war period.

[20] Geheime Staatspolizei, Staatspolizeistelle Dessau to Staatsministerium Dessau, 3 January 1938: 66–69; *Chronik der Stadt Rosslau* 1996: 67. For comparable examples of clearing Gypsies out of militarily 'sensitive' areas, see Hesse and Schreiber 1999: 224–25.

[21] Landrat Bernburg to Kripostelle Dessau, 2 December 1939, LAO, Kreisdirektion Bernburg II, no. 599/II: 6.

[22] In addition to the archival sources cited, the following account of Weltzel's and Lamperli's movements draws on two typescripts (11 pages in all) sent by Weltzel for publication in the *Journal of the Gypsy Lore Society*. Dora Yates deemed them inappropriate for publication. See Weltzel 1948 and 1949, and an earlier draft found among Weltzel's papers in SJL/WA, which differs in some details.

[23] Records of Berlin deportations in the files of the Oberfinanzdirektion Berlin (Landesarchiv Berlin), US Holocaust Memorial Museum microfilm series RG-07.008*1. On Marzahn, see Wippermann and Brucker-Boroujerdi 1987.

[24] Letter from Kiter to Weltzel, 10 August 1938, SJL/WA; *Memorial Book* 1993.

While Lamperli and his mother were being interrogated by the police about their family relationships, Weltzel was drafting a letter – the nearest he came to a public protest about Nazi policy towards the Romanies. It was occasioned by the publication of Otto Finger's study of 'two asocial Gypsy *Mischling* clans', and addressed to the director of the Giessen institute under whose imprint it was published. In the letter, he deployed his detailed knowledge of Sinti customs and individuals to challenge the scientific status of statements about their criminality, while acquiescing in the racialist language and deferring to the academic status of his addressee.[25] In retrospect, he accurately described himself as 'twisting myself like a snake' in the wording of the letter. During 1937 and 1938 Weltzel was also busy developing his career, applying for membership in the Reich Chamber of Literature, and in his application there is evidence of the same readiness to speak the language of the powerful. In another sense, too, the application contains reminders that the Nazi state created extraordinary pressures on all Germans, *gadje* and Sinti alike. While he was pursuing his personal research into the genealogy of his Sinti friends, Weltzel was gathering evidence for his own, since membership in an official organization depended on proof of Aryan status.

At the same time, Weltzel was pursuing a kind of normality, corresponding with philologists in Germany and completing the account of the lives of 'his' Sinti for publication in England. His letters to the editor of the *JGLS*, Dora Yates, made no direct reference to the hardships under which his subjects were living. The article, begun in 1936 and published in 1938, commented on the effects of poverty and legal constraints to travelling and peddling, but revealed nothing about the more sinister forms of harassment of which he was aware. He challenged 'the imputation that they are an inferior class of human beings', a veiled comment on official policy, while complimenting 'the present German government' on its campaign against urban crime.[26] By late 1938, though, the space for 'normality' in Sinti–*gadjo* relations was narrowing. Apparently as a result of the *JGLS* article, Weltzel received a visit from Robert Ritter, the criminologist who since 1936 had been responsible for the registration and classification of all German Romanies and who provided advice to the government on policy towards them. Ritter invited Weltzel to join his 'team', and specifically sought access to his genealogical records. By his own account, Weltzel refused to cooperate, beyond giving Ritter a few linguistic tips. He continued to visit and to correspond with his Sinti friends, and they with him.

[25] Weltzel to Heinrich Wilhelm Kranz, 16 November 1937, SJL/WA. On the Giessen institute, see Dalchow 1998.
[26] Weltzel 1938, Jubilee Supplement: 37–38. This last comment has been interpreted as signalling approval of Nazi policy towards the Romanies, but it is open to different readings; compare Zimmermann 1996: 431.

Lamperli was among the men identified as 'workshy' and sent to Buchenwald from Magdeburg in June 1938. He was released by order of the Berlin police headquarters the following February. The grounds for the release are not clear. In November, Max had asked a local pastor to intercede with the police on Lamperli's behalf, arguing that he was needed at home to support the family. The Magdeburg authorities, however, recommended against release. At the same time, Weltzel (by his own account) requested of Robert Ritter that Lamperli's release be arranged. Lamperli worked as a labourer until at least the end of 1939, when along with all other registered Sinti and Roma he was forbidden to leave his home city. During 1939 he visited Weltzel and corresponded with him; while other Sinti wrote of their sufferings and begged Weltzel for help, Lamperli's letters were studiedly light-hearted and scurrilous. In 1941 (according to Weltzel) he reported to his friend that he had been called up for military service.

Weltzel, too, was called up in 1941. He spent the war as a driver in a transport division, mainly on the Eastern Front. Even while on active service he kept an eye out for Romanies, asking after familiar family names among Sinti deportees whom he encountered in Poland and noting the circumstances of Romanies still travelling freely. He remembered being told by a soldier in the field about the massacre of Jews and Romanies in Kielce (August 1942).[27]

Lamperli's war was different. His call-up did not save him – officially certified since July 1941 as a predominantly 'Gypsy' *Mischling* – from being deported to Auschwitz-Birkenau in March 1943. Along with a handful of members of his extended family, he survived Auschwitz and was among the Sinti transported back into the Reich in April 1944. His first destination was Buchenwald, but the end of the war very likely found him labouring in Dora-Mittelbau or, like Otto Rosenberg, in Bergen-Belsen.[28]

Certainly, the next we hear of Lamperli is from north-western Germany. At the end of 1948, he wrote to Weltzel from Brake (near Oldenburg). He reported that he was doing well, travelling with his wife and sons and trading in violins. His principal reason for writing was to ask Weltzel for photographs of his family, most of whom had been killed: 'I know very well that you have all the pictures of our family you will show me the greatest friendship by doing this I will

---

[27] On Weltzel's military service: Deutsche Dienststelle Berlin to the author, 14 October 1999. On the Sinti deported to Poland in 1940, see Zimmermann 1996: 79–84; Hesse and Schreiber 1999: 245–51.

[28] Lamperli to Weltzel, 7 November 1939, SJL/WA; *Memorial Book* 1993. The date of arrival in Auschwitz and prisoner number indicate that he was deported with the inmates of the Magdeburg *Zigeunerlager*. On Romanies in the armed services, see Lewy 2000: 93–97.

visit you some time we two have a lot to discuss which is very important for you.'[29]

Lamperli was not the first of the surviving Sinti to make contact with his old associates. Weltzel reported that when he was demobilized he had found no Sinti in Rosslau, but in 1946 they began to return; the children of one of Lamperli's cousins visited Weltzel, and alerted Lamperli to the fact that he was still alive and at the old address. It is not clear whether Lamperli ever did visit Weltzel; Rosslau and Brake were on different sides of a zonal divide which most ordinary Germans had begun to see as a border by the end of 1948. In the Soviet Zone, returning Sinti struggled once again to scrape a living, sometimes formally acknowledged as victims of fascism and, more often than not, torn between the good intentions of the Soviet occupiers and sympathetic functionaries, the indifference of a weary and anxious population, and the routine hostility of the local police authorities.[30]

The memory and traces of persecution provided new sources of friction in an already suspicious time, as survivors tried to reclaim their homes and possessions. In these situations, the threat (at least) that individuals who had participated in or benefited from the Nazi persecution would be denounced to the authorities lay close to hand.[31] Perhaps this was what Lamperli meant to imply when he wrote to Weltzel of 'a lot of things to discuss which is very important for you'; or perhaps this is how Weltzel read it. In later years, one of the survivors (very likely Lamperli) claimed to have 'set the Russians on Weltzel'.[32] Members of Lamperli's family recalled twenty years later that they had reason to denounce Weltzel: they claimed that he had taken part in the deportations from Magdeburg, that he had been involved in interrogations at Buchenwald, and that he had been seen in company with the Nazi race scientists in Berlin.[33] At the time Lamperli wrote to him, Weltzel was conscious of being at risk, though it is not entirely clear whether that anxiety had specific grounds or was simply a reaction to the intensifying political tension in the shadow of the Berlin crisis of 1948; he asked Dora Yates

[29] Lamperli to Weltzel, 13 December 1948, SJL/WA. Weltzel to Dora Yates, 26 December 1948, Liverpool University Library, Gypsy Lore Society Archive (SGL/GLS), XIV.35.

[30] See Landespolizei-Abteilung Dessau to Landpolizeikreis Köthen, 12 July 1947, and Chef der Polizei Land Sachsen-Anhalt to Kreisrat Dessau-Köthen, 22 August 1947, LAO, Kreisdirektion Dessau-Köthen, no. 593: 143, 145. For an example of attempts of the Soviet military authority to suppress anti-Gypsyism see Befehl Nr 24 des Chefs der Verwaltung der SMA der Provinz Sachsen, 25 January 1946, ibid.: 146. See also Gilsenbach 2000: 93–118; Rosenberg 1999: 115–17.

[31] For examples of revenge-taking and denunciation, see Reinhardt 1999; Rosenberg 1999; Kiderlen 1997; Günther 1990.

[32] Georg Althaus to Dora Yates, 24 March 1964, SJL/GLS, XXXI.1.

[33] Reimar Gilsenbach to Siegfried Wölffling, 30 August 1968, Reimar Gilsenbach papers (courtesy of R. Gilsenbach). Compare Gilsenbach 1996.

to write to him under a different name care of a Berlin publishing house.[34] In the account that he wrote for English readers of the Nazi persecution he made a point of indicating that he knew of the suspicions of his Sinti friends. At the same time, he seemed relatively sanguine about the possibility of carrying on his writing. In the event he published no more, but found work that employed his peculiar skills: he was working as a technician in a local pharmaceuticals plant when he was arrested by the Soviet military authorities – now occupying the very barracks whose construction had actuated the expulsion of Lamperli's family. According to contemporaries, he also worked as an interpreter for the Soviets at some point after the war. Whether it was his link to the Sinti or a conflict arising from his interpreting work that led to his arrest remains unclear; the charge was a blanket one of espionage and anti-Soviet activities. Arrested in April, he was executed in September 1952. His widow, Klara, died in Rosslau in 1964; in her last years she eked out her income by selling Weltzel's photographs to Georg Althaus, a West German pastor who was as puzzled by the story of Weltzel and the 'Gypsies' as he was fascinated by the Sinti themselves.[35]

It is through the photographs, as they passed into Althaus's hands, that we are able to follow Lamperli's career to its end. In the early 1950s, Lamperli and his children were among a group of Sinti settled in Hildesheim when the pastor began to make regular visits on his motor-cycle, delivering second-hand clothes along with the gospel. (This would lead to the foundation of an official, though underfunded, mission in Braunschweig in 1957.) Althaus was often accompanied on these visits by one of his daughters, who were always welcomed by the Sinti. On one occasion, however, it emerged in the course of conversation that his eldest daughter was a midwife – a profession regarded in Sinti custom as taboo. Lamperli took on the role of spokesman for the community, ordering Althaus amid threats of physical violence to leave and never come back, and he later visited Althaus in Braunschweig to repeat the interdiction. At their first meeting, Lamperli accused Althaus of being a spy for the race scientists and a traitor, like Weltzel, whom he was sure Althaus knew. This was (by Althaus's account) the first time he had heard Weltzel's name; with the help of Dora Yates, he made contact with Klara Weltzel shortly thereafter. Meanwhile, Lamperli's

---

[34] Weltzel to Dora Yates, 26 December 1948.

[35] Elisabeth Hackel, MS memoir, Berlin 1997; rehabilitation certificate for Hanns Weltzel, issued by the Chief Military Court of the Russian Federation 29 March 1999 (both courtesy of Mr Klemens Koschig, Mayor of Rosslau); Klemens Koschig to the author, 19 November 1998; information from Mrs Dorothée Althaus-Pultke, Braunschweig, November 2001; Georg Althaus to Dora Yates, 19 June 1962, SJL/GLS, XXIX.3; Georg Althaus to Siegmund A. Wolf, 17 January 1964, Althaus papers in the possession of Mrs Dorothée Althaus-Pultke, Braunschweig (Althaus papers Braunschweig). On Althaus, see most recently Margalit 2000.

quest for photographs continued; he wrote to Weltzel again (apparently ignorant of his death), this time asking for a particular photograph, and when Klara suggested that he ask Althaus, the result was another meeting in Braunschweig. Althaus noted that Lamperli was no longer the 'splendid and approachable' character Weltzel had described; the experience of the camps had 'clearly transformed him' and as Althaus experienced him he was not only irritable and overbearing but – stereo-typically – deceptive and 'shallow'. The pastor also described 'a sort of friendship' that developed between the two men, fostered by mutual visits, strained by recurring moments of mistrust, but always refreshed by the display of the photographic images in which both men took delight, though for different reasons. Lamperli died in 1963 and was buried in Braunschweig.[36]

The Testimony of the Photographs

Photographs are the leitmotif and the cement of this story, binding together the braided lives of Weltzel and Lamperli and their respective 'families'. It is noteworthy that the end of the war brings a shift in their function, or at any rate we see them from different perspectives in the two periods. Objects of a negotiation between photographer and subjects after the war, as Sinti attempted to take possession of their relics, the photographs at their point of origin gave every impression of being fully under Weltzel's control, articles of exchange at best among Gypsiologists. This impression is in part an artefact of the way in which they have been archived, and the order in which they came into this his-torian's hands; I first became aware of Weltzel as a result of finding a selection of his photographs in the archives of the Gypsy Lore Society (GLS), and only several years later gained access to the complete set of over 200 images preserved among the papers of Georg Althaus. But the disposition of the photographs in space and time also reflects the differing intentions of the different people for whom the pictures were important.

In the 1930s, Weltzel selected about two dozen of his photographs to send to Dora Yates along with the manuscript of his 1938 article, invit-ing her to publish some of them as illustrations. The selection he made constituted an ethnographic collection. They were to be made available to a *gadjo* public, in illustration of those features of their Sinti subjects

---

[36] Georg Althaus, 'Aus der lutherischen Missionsarbeit an den verfolgten Zigeunern in Deutschland', MS Braunschweig 1959, Landeskirchliches Archiv in Braunschweig, Dienst an Israel 18; Georg Althaus to Hermann Langbein, 7 January 1964, Georg Althaus to Siegfried Wölffling, 11 February 1964, both Althaus papers Braunschweig.

which were of interest because they marked the Sinti as *different* from the viewers – fit objects of ethnographic research. No *gadjo* appears in any of these photographs, although there is of course one behind the camera. The selection actually published in the *JGLS* comprised the most emphatically exotic of the images. In the best tradition of colonial or orientalist photography, these pictures fix their subjects as objects of an alien gaze and seem reserved to the proprietorship of the photographer and the *gadjo* viewers rather than the Sinti. Weltzel's texts, too, emphasized the distance between photographer and subjects. He asserted that 'his' Sinti – 'a people living in the state of nature', though increasingly under threat from the encroachments of civilization – had no understanding of his own project and were unaware of being the objects of generations of academic study (cf. Rosenhaft 2001).

Even in the GLS set of photographs there are pictures that do not conform to the stereotypical image of the exotic. In a letter of 1938, Weltzel self-consciously pointed out to Dora Yates that he had included some 'pictures of my friends, taken in the way the *gadje* have themselves photographed, so you can see how this "damned race" can stand any comparison'.[37] When girls whom Weltzel has snapped sleeping under their caravans appear, like three of Lamperli's cousins, in fashionable dresses on Weltzel's terrace (Figs 1 and 2) or in studio portraits like the one of Lamperli's teenage niece (Fig. 3), Weltzel is revealed as an accomplished photographer with an eye for composition and an enthusiasm for the photographic process, as well as someone able to see his subjects (literally) in different lights. Weltzel's newspaper and magazine articles on local history and natural history were usually accompanied by his own photographs, but it is not clear what formal training he had. Images in the Althaus collection represent an even wider range of styles and genres, suggesting that Weltzel was aware of contemporary developments in art photography (Fig. 4).

But these photographs are not simply about Weltzel. His children of nature look quite at home in their city clothes. What Weltzel himself did not know, or did not admit to knowing, was that 'his' Sinti had considerable experience of being observed and photographed. In Berlin in the early 1930s, members of Lamperli's family not only encountered and interacted with *gadje*, but were given a prominent role in *gadjo* accounts of 'Gypsy' life. In 1931, they featured as characters in *Ede und Unku*, a novel inspired by a chance meeting between the Communist writer Grete Weiskopf ('Alex Wedding') and one of Lamperli's young cousins, Unku. A few years later the missionary Frieda Zeller-Plinzner described Unku and her brothers and sisters in some detail in her account of the Berlin 'Gypsy'-mission. Both accounts were illustrated

---

[37] Hanns Weltzel to Dora Yates, n.d. [1938], SJL/GLS, IX.53.

Figure 1. Unku, Rosslau, probably 1936 (sent by Hanns Weltzel to Dora Yates).

with photographs.[38] Weltzel's friends not only had extensive experience of commercialized urban life, but belonged to a performance culture; some of their friends and relations worked periodically as extras in the Berlin film studios.[39] Most of Weltzel's subjects look happy to be photographed, and when not caught off guard their poses and dress suggest elements of self-fashioning in which some, at least, felt free to draw on the products of *gadjo* culture as well as their 'own'. The line was in any case easily crossed, since popular culture had long since incorporated elements of dress and hairstyle that signified 'Gypsiness' into the visual vocabulary of glamour deployed in advertising, fashion and the cinema. This kind of iconic self-consciousness seems most obvious in the case of the young Sinti women, but it is not exclusive to them.[40]

The full archive shows Lamperli, too, in a number of 'roles'. Weltzel sent no photographs of Lamperli to Liverpool before the war; although Weltzel's chief informant figures by name and in considerable detail in

[38] Wedding 1931; Zeller-Plinzner 1934. The photographs illustrating *Ede und Unku* were taken by the pioneer of political photomontage, John Heartfield.
[39] On the implications of performance in Romani culture and its relation to notions of authenticity and Romani–*gadjo* relations, see Lemon 2000, esp. chapter 3.
[40] On the 'exchange of fantasies' across the sexual divide between *gadje* and Romanies, see Okely 1996.

Figure 2. Unku (centre), Lotte (left) and Puppchen (right) on the Weltzels' terrace, Rosslau, 1936 (sent by Hanns Weltzel to Dora Yates).

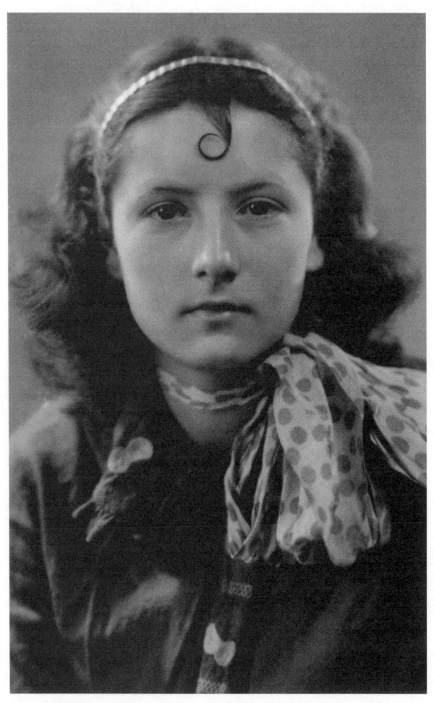

Figure 3. Portrait of Tsiga, 1935/36 (sent by Hanns Weltzel to Dora Yates).

Figure 4. Tsiga: an 'art-shot', 1937 (Althaus papers).

the *JGLS* article, the only graphic representation of him there is a self-portrait drawing of Lamperli as a knight in armour. The sole photograph of Lamperli in the GLS archives (Fig. 5) shows a man not easily identifiable as a Sinto; it is dated 1939, and Weltzel sent it to Liverpool in 1948.[41] The Althaus collection yields more 'typical' images, including one of Lamperli tucking into a hedgehog (Fig. 6), and clearly putting on a show for the camera.

If Weltzel was looking, then, his subjects were emphatically looking back. But the photographs of Lamperli are also characteristic of the way in which the full archive exposes the extent of the interaction between photographer and subject. The Althaus collection allows us to see Weltzel himself among the Rosslau Sinti (Fig. 7). Moments of intimacy between Weltzel and his friends give the lie to the ethnographer's assertions of distance and reinforce the impression conveyed in his writings that he was aware himself that his romantic vision was unstable. At the same time these images throw into relief the moral and empirical question of what kind of relationship Weltzel thought he was maintaining

---

[41] Compare the comment of Luc de Heusch, *The Cinema and Social Science* (1962): '[Sometimes] an ethnographer goes so far as to publish pictures of men he has known and liked but does so with considerable reluctance, as if the emotive power of the picture, being foreign to his purpose, embarrasses him.' Cited in Pinney 1992: 81.

Figure 5. Lamperli in front of Weltzel's house, Rosslau, 1939 (sent by Hanns Weltzel to Dora Yates in 1948).

with his friends once they were in the grip of full-blown persecution. The photograph of the three young women sent to Liverpool in 1937–38 (Fig. 2) was in fact one of a series, taken during a social visit to the Weltzels; other photographs in the series include Klara Weltzel (Fig. 8). These photographs also make it possible to identify the location of the

Figure 6. Lamperli preparing to eat a hedgehog (Althaus papers).

'first' Lamperli photograph as Weltzel's house; taken together with a photograph of Lamperli in Weltzel's living room (Fig. 9), that 'first' Lamperli picture becomes recognizable as part of the record of another social visit, this time on Lamperli's part. By 1939, though, Lamperli was on leave from Buchenwald and subject to police and employer pressure to maintain a steady job or be reincarcerated. Weltzel knew this, and our knowledge of it demands a re-reading – necessarily inconclusive – of both the photographic act and Lamperli's hyper-respectable self-presentation.

Lamperli's sister, Repina, appears in both series in a similarly discomfiting range of contexts. Among the GLS pictures, she is portrayed with her husband, Kiter, among the family caravans (probably) in Rosslau (Fig. 10). The Althaus photos show that she was one of the Sinti whom the Weltzels entertained at home (Fig. 11), but they also include the record of another kind of visit. This is one of a series of photographs that Weltzel took in the Magdeburg 'Gypsy camp', and the

Figure 7. Hanns Weltzel with an elderly Sintezza in Rosslau (Althaus papers).

only one to contain human figures. It shows Repina and her (and Lamperli's) brother, Biku (Fig. 12). The photograph confirms what is also clear in the manuscript sources: Weltzel told Dora Yates of his intention to visit Lamperli in the camp in 1938, and his post-war account described his first visit and the shock of seeing his friends 'desperate, worn out, depressed and all somehow ugly'. Weltzel went on to make a comment that reflects his sense of complicity and also of helplessness; referring to the last *gadjo* to have a responsible role in the Friedrichslohra experiment, and the one who recorded its failure, he wrote: 'I now understood the teacher [...] who must have found the Friedrichslohra Sinti in a similar condition back then'.[42] This was also the occasion when

---

[42] Weltzel 1949: 2; Weltzel to Dora Yates, 28 June 1938, SJL/GLS, XIV.51.

Figure 8. Unku, Lotte and Puppchen with Klara Weltzel (second from left) at the Weltzels' house, Rosslau, 1936 (Althaus papers).

many of 'his' Sinti first reproached him with betrayal. Perhaps their absence from most of the Magdeburg pictures records a positive act of refusal.

Conclusion

This essay began with the assertion that it is both possible and necessary to see the history of Sinti and Roma in Germany as part of a shared history, and with a plea that scholars direct their vision to the moments of normality in a chronicle of actions and interactions to which both Romanies and *gadje* were party. In the case of Weltzel and Lamperli and their respective 'families', the harder we look the more questions present

Figure 9. Lamperli in the Weltzels' house, Rosslau, 1939 (Althaus papers).

themselves. This is not simply because the circumstances, with the Holocaust at their centre, were anything but normal. One thing that the textual and photographic evidence does document is the struggle of both Sinti and *gadje* to maintain or recover ordinary lives in extraordinary times. The more closely we inspect the photographs, though, and the more attentive we are to the presence of multiple 'significatory frameworks', the harder it becomes to 'fix' the nature of what they are recording. We become aware of negotiations at every point in the life of each image, starting *within* the frame, as subjects and photographer bring their own intentions to the making of the picture. To say that Weltzel's photographs record a relationship, then, is not to say that they lead us to any firm conclusions about (for example) what Weltzel and Lamperli expected from each other, or what either of them meant when he addressed the other as *mala*, 'friend'. But it is one of the features of social interaction in a complex society that relationships are not easily read.

Figure 10. Repina (Lamperli's sister) and her husband Kiter, Rosslau, 1936/37 (sent by Hanns Weltzel to Dora Yates).

Figure 11. Repina (right) and Lulu (left) on the Weltzels' lawn, Rosslau, 1937 (Althaus papers).

Figure 12. Repina and her brother Biku in the Magdeburg 'Gypsy camp', 1938 (Althaus papers).

They *happen*, and so are inherently unstable; they are ambivalent, and thus subject to negotiation. The same is true of identities. The lore of both Sinti and *gadje* tended to deny complexity, insisting that these two men stood on opposite sides of a significant cultural divide, that they lived in different worlds. In these documents, by contrast, Sinti and *gadjo* alike appear as engaged in a continuous labour of balancing distance and intimacy, simultaneously reaffirming difference and enacting hybridity. We have everything to gain by being attentive to the specific rhythms and outcomes of that process, in which both parties have always had an active role.

References

Adler, Marta. 1960. *Mein Schicksal waren die Zigeuner*. Bremen: Schunemann.
Block, Martin. 1936. *Zigeuner: Ihr Leben und ihre Seele*. Leipzig: Bibliographisches Institut.
Chronik der Stadt Rosslau. 1996. Köthen: Micado.
Clifford, James. 1988. 'On Ethnographic Authority', in *idem*, *The Predicament of*

Culture: Twentieth-Century Ethnography, Literature, and Art. Cambridge, MA: Harvard University Press.

Dalchow, Stephan. 1998. *Die Entwicklung der nationalsozialistischen Erb- und Rassenpflege an der medizinischen Fakultät der Ludwigs-Universität Giessen*. Giessen: Wilhelm Schmitz.

Devereux, Leslie, and Hillman, Roger (eds). 1995. *Fields of Vision: Essays in Film Studies, Visual Anthropology, and Photography*. Berkeley: University of California Press.

Edwards, Elizabeth (ed.). 1992. *Anthropology and Photography 1860–1920*. New Haven and London: Yale University Press.

Eiber, Ludwig. 1993. *'Ich wußte, es wird schlimm.' Die Verfolgung der Sinti und Roma in München 1933–1945*. Munich: Buchendorfer.

Eitel, Peter (ed.). 1997. *Ravensburg im Dritten Reich*. Ravensburg: Oberschwäbische Verlagsanstalt.

Franz, Philomena. 1992. *Zwischen Liebe und Hass*. Freiburg: Herder.

Gilsenbach, Reimar. 1996. 'Mit den Augen der Sinti', *Die Tageszeitung* (Berlin), 6 June: 14.

— 2000. *Von Tschudemann zu Seemann: Zwei Prozesse aus der Geschichte deutscher Sinti*. Berlin: Centre de recherches tsiganes/Edition Parabolis.

Ginsburg, Faye. 1995. 'Mediating Culture: Indigenous Media, Ethnographic Film, and the Production of Identity', in Devereux and Hillmann (eds) 1995: 256–91.

Günther, Wolfgang. 1990. *'Ach, Schwester, ich kann nicht mehr tanzen...': Sinti und Roma im KZ-Bergen-Belsen*. Hanover: SOAK.

Hägele, Ulrich. 1998. 'Der zerstörte Blick: Fotografie im Dienste unmenschlicher Wissenschaft', in Hägele (ed.) 1998: 94–121.

Hägele, Ulrich (ed.). 1998. *Sinti und Roma und Wir: Ausgrenzung, Internierung und Verfolgung einer Minderheit*. Tübingen: Kulturamt Stadt Tübingen.

Hesse, Hans, and Schreiber, Jens. 1999. *Vom Schlachthof nach Auschwitz: Die NS-Verfolgung der Sinti und Roma aus Bremen, Bremerhaven und Nordwestdeutschland*. Marburg: Tectum.

Kenkmann, Alfons, and Rusinek, Bernd.-A. (eds). 1999. *Verfolgung und Verwaltung: Die wirtschaftliche Ausplünderung der Juden und die westfälischen Finanzbehörden*. Münster: Oberfinanzdirektion.

Kiderlen, Dorothea. 1997. ' "Duesch halt fescht d'Zähn' zammabeißa...": Verfolgung und Vernichtung der Ravensburger Sinti', in Eitel (ed.) 1997: 342–60.

Krausnick, Michail (ed.). 1983. *Da wollten wir frei sein! Eine Sinti-Familie erzählt*. Weinheim: Beltz.

Lee, Ken. 2000. 'Orientalism and Gypsylorism', *Social Analysis*, 44.2: 129–56.

Lemon, Alaina. 2000. *Between Two Fires: Gypsy Performance and Romani Memory from Pushkin to Socialism*. Durham, NC: Duke University Press.

Lewy, Guenter. 2000. *The Nazi Persecution of the Gypsies*. New York: Oxford University Press.

Margalit, Gilad. 2000. '"Großer Gott, ich danke Dir, daß Du kleine schwarze Kinder gemacht hast." Der "Zigeunerpastor" Georg Althaus', *Werkstatt-Geschichte*, 25: 59–73.

Maxwell, Anne. 1999. *Colonial Photography and Exhibitions.* London: Leicester University Press.

Memorial Book: The Gypsies at Auschwitz-Birkenau. 1993. Munich: K.G. Saur.

Mettbach, Anna, and Behringer, Josef. 1999. *'Wer wird die nächste sein?' Die Leidensgeschichte einer Sintezza, die Auschwitz überlebte.* Frankfurt: Brandes & Apsel.

Okely, Judith. 1996. 'Gypsy Women: Models in Conflict', in *idem., Own or Other Culture.* London: Routledge.

Opfermann, Ulrich F. 1999. 'Zigeunerverfolgung, Enteignung, Umverteilung: Das Beispiel der Wittgensteiner Kreisstadt Berleburg', in Kenkmann and Rusinek (eds) 1999: 67–86.

—2001. 'The Registration of Gypsies in National Socialism: Responsibility in a German Region', *Romani Studies*, 5.11: 25–52.

Pinney, Christopher. 1992. 'The Parallel Histories of Anthropology and Photography', in Edwards (ed.) 1992: 74–96.

—1997. *Camera Indica: The Social Life of Indian Photographs.* Chicago: University of Chicago Press.

Reemtsma, Katrin. 1996. *Sinti und Roma: Geschichte, Kultur, Gegenwart.* Munich: Beck.

Regener, Susanne. 1999. *Fotografische Erfassung: Zur Geschichte medialer Konstruktionen des Kriminellen.* Munich: Fink.

Reinhardt, Lolo. 1999. *Überwintern: Jugenderinnerungen eines schwäbischen Zigeuners.* Gerlingen: Bleicher.

Ribbe, Wolfgang (ed.). 1987. *Berlin-Forschungen II.* Berlin: Colloquium.

Rosenberg, Otto. 1999. *A Gypsy in Auschwitz: As Told to Ulrich Enzensberger.* Trans. Helmut Bögler. London: London House.

Rosenhaft, Eve. 2001. 'Gefühl, Gewalt und Melancholie in den Humanwissenschaften. Der "Zigeunerforscher" Hanns Weltzel und die Ambivalenz des ethnologischen Blicks', *Sozialwissenschaftliche Informationen*, 3/2001: 22–34.

Sekula, Allan. 1984. 'The Traffic in Photographs', in *idem, Photography against the Grain: Essays and Photo Works 1973–1983.* Halifax: Press of Nova Scotia College of Art and Design: 77–101.

Sontag, Susan. 1982. *On Photography.* Harmondsworth: Penguin.

Spyer, Patricia. 2001. 'Photography's Framings and Unframings', *Comparative Studies in Society and History*, 43: 181–92.

Stojka, Ceija. 1988. *Wir leben im Verborgenen.* Vienna: Picus.

—1992. *Reisende auf dieser Welt.* Vienna: Picus.

Stojka, Karl. 1994. *Auf der ganzen Welt zu Hause.* Vienna: Picus.

Tagg, John. 1988. *The Burden of Representation: Essays on Photographies and Histories.* London: Macmillan.

Trumpener, Katie. 1992. 'The Time of the Gypsies: A "People without History" in the Narratives of the West', *Critical Inquiry*, 18: 843–84.

Wedding, Alex (Grete Weiskopf). 1931. *Ede und Unku*. Berlin: Malik.

Weltzel, Hanns. 1934. *Von Ottern und Nattern: Ein Schlangenbuch*. Braunschweig: Wenzel.

—1936. *Erk Alburger*. Berlin: Rowohlt.

—1938. 'The Gypsies of Central Germany', *JGLS*, Third Series, 18: 9–24, 73–80, 104–09, and Jubilee Supplement: 31–38.

—1941. *Der Vormittagsreiter*. Berlin: Herbig.

—1948. 'Wie das Unheil hereinbrach'. Typescript. Liverpool University Library, Gypsy Lore Society Archive, XIV.40.

—1949. 'Fortsetzung'. Typescript. Liverpool University Library, Gypsy Lore Society Archive, XIV.39.

Willems, Wim. 1997. *In Search of the True Gypsy: From Enlightenment to Final Solution*. Trans. Don Bloch. London: Frank Cass.

Winter, Walter Stanoski. 1999. *WinterZeit*. Hamburg: Ergebnisse.

Wippermann, Wolfgang, and Brucker-Boroujerdi, Ute. 1987.'Nationalsozialistische Zwangslager in Berlin III. Das "Zigeunerlager" Marzahn', in Ribbe (ed.) 1987: 189–201.

Wittich, Engelbert. 1911. *Blicke in das Leben der Zigeuner von einem Zigeuner*. Striegau: Huß.

Zeller-Plinzner, Frieda. 1934. *Jesus im Zigeunerlager*. Neumünster: Ihloff.

Zimmermann, Michael. 1996. *Rassenutopie und Genozid: Die nationalsozialistische 'Lösung der Zigeunerfrage'*. Hamburg: Christians.

Ritual of Memory in Constructing the Modern Identity of Eastern European Romanies

Slawomir Kapralski

Since the fall of Communism, the Romanies of eastern Europe have become both the subjects and the objects of a process of *ethnogenesis*: a conscious attempt to achieve the accepted status of a non-territorial, ethnic-national group. One of the most important aspects of this process is the development of an identity that could function in the contemporary world and unite different groups of Romanies. Such an identity must also be powerful enough to counteract the influence of traditions, both internal and external, denying the Roma a distinct national identity and hindering attempts directed towards the formation of such an identity. In this chapter, I argue that the viable foundations of such an identity can be found in the memory of the persecution of the Roma during the Second World War. This memory is generalized in the narrative of the Holocaust, and symbolized by the site of the Auschwitz-Birkenau death camp, which can be thus understood in Bakhtin's terminology as a *chronotope* of modern Romani identifications. However, for several reasons which are discussed in this chapter (e.g., the lack of identification with the Holocaust and/or its generalized symbols by some Romani groups), the tradition based on such memory, narrative, and symbol must be – to a large degree – 'invented'. In the last part of this essay, I will present a case study of a ritualized practice which bears great potential in making this tradition a part of living memory and an identity-building factor. The practice in question is the 'Romani Caravan of Memory', an annual event in which the members of the Bergitka Roma group from Tarnow in Southern Poland make a pilgrimage to places where Romanies were murdered during the Second World War.

Towards a Modern Romani Identity

Nicolae Gheorghe (1991), advocating the political rather than cultural character of Roma ethnogenesis, stresses the fact that Roma ethnicity should not be perceived as an independent variable. It is, in his opinion, a consequence of political actions taken to secure the existence of the Roma and to provide them with recognition. Of course, this process does not mean an abandonment of ethnic identity. It is rather conceived as an adherence to a different type of nationalism from the ethnic one dominant in eastern and central Europe. This new political nationalism means, first of all, political organization and participation in political life; it strives to create a common arena in which people of different ethnicities can cooperate in solving their problems, without allowing the differences between them to become a dominant issue precluding communication. In such a project, 'culture moves to politics' (Gheorghe 1991: 842): the most secure place for cultural difference seems to be the sphere of interaction between equal political agents in which political homogenization protects ethnic heterogeneity.

The politicization of ethnogenesis, therefore, implies a stress on the external activities of Romani organizations and movements, supported by various ideological currents of Romani nationalism. These organizations, not the ethnic constructions of identity, are becoming the foci of the Roma collective emancipation and the political agents of the nation-building process (Gheorghe 1991: 842–44). Their activities, however, have to confront the opposite traditions of imagining the Roma political potential, both within and outside the Roma community. The first type of resistance is found among the more traditionally minded Romanies for whom any attempts at political organization of the Roma may seem irrelevant or even contradictory to the principle of *Romanipen* (the Romani 'way of life'), since they require close contacts with the non-Romani world and use methods that might be regarded as 'alien' to the Roma. The second type of resistance – it almost goes without saying – is expressed by those who perceive the Roma as a 'social problem' which has to be 'solved' through coercive assimilation or by administrative means.

Yet another voice against Romani political nationalism comes, surprisingly, from the ranks of scholars who study Romani culture. According to Ian Hancock, 'the former sub-editor of the *Journal of the Gypsy Lore Society*, Brian Vesey-Fitzgerald, scorned the Romani nationalist movement as "romantic twaddle" [...], echoing the words of Dora Yates, honorary secretary of the same society, [...] who, referring to the same movement, asked "except in a fairy tale, could any hope ever have been more fantastic?"' (Hancock 1987: 127). In a book that appeared two years after the first World Romani Congress, Werner Cohn claims that 'the Gypsies have no leaders, no executive committees, no nationalist movement. [...] I know of no authenticated case of genuine Gypsy allegiance to political or religious causes' (quoted in Hancock 1987: 127). Such a nostalgic portrait of the Roma results from a cultural projection of romantic, anti-modernist ideals, with Romanies as the personification of a longing for a life uncontaminated by civilization. In such a context, Ian Hancock observes, the political organization of the Roma may be considered as '[giving the] lie to non-Gypsy perceptions of the Gypsy as happy-go-lucky wanderer. If Gypsies have expressed such aspirations, they are charged with having been contaminated by the outside world, and with no longer being "proper" Gypsies. [...] When non-Gypsies go from wagon to automobile, it is called progress; when Gypsies do the same thing, it is disappointment' (Hancock 1991b: 138).

Criticism of the politicization of Romani ethnogenesis expresses an important point: genuine Roma ethnic tradition is often perceived as essentially anti-modern and incapable of supporting attempts to achieve modern national identification. To counteract such a view, and to legitimize the Roma nation-building process, one may turn to the indigenous tradition of Roma nationalist movements. This tradition, respectable as it is, may nevertheless be insufficient. First, it may be perceived as not encompassing a historical perspective of suitable duration. Secondly, it is doubtful whether this tradition possesses a sufficient unifying strength and power to bring together different groups of the Roma. Thirdly, it might be argued that this tradition does not carry enough emotional appeal, either internally or externally, to become a symbol of identity to the Roma and to justify Roma emancipation to the non-Romani world. Therefore, I would argue that the nationalist tradition has to be accompanied by yet another tradition possessing attributes that the former lacks. This is the tradition of the Roma as a persecuted people: a continuous history of suffering stretching back more than a thousand years; a tradition to which all Romanies alike were exposed and which corresponds with the Roma versus *gadze* opposition around which Roma ethnic identity has been established, thus making it acceptable for all Romanies; and a tradition that has enormous emotional appeal and can present the emancipation of the Roma as moral compensation for, and political protection against, the perpetuation of persecution.

The emotional appeal of the tradition of persecution is partly dependent on this tradition finding its representation in the narrative of the Holocaust, a part of which was the attempted extermination of the Roma during the Second World War (here I leave aside the controversy about the uniqueness of the Holocaust). The history of the Romani Holocaust is a developing branch of scholarship, but the writings of Kenrick and Puxon (1972), Hancock (1987, 1991a), Huttenbach (1991), Tyrnauer (1991) and others, aside from serving an academic function, play a significant role in the attempt to draw the contours of the Roma collective memory as the historical representation of their tragic fate. The Romani Holocaust is thus presented as the culmination of the persecutions the Roma have experienced since their arrival in Europe and as a condensation of different forms of discrimination to which they have been subjected. As such, the Holocaust creates a chronological linearity of Romani history, dividing it into periods 'before' and 'after'. Moreover, it endows this history with meaning as the continuous unfolding of this persecution pattern.

The Roma and the Holocaust

The Roma narrative of the Holocaust, in order to exercise its extra-academic influence, needs a symbol that can serve as a condensation of meanings and messages integrating the nationalist tradition with the persecution tradition. For a number of reasons, including the growing visibility of Romanies in the area of Auschwitz-Birkenau (in the form of both individual or group visits, or participation of Romani representatives in public commemorative ceremonies held, for instance, on the anniversary of camp liberation), as well as the efforts of international Romani organizations to set up large-scale ceremonies commemorating the liquidation of the 'Gypsy camp' on 2 August 1944, one could expect that such a powerful symbol might be – as for the Jews – Auschwitz.

As a symbol, Auschwitz-Birkenau can best be described by the concept of *chronotope*, introduced into literary theory by Mikhail Bakhtin. For Bakhtin, a chronotope represented 'the intrinsic connectedness of temporal and spatial relationships that are artistically expressed in literature' (Bakhtin 1981: 84). Borrowing this concept, we may say that, in the field of collective identities, a chronotope is a locus in which time has been condensed and concentrated in space (Gillis 1994: 14). In other words, a chronotope means a real but symbol-laden and often mythologized place in which events important for the construction of a group's identity either actually happened according to the group's vision of the past, or are symbolically represented by, for instance, monuments or the very arrangement of space, and the social functions of those monuments or space.

Thus, the most important question, regarding the capacity of the tradition symbolically represented by Auschwitz to function successfully, is whether Auschwitz is a widely accepted identity chronotope among the Romanies of different eastern European countries. The narrative of the Holocaust bears huge potential to serve as a cornerstone for Romani national identity. The question is, however, whether this narrative emerges from among those relaying the memory of concrete groups, or whether it is the symbol of an elite's politics of identity. A related question is to what extent Auschwitz can act as a commonly accepted symbolic site that condenses the meaning of the Romani Holocaust. In order to answer these questions I would like to refer to the results of my research project 'Violence and Memory: The Holocaust and the Construction of Romani Identity in Eastern Europe' in the framework of which mid-level activists from Romani organizations and journalists of Romani media in several eastern European countries were asked questions regarding the importance for them of Auschwitz and the Holocaust more broadly.

In general, the consolidating function of memory is widely recognized among the Roma elites in central and eastern Europe. Collective memory has, for instance, been explicitly mentioned as equivalent to having a state: 'Of course, we remember [the extermination] and we will remember,' said a Rom from Moscow. 'You know, we do not have our statehood, and the only things which hold us together are our memories and our traditions'. The experience of consolidation may be the outcome of a visit to Auschwitz. For a Polish Romani woman, such a visit made it clear to her that the Roma were targeted for total annihilation, and not for selective murder: 'Before [the visit] I had thought that they [the Germans] wanted to kill only the important people of our nationality, but after the visit I realized that they wanted to kill every ordinary Roma' (Tarnow, Poland). There is also a widespread awareness of the racist motives behind the Nazi persecutions – motives still present in contemporary attitudes towards Roma. According to a Serbian Rom, the murder of the Roma was possible not just because of the racist idiosyncrasies of the individual Nazi leaders, but because of the strong racist consciousness of ordinary people, Germans and their local accomplices. This fact makes the issue of persecution and extermination a very contemporary one. The above-mentioned Serbian Rom observed that fear of persecution can be a reason for Roma to deny their identity: 'I heard them saying: "What if one day a new Hitler appears?"' (Belgrade, Yugoslavia). According to a Romani woman from the Czech Republic, 'It is understandable that the Roma sometimes behave impulsively, having had this experience in the past. Maybe they are afraid that the situation is becoming similar to that of the 1930s. We cannot be surprised that they sometimes deny their nationality' (Prague, Czech Republic). It is a bitter paradox that the very same factor that helps build Roma identity – the collective memory of attempted genocide – becomes a reason to deny it. It only emphasizes the significance of that memory in the contemporary context and the extent to which it is a living memory with continuous reference to the present.

This general remark finds its concretization in the context of Auschwitz as well. Some time ago, after a Bacs-Kiskun County Roma Festival had come to a close, a group of Roma participants from Budapest found their bus painted with the slogan 'Gypsies, go to Auschwitz' (Budapest, Hungary). Experiences like that, supported by very common graffiti on the walls of eastern European cities saying

'Gypsies to the gas chambers', must evoke a feeling of discomfort and unease about making the actual trip to Auschwitz, and must supply this Holocaust-related identity with an ambiguous mixture of pride and fear. Sometimes, however, a visit to Auschwitz, especially combined with participation in commemorative ceremonies, can be a very rewarding experience. As a female Romani activist from Slovakia said,

> Often when I'm losing energy and I don't know what to do, it is very good to visit a Romani colony where I can see the poverty people live in, and it somehow recharges me with energy so that I know that I can and I have to work further. *It was something like this in Auschwitz.* Many people, many Romanies were there from all around Europe and some from the United States. [...] I saw that it is a huge nation, [but a nation] which has such a [low] position in the world as it has, [...] that I [must] do something to change it. (Bratislava, Slovakia; my italics)

According to the same person, if one wants to create one's own nationality, one has to build on the principle of identity. In order to accomplish this, '[it] is important that we know [...] who we are, where we come from, and for this we must know that we have language as well as history, [...] what happened during the war and why it happened'.

Nevertheless, knowledge of 'what happened' seems to be widespread only among those more active or more involved in the life of Romani organizations. Furthermore, the level of knowledge also depends on access to the personal experiences of survivors: when there is a lack of communication between family memories and the knowledge recounted in public discourses, the acquaintance of respondents with the situation of the Roma during the Second World War is much lower. In order to illustrate this point, I would like to look more closely at the situation of Bulgarian Roma. Among our informants, the word 'Auschwitz' did not seem to evoke any strongly defined associations. Although only one person had not heard of Auschwitz at all, the knowledge the remainder had of this place was rather vague. For instance, for one person Auschwitz was a place 'where minorities were exterminated'; only two knew a bit more than the others. Generally speaking, respondents were more familiar with the word 'Buchenwald' than with 'Auschwitz', even if their knowledge of the Buchenwald camp was as limited as their knowledge of Auschwitz-Birkenau. One might say that, in the case of Buchenwald, the name of this camp serves as a label for all atrocities committed against the Roma during the war and not as a sign of any historical knowledge of special sites. For one of the respondents, Buchenwald was a place 'in which Nazis killed 500,000 Romanies with tear gas and burned them in furnaces'. This figure – probably given as the total number of Romani victims – was also mentioned in a different interview. Yet another Bulgarian informant had heard of it, as of the

Romani Holocaust in general, only a couple of years ago. His knowledge was derived exclusively from the media and literature distributed by international Romani organizations; this was also the case with all the others who knew something about this matter. In addition to media in general, respondents sometimes added concrete influences, such as a documentary shown on television, and in addition to literature received from Romani organizations, conference materials as well as books and articles about the war in general all appeared to be sources of my informants' knowledge.

None of the respondents had any personal experiences such as family histories related to the period of the Second World War. It seems that this was not a particularly distinct period in the history of Bulgarian Roma. During most interviews, these informants claimed that the Roma in Bulgaria were relatively safe. One person mentioned Bulgarian Jews in this context, claiming that they were in a similar situation to that of the Roma, both relatively unaffected by the atrocities of the Holocaust. Another person claimed that the Bulgarian Roma were saved thanks to King Boris, who had apparently developed a sort of sympathy towards the Roma. According to her, King Boris

> managed to save his Roma and Jews – mainly the Jews, since there was a special order to deport the Jews from Bulgaria [...] Our country, Bulgaria, is proud of this, of the noble act of that monarch [...] I know from my parents that he loved the Roma very much, he loved them very much; he used to go shopping at the market place in an absolutely natural manner; he didn't move around in such cars as today's politicians do – making people resentful of them [...] He was close to the people, he walked among people, he loved and appreciated them. Maybe for this reason he was killed by the Germans: there is such a rumor among people that he gave his life, he was poisoned [by the Germans] because of that, but he saved not only the Jews but the Roma as well. The Roma were his favorite nation – at least, this is what I know from my parents.

A different version of the myth of a 'good king' (or rather, in this case, of a 'good king's wife') was noted by Marushiakova and Popov (1999: 93):

> This happened in the time of the King. The King decided to exterminate all the Gypsies and said to himself: 'Today I'll kill them!', but he lay down and went to sleep. Then his wife went to a meadow where she picked lots of different kinds of flowers and returned to the King. She woke him up, and when he saw the flowers she told him: 'There are lots of different flowers just as there are lots of different people. Don't kill them!' So the king decided to spare them and ever since the Gypsies paint their houses in different bright colours.

In spite of the differences of detail, the stories are very similar and contain a number of features commonly attributed to rulers in their mythological representations. It is rather significant that it is precisely within this mythological structure that some Bulgarian Roma place the story of their suffering and survival. This reflects a lack of real personal experiences and/or lack of a relevant discourse passed down to them and through which a realistic description of the Holocaust could be produced. Therefore, we have here an interesting case of two knowledge frameworks that engender the way the Holocaust is conceptualized: media and myth.

When, however, our respondents switch from discussion of the past to that of its possible consequences in the present, their language becomes more realistic, although the media definitely remains one of its sources, in addition to the language of the official documents of Romani organizations. Even those who do not possess sound knowledge of the Holocaust do understand the importance of Auschwitz. In their opinion, the visits to Auschwitz by different Roma groups perform the important role of reminding the whole world that Roma, too, were persecuted. Beneath the surface of such opinions lies a more or less explicit claim that the Roma still do not hold a recognized place in the narrative of the Holocaust, that they are not perceived as victims of the Holocaust along with Jews. 'Everybody talks only about the Jews', as one respondent said. In the opinion of this person, the Roma claim to a legitimate place in the narrative of the Holocaust has been symbolically expressed by the visits of the Roma to Auschwitz. They go there in order to keep their memory alive because there are no monuments that would otherwise memorialize their suffering. The act of 'going there' is thus a 'memorial performance', necessary for people who do not have their own 'memorial sites'.

Similarly, the belief of another respondent that the numbers of Roma murdered during the war equalled the numbers of Jewish or Polish victims reveals her desire for the Roma to be accepted as having suffered equally, for their tragedy to be known by the world, and, by the same token, for their recognition as a legitimate part of the tragic history of our times. The struggle to win the Roma a place in the landscape of suffering turns out to be an attempt to change their status from that of outsiders to European history and culture to that of one of its main victims.

Such attempts can easily be included in the universal message of history as well. In the following statement, by a respondent replying to the question 'Why do the Roma visit the site of Auschwitz-Birkenau?', no reference has been made to a particular situation or group memory of the Roma: 'The Roma go there, and return there, in memory of the dead, because people who survived this horrible thing try to explain it and render it to us in the most tangible manner. And the aim is to awaken human conscience so that such crimes would not be allowed any more.' This statement, together with those quoted earlier, indicates that, in assessing the importance of Auschwitz as a symbol, our respondents refer to two types of discourse: the particular one that underlines Roma suffering and aims at improving their status, and the universal one that emphasizes the meaning of Auschwitz for humankind in general. Nevertheless, in the latter case, by making the Roma participate in the universal meaning of Auschwitz, the objectives of the first discourse can also be achieved.

Although only one informant had actually visited Auschwitz, on the occasion of his stay in Poland, his recollection may serve as proof that such visits bear great potential for revitalizing memory and building a sort of relationship with the past that could earn the respect of others. When in Auschwitz, he saw a group of Polish peasants – ordinary people, rather poorly dressed, and guided by a priest. They lit candles and started to sing a solemn ('probably religious') song. The informant recounted the reactions:

> This shattered me. Immediately all the noise around stopped, even cameras stopped, as if people sensed that they should not [do anything], that there are things that are sacred. Perhaps for about three minutes this ceremony made the whole place, full of people, shut up as a sign of respect for the way those Poles commemorated events that had happened many years ago. The lesson given by those ordinary peasants was something that I remember and it will remain in my memory.

For those who – like this respondent – want the Roma to be granted their rightful and deserved place in the memory of the Holocaust, such an emotional experience can indeed act as a stimulus for the organization of visits by Roma to Auschwitz – to perform rituals of memory even when there are no individual memories of persecutions during the war. And it comes as no surprise that, according to this respondent, Bulgarian Roma should visit Auschwitz-Birkenau, the place where other European Roma perished.

Still, for the Bulgarian Roma, the Holocaust does not seem to be, generally speaking, an event that could create a message powerful enough to unite the Roma around its meaning. Although there is a genuine interest in history among the mid-rank activists, it is difficult to imagine the memory of the Holocaust as a spontaneous identity-building factor because it is not rooted in private memories. One can, however, imagine that institutional attempts to spread the knowledge of Romani history among the broad masses of the Roma, and to convince them (as well as outsiders) that the Roma were at the centre of world history, might be successful.

In Romania the situation is slightly different. The Romanian Romanies have their private memories of persecutions during the Second World War and this makes them different from the Roma in Bulgaria. Still, even in their case it is difficult to speak of a generalized memory of the Holocaust as a factor that could unite them with Roma from different countries. Their memory of their sufferings during the war is firmly placed within the Romanian context and focuses on events and places that are peculiar to the history of Romania. For instance, the word 'Auschwitz' does not, as a rule, evoke any particular emotions, even if our respondents do possess certain knowledge of what happened there. For some of them, commemorative ceremonies held in Auschwitz are, for example, only an opportunity for their leaders to 'rub shoulders with celebrities', instead of staying at home and working to improve the living standards of their people. On the other hand, there is widespread knowledge of the local site of persecutions, that is, the Transnistria region, located between the Dniester and Southern Bug Rivers – the territory that Hitler gave the Romanian Nazi-allied government of Marshal Antonescu in 1941 in compensation for Transylvania's transfer to Hungary. In the camps and forced settlements of that area, 20,000 of the approximately 25,000 Romanian Romanies deported there in 1942 died due to maltreatment, disease and harsh conditions (cf. Kelso 1999). All of our respondents had heard of 'the camps at the Bug River' and it appears that, for the time being, it is the Transnistria region that is capable of performing the role of a symbol of Romanian Roma suffering during the war.

Even in those Romani communities in which knowledge of Auschwitz is more detailed and whose members more frequently participate in organized commemorative visits to Auschwitz – that is, for instance, those in Hungary or in the Czech Republic – no pattern of communicating memory of the sufferings of the war has been elaborated, even within families. Sometimes it is only recently that the silence has been broken and the younger generation of Roma have learned that their relatives were victims of Nazi persecutions. In such a situation it is difficult to speak of a communication between family memory and generalized knowledge, even when the latter has been supported by the recognition of the symbolic or 'political' importance of commemorative ceremonies.

To summarize, it seems that the memory of the Romani Holocaust cannot easily be used as a ready-made identity-building factor to unify different groups of the Roma. There is a big difference between those groups who were victimized and those who survived the war relatively unaffected. Furthermore, those who did become the objects of persecution often have their own places which denote their fate for them; hence, they may be reluctant to accept a single general symbol, such as

Auschwitz. In any case, among those who are prepared to accept such an encompassing symbol, their private memories and/or ways of communicating them have not been elaborated as yet. This does not mean that the symbolized and generalized memory of the Holocaust cannot become an important factor in constructing modern Roma identity. It does mean, however, that such a memory does not exist as a widespread phenomenon that can simply be employed as part of identity-building strategies. Rather, it must be interpreted in terms of a 'project' that may be implemented through such strategies undertaken by the Romani elites.

Constructing Romani Identity through Ritualized Practice: The Case of the 'Caravan of Memory'

As we can see, the tradition on the basis of which the modern identity of Romanies could be built must be 'invented' rather than simply maintained and perpetuated. 'The element of invention is particularly clear,' Eric Hobsbawm writes, '[where] the history which became part of the fund of knowledge or the ideology of nation, state or movement is not what has actually been preserved in popular memory, but what has been selected, written, pictured, popularized and institutionalized by those whose function it is to do so' (Hobsbawm 1983: 13). Construction here means standardization of the symbolic meanings of what has happened to a group, and presentation of a stream of historical events as representing the particular logic or principle that has formed the group's past, has an influence on its present, and will determine its future.

Yet there is no single, generally accepted experience of the Holocaust at the level of a popular memory of eastern European Roma. There is also a lack of a generally accepted singular symbol of the Holocaust among those who share a belief in the importance of its experience (Auschwitz is much less known among the less educated and among those who come from countries that had their own camps for the Roma). For these and other reasons a gathering together and unification of Romanies around the experience of the Holocaust and Auschwitz as its symbol will entail a rather long process administered by the Romani elites.

Moreover, the traditional Romani identity, according to Andrzej Mirga and Lech Mroz, was created in the framework of culture, not history. It rested in manifestations of an atemporal value-pattern of *Romanipen* – 'being a Rom' in the surrounding world of 'others' – and in maintaining 'horizontal' kinship relations, ways of life, and patterns of interaction with non-Romanies. While national communities of Europe defined themselves with reference to their respective histories, 'the need of history was alien to the Roma and has appeared only recently due to the Roma elites [...] attempting to create, in a divided and sub-ethnically differentiated [Roma] population, a sense of national community' (Mirga and Mroz 1994: 31–32). Such an atemporal identity is by no means weaker than an identity based on the collective memory of a group's history. The persistence of Roma identity despite all the constraints, hostile environments, and deliberate attempts at its destruction is a well-known fact which proves that a viable identity can be achieved and perpetuated in a non-historical dimension. However, it is not the kind of identity that could easily be transformed into a national one: the latter needs historical tradition, something that the former cannot provide. Therefore, efforts directed at establishing a sense of national identity among Romanies would necessarily involve the invention of such a tradition as could minimize conflict between the old frameworks within which Romanies identified themselves and the requirements of modern identifications.

Applying the model of national memory formation presented by James Fentress and Chris Wickham to the process of inventing traditions, we may distinguish the following stages: first, the construction of tradition by elites; secondly, the creation of a 'rhetorical discourse', related to a given tradition and 'directed at internal or external opponents'; thirdly, the conveyance of the tradition to the collective memory and creation of popular discourses that 'make up the substructure of national historical consciousness' (Fentress and Wickham 1992: 129). If the first two tasks already seem to have been accomplished successfully by Romani organizations and intellectual elites, the third remains an assignment for the future.

In order to make the memory of the Holocaust an important part of popular discourse, one must refer to that quality of social memory that Paul Connerton has called its performative nature (Connerton 1989: 4–5); it has to be implemented through 'bodily practices' and then further requires these for its maintenance. Therefore, the Romani presence in Auschwitz may be interpreted not only as a manifestation of Romanies' claim to the place they deserve in the history of the Holocaust and to participation in the symbolic meaning of Auschwitz. The Romani presence proclaims their suffering to the outside world, but it is also a ritual practice that transforms the disparate individual memories of survivors and their families into a collective memory, revitalizes the past of the Holocaust in the present, and creates a historical tradition to which the Roma may adhere.

In the final part of this essay, I would like to present a particular case of such 'bodily practice' or ritual of memory – namely, the annual 'Tabor Pamieci' (Caravan of Memory) of the Roma community in Tarnow, a city in southern Poland.[1] Here, instead of applying the concept of ritual in its strict sense (if we can speak of a strict sense of this notoriously vague and variously defined term), I would refer rather to the concept of 'ritualized practice', which is, according to Catherine Bell, 'a type of social strategy' that emerges 'for the purpose of social control and/or social communication' (Bell 1992: 89). I shall focus here exclusively on the communicative functions of ritualized practice, those which, according to Bell, contribute to legitimation and internalization of certain values.

'Ritualization,' Bell writes, 'is a particularly "mute" form of activity. It is designed to do what it does without bringing what it is doing across the threshold of discourse or systematic thinking' (Bell 1992: 93). The aim of this section will be to 'give voice' to the Caravan of Memory as a ritualized activity, to make it speak of the ideas, symbols and values that it communicates in a pre-discursive way to its participants.

Tarnow is, in many respects, a unique place. One of the first – if not the first – organizations of Romanies in Poland was established here. Its members were Romanies from the Bergitka Roma group, who primarily lived a sedentary life in the Carpathian Mountains until they moved to urban centres in the 1950s, attracted by the opportunities offered by huge Communist industrial projects. For the extremely poor mountain Roma the possibility of obtaining permanent jobs and apartments in blocks of flats meant a radical improvement in their living conditions. The 'Socio-Cultural Association of the Roma' in Tarnow performed an important role in integrating newcomers with the local community and securing their status and situation. On the other hand, the organization has been criticized by more traditional Romanies as collaborating with the Communist regime, and therefore betraying the Romani way of life.

The Romanies who settled in Tarnow received help from the curator of the regional museums, Adam Bartosz. He is an ethnographer and a specialist in Romani Studies who set up the first permanent exhibition in Poland devoted to Romani culture. This exhibit is displayed at the ethnographic branch of the local museum. The exhibition is probably the only one of its kind in eastern-central Europe and the museum has become a place in which local Romanies present Roma culture to a non-Romani audience.

The two institutions – the 'Social-Cultural Association of the Roma' and the local museum – are behind the idea of 'reconstructing' a Romani *tabor* (caravan). The element of 'reconstruction' – or rather, we should say, 'invention' – is clearly visible here not only because the idea came from a non-Romani ethnographer, but also because the caravan, an inte-

---

[1] In my account of the 'Caravan of Memory', I refer to my own observations as a participant in the summer of 2000, to personal communications from its organizer, Adam Bartosz, and to his article in which he presents the history and main ideas of this project (Bartosz 1999).

gral element of a nomadic lifestyle, does not belong to the tradition of the Bergitka Roma, who, since settling in the Carpathians, have been a static population. Nevertheless, for the participants, the caravan may signify the generalized Romani values to which they may want to adhere.

Adam Bartosz began to organize the Caravan of Memory in 1996. After a few years, its structure became defined and established and is now, with slight changes, repeated year after year. The Caravan departs from the ethnographic museum that houses the Romani exhibition. Before embarking, the participants receive a blessing from the Polish Romani chaplain, a non-Romani priest, Reverend Stanislaw Opocki. Elements of Roman Catholicism, the dominant religion in Poland, are evident in many other situations during the Caravan. Apart from the central role that Father Opocki plays, local parish priests usually welcome the travelling group wherever it arrives; these clergymen also attend commemorative ceremonies at the sites of mass executions and pray there together with the participants of the Caravan. They also perform the wedding or christening ceremonies that sometimes take place during the Caravan.

The first stop the Caravan makes is at the Monument of the Victims of Auschwitz in Tarnow, on the site from which on 14 June 1940 the first transport of Polish (non-Romani) prisoners to Auschwitz departed. The Caravan participants light candles and musicians play a sorrowful tune. Occasionally, there are speeches given by more influential persons accompanying the Caravan. From the site of this monument the Caravan moves to a cemetery in the Krzyz district of Tarnow where the city's Romanies bury their dead. The participants of the Caravan commemorate their deceased just as they would during All Souls' and All Saints' Days: through prayer, music, and pouring vodka on the graves.

The next step is Zabno, where there is a mass grave of Romanies murdered here in the summer of 1943. The participants pray at the gravesite, light candles and lay flowers on it, and sing mourning songs and the Romani anthem.[2] The Romani flag is displayed there, as it is in all other

[2] The Romani flag was adopted in 1933 at the international conference 'United Gypsies of Europe', organized in Bucharest by the General Association of Gypsies of Romania. It originally consisted of two horizontal bars, the lower green and the upper blue. In 1971, the 1st World Romani Congress decided on the embellishment of the flag with the red, 16-spoked chakra and reaffirmed it 'as the national emblem of the Romani people' (Hancock 2002: 120). The symbol of chakra, to which Grattan Puxon refers as 'the ashok chakra of India', indicated one of the Congress's aims: to symbolically re-unite the Roma with their ancient homeland – India (Puxon 2000: 110, 113). At the same Congress the Romani anthem was adopted, with words by a Yugoslav Rom, Zarko Jovanovich, to a traditional Romani tune. In the academic literature and in documents by Romani activists the flag and the anthem have been referred to as national symbols. This emphasizes their symbolical function in integrating various Romani groups living in different countries, providing an emotional appeal and winning respect and recognition by the non-Roma.

commemorative ceremonies during the Caravan. The local priest, together with Father Opocki, leads prayers; the mayor of the town, together with some of the more important participants of the Caravan, makes speeches. Sometimes the Caravan stops overnight at a campsite near Zabno and the Caravan's participants invite local residents to a musical concert which is held as a sign of gratitude for taking care of the Romani grave at the cemetery.

From Zabno the Caravan moves to its final destination, Szczurowa. In this village, on 3 August 1943, 93 Romanies, including women, children and the elderly, were killed by the German police. As such, Szczurowa is the largest known site of mass executions of the Roma in the vicinity of Tarnow. Relatives of the murdered have always visited Szczurowa and their visits have unconsciously taken on ritual form, involving a walk from the site of the former settlement of the Szczurowa Romanies to the local cemetery where they were executed and buried. We may thus say that even if the Caravan of Memory belongs by and large to the category of invented tradition, it is nevertheless based on spontaneous family and group rituals.

In Szczurowa, the participants of the Caravan are welcomed by the local parish priest who subsequently leads the visitors to the grave of the murdered Romanies. After a prayer, the names of the murdered Romanies are read out. From the cemetery the group moves to the church for a religious service, sometimes accompanied by other ceremonies: for example, in 2000 there was the christening of a newborn child. These ceremonies are followed by private celebrations held at the campsite in Dolega near Szczurowa where the Caravan stays for the last one or two nights. In Szczurowa itself, there is a public celebration: a concert for the local audience, including the local authorities, which is a form of expressing the gratitude of the Tarnow Romani community to the people of Szczurowa for the upkeep of the grave of the murdered Romanies. The next day the Caravan returns to Tarnow, sometimes visiting other cemeteries en route where Romanies have been buried.

This is a synthetic picture of the Caravan, more or less adequately describing its course as it was established in the first two trial years. There may be small changes which depend, for instance, on the weather, but generally the activities that take place during the Caravan are as described above. The Caravan's participants are likewise established: mainly Romanies from Tarnow and other Bergitka Roma from southern Poland. Sometimes Romanies from abroad participate: for instance in the 2000 Caravan there was a group of Roma musicians from Hungary. The organizers are very keen on inviting important members of the Polish Romani community from outside the Bergitka group of Roma, as well as important activists from international Romani organizations. In this way, the organizers try to secure recognition of the Caravan within the two most important frameworks out of which contemporary Romani authority emerges: the 'traditional' and the 'modern'. Those persons not only add prestige to and legitimate the Caravan in various Roma circles, they also fulfil an important educational role as well as an integrative function. The traditional leaders educate the younger participants of the Caravan about Romani customs and culture, and, in a way, integrate them with the larger, stronger, and more respected groups of Romanies living in Poland – something that is particularly important in the case of the small, poor, and relatively isolated Bergitka Roma. The modern leaders educate the participants about the perspectives of Romani political activity and therefore integrate them with the discourses of modern Romani identity. The presence of these two categories of people, discourses and identities during a single event shows that it is possible to synthesize tradition with modernity – the elements of the traditional Romani identity with the demands of a modern, politicized identity of the Roma as a political nation.

Among the non-Romani participants of the Caravan one should list the staff of Tarnow's museum, scholars who are interested in researching the Romani community, and, perhaps foremost, journalists. There has been growing interest in the Caravan in the media and in 2000 two television crews, five radio broadcasters and a few print journalists participated in the event, providing quite extensive coverage in the local and national media. A certain number of non-Romanies, including priests, representatives of local authorities, and occasional spectators, have also participated in some of the events during the Caravan. The Caravan is actually very popular among the local population: the concerts in particular are well attended, but there is a friendly and interested audience of local people at all stages of the Caravan.

We may thus say that there are four groups of participants in the ritual: in addition to the main group, the Bergitka Roma from southern Poland, three others help to create the communication channels leading to the external frames of reference within which the Caravan of Memory can be placed. Thus, the presence of influential members from Roma groups other than the Bergitka refer the Caravan to the overall Romani tradition and legitimize it within the framework of traditional authority in the broader community of Polish Romanies. The members of the international Romani organizations provide the main group of Caravan participants with a link to modern ways of defining 'being a Rom' in the contemporary world. Finally, the participation of non-Romanies symbolizes a certain recognition of the Roma in their Polish environment.

There are basically three symbol-laden places that the participants of the Caravan visit during the event. The most important are, of course, the sites of mass executions of Romanies, which thus become 'condensation' points for the group memory of the Holocaust and therefore become chronotopes for the group identity. Visiting the graves of relatives at the Tarnow cemetery, on the other hand, evokes the private memories of the participants, while the stop at the Auschwitz monument involves a reference to a generalized discourse of the Nazi Holocaust. In such a way, the group memory of the wartime annihilation draws on the resources of individual memories, on the one hand, and on the symbolism of the Holocaust on the other. In a way, the concurrence of these three different sites in one ritualized activity – their spatial proximity and symbolic similarity – helps to synthesize their different meanings into a coherent message even for those who do not perceive the generalized symbols of the Holocaust (such as Auschwitz) as having an emotional appeal or as chronotopes of Romani identity.

The three main symbolic frameworks of the Caravan perform a similar synthesizing function. The symbolism of traditional Romani life is contained in such elements of the Caravan as camping, meetings with the 'elders', family reunions and celebrations (weddings, christenings), and playing music together. The national symbolism is brought into the ritual by displaying the Romani national flag and performing the Romani anthem during commemorative ceremonies. Finally, religious symbolism is continuously present at the different stages of the ritual.

In this way we can speak of three interwoven processes that occur in the course of the Caravan. First, a real agent of ritual emerges: a group of Romanies from southern Poland, open to the traditional Romani life, as well as to the modern possibilities of being Roma, and to the non-Romani environment. Secondly, the ritual process symbolically invests this group with a collective memory which refers to the fate of Romanies during the Second World War and which integrates the individual and family memories of participants with the generalized memory and symbolism of the Holocaust. Last of all, in the ritual, the memory of our group finds its expression in three different symbolical frameworks: traditional, national, and religious. These three processes – connected by ritual and transformed into a symbolic message in the course of it – create a chance to transmit comprehensively the 'invented tradition' of the Holocaust victims to the collective memory and popular discourses of Romanies and thus to make it a cornerstone of their modern identity.

References

Bakhtin, Mikhail M. 1981. 'Forms of Time and of the Chronotope in the Novel: Notes toward a Historical Poetics', in Michael Holquist (ed.) *The Dialogic Imagination: Four Essays by M.M. Bakhtin.* Austin: University of Texas Press.

Bartosz, Adam. 1999. 'Cyganski Tabor Pamieci' (Gypsy Caravan of Memory), *Pro Memoria*, 10: 53–55.

Bell, Catherine. 1992. *Ritual Theory, Ritual Practice.* Oxford: Oxford University Press.

Connerton, Paul. 1989. *How Societies Remember*. Cambridge: Cambridge University Press.

Fentress, James, and Wickham, Chris. 1992. *Social Memory*. Oxford: Blackwell.

Gheorghe, Nicolae. 1991. 'Roma-Gypsy Ethnicity in Eastern Europe', *Social Research*, 58.4: 829–44.

Gillis, John R. 1994. 'Memory and Identity: The History of a Relationship', in *idem* (ed.), *Commemorations: The Politics of National Identity*. Princeton, NJ: Princeton University Press.

Hancock, Ian. 1987. *The Pariah Syndrome: An Account of Gypsy Slavery and Persecution*. Ann Arbor, MI: Karoma Publishers.

—1991a. 'Gypsy History in Germany and Neighboring Lands: A Chronology Leading to the Holocaust and Beyond', in David Crowe and John Kolsti (eds), *The Gypsies of Eastern Europe*. Armonk, NY, and London: M.E. Sharpe.

—1991b. 'The East European Roots of Romani Nationalism', in David Crowe and John Kolsti (eds), *The Gypsies of Eastern Europe*. Armonk, NY, and London: M.E. Sharpe.

—2002. *We are the Romani People / Ame sam e Rromane dzene*. Hatfield: Centre de Recherches Tsiganes (Gypsy Research Centre) and University of Hertfordshire Press.

Hobsbawm, Eric. 1983. 'Introduction: Inventing Traditions', in Eric Hobsbawm and Terence Ranger (eds), *The Invention of Tradition*. Cambridge: Cambridge University Press.

Huttenbach, Henry R. 1991. 'The Romani Porajmos: The Nazi Genocide of Gypsies in Germany and Eastern Europe', in David Crowe and John Kolsti (eds), *The Gypsies of Eastern Europe*. Armonk, NY, and London: M.E. Sharpe.

Kelso, Michelle. 1999. 'Gypsy Deportations from Romania to Transnistria 1942–44', in Donald Kenrick (ed.), *In the Shadow of the Swastika: The Gypsies during the Second World War*, II. Hatfield: Centre de Recherches Tsiganes (Gypsy Research Centre) and University of Hertfordshire Press.

Kenrick, Donald, and Puxon, Grattan. 1972. *The Destiny of Europe's Gypsies*. London: Chatto-Heinemann for Sussex University Press.

Marushiakova, Elena, and Popov, Vesselin. 1999. 'The Bulgarian Romanies during the Second World War', in Donald Kenrick (ed.), *In the Shadow of the Swastika: The Gypsies during the Second World War*, II. Hatfield: Centre de Recherches Tsiganes (Gypsy Research Centre) and University of Hertfordshire Press.

Mirga, Andrzej, and Mroz, Lech. 1994. *Cyganie: Odmiennosc i nietolerancja* (*Gypsies: Distinctiveness and Intolerance*). Warsaw: Wydawnictwo Naukowe PWN.

Puxon, Grattan. 2000. 'The Romani Movement: Rebirth and the First World Romani Congress in Retrospect', in Thomas Acton (ed.), *Scholarship and the Gypsy Struggle*. Hatfield: University of Hertfordshire Press.

Tyrnauer, Gabrielle. 1991. *Gypsies and the Holocaust: A Bibliography and Introductory Essay*. Montreal: Montreal Institute for Genocide Studies.

'Severity has often enraged but never subdued a gipsy':[1] The History and Making of European Romani Stereotypes

Colin Clark

The Context: Back in 1886...

Picture the scene. It is a 'chilly English summer day' in July 1886 and by a patch of waste ground near Liverpool Lime St. station there are some 100-plus 'Greek Gypsies' who have been abandoned by the London train. Their desired progress to New York via a steamer has been delayed; they are eventually moved to a less visible part of Liverpool, an area known as Walton where the Zoological Gardens are. The usual questions are being asked. How long are they to be here? What is to be done with them? It seems they are fixed to remain in the 'garrets and caverns of Europe' – so predicts our erstwhile reporter for the *Chambers' Journal*, one David MacRitchie. He warily approaches the camp with a Greek gentleman there to represent a wealthy merchant of Liverpool, who has taken an interest in the situation of his compatriots. On his instructions, all begging is to stop – it may harm their chances of admission to the New World. MacRitchie, as he walks forward, observes the 'distinct lack of qualities' such as 'cleanliness, industry or wealth' around the encampment; he notes the 'dingy' 15 to 20 tents and the 'swarthy' and 'tawny' faces and complexions of the men, women and children who busy themselves around their temporary homes. Following a few sentences in Greek from his companion, our man in Liverpool has their attention:

> As soon as the leading men of the band who were then present – the chief himself had gone into town with two of his followers – understood that one of their visitors was a fellow-countryman, representing their patron, they thronged around him with a hundred questions, gesticulating violently the

[1] Henry Woodcock, *The Gipsies* (London, 1865), quoted by Macfie (1943: 78).

while; and the burden of their complaint was: 'How long must we remain here?' 'Why should we be detained when our journey is half over?' 'Why will the Americans not let us come?' Their case was really a hard one. Three hundred napoleons had they spent on their journey from Greece – on the clear understanding that they were to obtain a passage across the Atlantic from Liverpool, the money for which they had in their possession. Then came the word that they would not be allowed to land; when immediately the steamship companies unanimously refused to take them as passengers. Nor was Canada a bit more friendly than the States, so that only South America remained open to them. This, indeed, was where they specially wished to go – among the Southern Europeans and their fellow-gypsies. But a voyage to Brazil means a great deal more money than the short passage to New York. The other alternative held up to them – to return to their native country – they indignantly repelled. They had left it for want of employment, and in the hopes of making more money in the New World; for the reasons, in short, which induce other people to emigrate; and they had no wish to waste their substance on a fruitless journey to and from Liverpool. (MacRitchie 1886: 578)

Such were the reflections of David MacRitchie, the first Secretary and later President of the Gypsy Lore Society, on the arrested progress in Liverpool of a group of 'Greek Gypsies' who were attempting to sail to the New World over 100 years ago. The refusal of the shipping companies to transport them to their preferred American destination and Canada's similar refusal to give them leave to enter its territories have many echoes in events past and events we have recently witnessed at the close of the twentieth century. Yet, as the title of this chapter puts it, in a quotation from Woodcock to be found in his 1865 book *The Gipsies*, 'severity has often enraged but never subdued a Gipsy'. As in 1886, so more recently the harsh restrictions on the movement and settlement in various European territories of those whom we now properly call Romanies have not prevented them from seeking shelter in states that do their best to close their borders when faced with the persecuted and oppressed seeking sanctuary.

But why do such 'dark-skinned strangers', to borrow another of MacRitchie's phrases, meet with this reception? What is it that provokes the reaction? Is it their number? Is it their appearance? Is it their perceived manners, customs, beliefs and traditions – in essence their very 'Otherness' from what we believe to be a 'true European'? Is it their very 'Gypsy-ness' or 'Romani-ness' that causes the furore in the first instance? Is their ethnicity or identity a factor at all here? Could MacRitchie's Liverpool 'squatters' (another term he invokes) have been a different ethnic group entirely and still received the attention and the hostility they encountered during their short stay in the city? It is the purpose of this chapter to build on an earlier, more specific case-study article that examined the way in which British newspapers greeted the arrival of Czech and Slovak Romani asylum seekers at Dover during late 1997 and early 1998.[2] In a sense, this chapter comes first, rewinding *theoretically* to make sense of the larger, more general questions that need to be addressed before looking at any individual time period or context.

I am principally arguing that the portrayals of groups and individuals known or identified as 'Gypsies' in nineteenth- and twentieth-century European historical discourses provide little meaningful insight into the identities, histories, cultures and lifestyles of such a population. Instead, particularly by examining the British situation, I shall show that they constitute a montage or a scrapbook of exposures of the ideology that produces (and reproduces) them. I shall provide an explanation of how such images and discourses were arrived at and continue to be reproduced. I shall also argue that historical (and, indeed, contemporary) representations can be regarded as part of a much wider political process of introducing repressive legislation to neutralize the supposed disruptive 'threat' of 'Gypsies' (in their many varied forms) to particular state interests.

Introduction

For centuries, groups and individuals 'known' as Gypsies have had identities forced onto them from 'outside' – identities that conveniently coincided with the particular roles into which they were being placed: the *bogeyman* and the *noble savage* typify the archetypes, and correspond to political attempts to repress or assimilate them. In a sense, the duality of these characterizations is also detectable in more recent mediated images of 'New Age' Travellers, although the 'positive' attributes are scarcer and less well embedded than the romanticized 'traditional Romany' stereotypes that are also found in nineteenth- and twentieth-century literary representations (Hetherington 2000).

In this chapter I aim to outline some of the more typical and persistent components of the stereotypes of Gypsies; to connect these qualities with the interests and fears of their producers/consumers; and to relate the generation of (overwhelmingly) negative press representations to the genesis of political and legislative reaction.[3] Indeed, I would agree that the British press has historically provided such a medium when

[2] Clark and Campbell 2000. This is a 'snapshot' of press coverage in Britain over nearly three weeks and a critical structuralist engagement with the issues that arose out of that coverage.

[3] I am keen here to point out the danger of stereotyping stereotypes. This is sometimes not easy to avoid and one should be aware of this at all times. For example, we should be aware of the ways in which various stereotypical elements are framed in some essential, overarch-

required, as evidenced in the late twentieth century by the Criminal Justice and Public Order Act of 1994 in the United Kingdom. This is an Act, according to one text, that has effectively criminalized nomadism and has sought to 'ethnically cleanse' Gypsies from British society (Hawes and Perez 1996: x–xiii).

In existing British records, groups of Romanies, Gypsies and Travellers as distinct ethnic groups are first mentioned in the sixteenth century.[4] Since that time, they have survived on the fringes of settled society as an 'outsider' group, both by retaining their own sense of distinct cultural identities (by means of self-defining taboos, rituals and language) and by adapting to changes in the major economy and society. They have resisted assimilation into contemporary norms, from feudalism to post-industrial capitalism, while successfully exploiting economic opportunities – the 'commercial nomadic niche' – as these have presented themselves.

To Gypsies, non-Gypsies are *gadjos* – 'outsiders' or 'strangers' – to be understood and related to in the light of Gypsies' own cultural and personal experiences of the (oppressive but exploitable) majority society.[5] Non-Gypsies are a contradictory source of both economic opportunity and social persecution (Clark 2002). The Gypsies, by necessity, are in regular contact with members and representatives of the sedentary pop-

---

ing stereotype which is fixed in time and place. Some I discuss here, for example the later literary stereotypes, are born out of sixteenth- and seventeenth-century crises of genocide and enslavement. In other words, they were a product, not an explanation, of these crises. Likewise, this chapter mainly deals with north-western European stereotypes. These are different from the kinds of historically produced and recurrent stereotypes we see in the Balkans – here being based around notions of Gypsies being feckless, ignorant and lazy. The north-western European stereotype, as is shown, is a version of the Jewish 'sly and cunning fox' type – the eternal wanderer and, in the Gypsy case, illiterate. To this day, Iberian and Baltic stereotypes are again different and local or regional differences also abound throughout the world. General statements are thus very problematic – there is no fixed set of universal genetic or ethnic characteristics that can or should be applied to Gypsies (even though Heinrich M.G. Grellmann encouraged this kind of thinking, of course). Stereotyping is a moveable feast and needs to be located in its specific historical context – difference rather than ideal-types is the methodological and theoretical way forward. I am grateful to Thomas Acton for an exchange of ideas on these issues.

[4] Although, as Okely (1983: 3) notes, quoting Jean-Paul Clébert, in fourteenth-century Europe, 'all mountebanks and travelling showmen found themselves dubbed "Egyptians"'. Indeed, the point here is that early references might not all have been to the same ethnic group. Some linguistic evidence points to the immigration of at least two dialect groups during this period.

[5] *Gadjo* is, of course, the Angloromani term. Equally we can speak of *gajji, gaje, gadzhe, buffer, flattie, josser* etc. It all depends which specific ethnic group one is speaking about. The terms mean roughly the same, though we should resist generalizations in this context. Indeed, some – particularly wealthier – Gypsies reject their Romani brothers and sisters while engaging with influential *gadjos* for economic or political purposes.

ulation. For modern house-dwellers, the earliest and most sustained contacts with Gypsies are generally experienced through some represen- tative medium: Gypsies appear in nursery rhymes that they heard as chil- dren and now tell their own children. Likewise, playground lore, gossip, folk stories and tales, and songs that are orally transmitted also feature 'Gypsy' characters. Fiction, textbooks, art, printed and broadcast media contain recorded references with varying degrees of accuracy and truth. Bundled together, they provide the means by which stereotypes are cast, reinforced and disseminated. We now move on to look at just a few of the themes that are constant throughout these media.

Recurrent Themes in Stereotyped 'Gypsy' Identities

In order to unpack these portrayals, and their bearing on social and political responses, we shall first look at the major themes that charac- terize the stereotypes before the nineteenth century. These divisions of the material may seem somewhat arbitrary, in that they are identified by terms that may not be explicit in the texts themselves. However, these themes are implicitly woven through most historical representations, which tend to crystallize around one or more of the following types.[6]

Theme 1: Blackness Equals Savagery Equals 'Other'

The *Oxford English Dictionary* (1933) states that 'Gipsies' (sic) 'have a dark tawny skin and black hair'. More recently, the *New Shorter Oxford English Dictionary* (1993) defines Gypsies as 'member[s] of a travelling people in Europe and N. America', although it still goes on to insist that they 'have dark skin and hair'. To be a 'real Gypsy' one must be 'dark', it seems, whether 'tawny' or not. In medieval Europe, the colour black of course symbolized a potent fear of the primeval unknown, of disease, death and decay, poverty, sorcery, evil and the devil, in opposition to white, which represented life and growth, health, goodness, truth, clean- liness and God. The Gypsies' physical appearance as black-skinned is a common theme in the early records, such as this from France in the early fifteenth century:

> The men were very black, with curly hair. The women were the ugliest and blackest that have ever been seen. Their faces were all furrowed, their black hair like a horse's tail [...] they were the most wretched creatures that had

---

[6] For reasons of space, I am not dealing in this chapter with the contested view on what the impact has been of the assumption of individuals, institutions and governments that 'Gypsies' equals 'nomads'. This I see as an entire article, or even book, in its own right and a few pages here would not do the complex issue any justice at all (see n. 3).

been seen in France in living memory. (Quoted in Kenrick and Puxon 1972: 16)

Blackness also reinforces exotic connotations: the Gypsies are distinguishable by the colour of their skins, and, as with other non-white immigrants, their blackness was also associated with an essentially primitive, animal-like relationship to nature, which could be romanticized as a lost ideal, or denigrated as a throwback anachronism. Fraser quotes from a Swiss chronicle of 1422: 'Note that they were the ugliest brood ever seen in these parts. They were thin and black and ate like pigs' (1992: 72).

Another example of the equation of the Gypsies' 'blackness' with 'primitive' attributes occurs in one of the earliest attempts at scholarly investigation, *Dissertation on the Gipsies*, by Grellmann (first published in 1783): 'Let us reflect how different they are from Europeans; the one is white, the other black. This cloaths himself, the other goes half naked. This shudders at the thought of eating carrion, the other prepares it as a dainty' (1787: xiii). Okely, however, suggests that this black appearance may, at least for some indigenous nomads, have been a disguise to project an exotic aura as an aid to commerce, such as fortune-telling, entertaining, and so on: 'Thompson [...] reveals specific examples of persons recorded as vagabonds but convicted of felony for calling themselves by the name of an "Egyptian" [...] in 1549 a John Roland was recorded in County Durham as "oon of that sorte of people callinge themselves Egyptians" [...] Around 1610 a pamphleteer declared that "they goe alwais never under an hundred men or women, *causing their faces to be made blacke, as if they were Egyptians*"' (1983: 4, Okely's emphasis).

Theme 2: Nobility and Leadership

Accounts of the Gypsies have tended to suggest the existence of an aristocracy within the culture, who ruled over their 'subjects'. Vesey-Fitzgerald has an 'exploring band' in fifteenth-century Germany:

> At their head rode a duke and a count, richly dressed wearing belts of silver and leading hunting dogs in the manner of European nobles. Behind these nobles come a motley ill-dressed crowd of men on foot, and the women and children came in the rear, riding wagons. (1973: 13)

This notion persists to this day (see, for example, Jarman and Jarman 1991: 12–13, 50, regarding Welsh Gypsies), and is a recurrent theme in newspapers, although Okely quotes a modern-day Traveller as follows: 'If any Traveller dared say he was a leader, there'd be a line of men all the way to London to take him on. Before he said he was "King of the Gypsies", he'd have to get through that lot!' (1983: 172).

Liégeois confirms scepticism concerning this old component of the stereotype: 'The "King of the Gypsies" is a figment of the imagination of the gadze (non-Gypsies), and neither Roma as a whole nor any of the sub-groups have a formal leader [...] These terms [...] do not reflect a social hierarchy, but were an instance of superficial adaptation to local conditions and customs' (1986: 58–63). One such adaptation is instanced in the early records of Gypsies in Scotland, when an 'Egyptian' had extraordinary powers conferred on him by a writ of James V: '[the writ] granted considerable privileges to John Faw, "lord and erle of Litill Egipt" [...] enjoining all those in authority in the kingdom to assist John Faw in executing justice upon his company, "conforme to the lawis of Egipt" and in punishing all those who rebelled against him' (Fraser 1992: 118). It may be, as Liégeois suggests above, that this notion of nobility was a means of interaction with local populations, power-structures and kings and queens. The appearance of a band of 'foreign' nomads might appear to constitute less of a threat if they manifested themselves as an ordered microcosm of the dominant European society, and this would enable their 'nobility' to mix with the local and national nobility (see Crofton 1888).[7]

Theme 3: Occultism and the 'Dark Arts'

Gypsies have consistently been associated with the supernatural: fortune-telling, casting spells, magical healing powers and rituals are essential characteristics of this stereotype, which, again, persist in modern representations: 'A magistrate, who yesterday fined a gypsy [sic], asked at Marlborough Street Court in London to remain anonymous. "No names please," he said, "I don't want a curse at the end of the day"' (*The Times*, 15 August 1984). Fortune-telling appears to be the most frequently mentioned occult attribute, and the earliest accounts describe Gypsies, usually – but not always – women, who could read an individual's past, present and future by the art of palm-reading. Indeed, the earliest accepted reference to Gypsies in England alludes to 'an "Egypcyan" woman [...] who could tell marvellous things simply by looking into a person's hand' (Fraser 1992: 114). Fraser also quotes a fifteenth-century chronicle:

> Many people went to see [the Gypsies] on account of the [Gypsy] duke's wife who could tell fortunes and predict what would transpire in a person's life, as

---

[7] See Hancock 2000. Hancock argues that the social organization of the earliest Romani immigrants may have been that of an army – with very different standing for members based on internal class divisions. In other words, the anti-hierarchical organization of Romanichals and the democratic/consensual organization of the Kalderash Kris tribunal system are not [the only models we find in the literature.

well as what was happening in the present and how many children they had and whether a wife was good or bad, and other things. In many cases she told truly. (1992: 72)

Others, especially the Church, were less keen on such activities, and many of the portrayals depict palm-reading as a means of talking the 'credulous and dim-witted' out of their money, and, often enough, merely as a distraction technique to enable a child to pick the hapless punters' pockets or cut their purses. Another story of Gypsy 'supernatural magic' comes from Sweden:

> There was a Gypsy woman who came to a place where a woman lay about to give birth. 'Perhaps you would like me to give the pains to your old man,' said the Gypsy woman, 'Yes,' thought the woman. 'That's a good idea.' In a few moments the husband began to have strong pains in his stomach. Meanwhile the mother gave birth without any pain. (Quoted in Kenrick and Puxon 1972: 31)

Theme 4: Crime Equals 'Gypsy'

Alongside the aura of occultism, the stereotype of the '(dirty) thieving Gypsies' is deeply embedded in the popular consciousness, and is another factor underlining their 'otherness':

> dyverse and many outlandyshe People calling themselves Egyptians [who] usyng no Crafte or faicte of Merchandyce had comen into this Realme an gone from Shire to Shire and Place to Place in greate Company, and used great subtyll and crafty means to deceyve the People, beryng them in Hande that they by Palmestre could telle menne and womens Fortunes and so many tymes by crafte and subtyltie had deceyved the People of theyr Money and also had comyted many and haynous Felonyes and Robberies to the great Hurte and Deceyte of the People that they had comen amonge. (22 Henry VIII, c.10, 1530, cited in Thompson 1923)

Early records refer to frequent petty crimes and deceptions, such as shoplifting and purse-cutting, horse-stealing, poaching, and so on. However, these were, perhaps, not uncommon transgressions in their time: the great significance lies in their attachment to an identifiable ethnic group, as an embedded and defining characteristic – a supposedly inherent trait. For example, Grellmann notes that 'these people are famed, and were even from their first appearance in Europe, for being plunderers, thieves and incendiaries: so that the European not only dislikes, but hates them' (1787: xv). This 'fame' has been passed down through the centuries. De Marly describes the clothing of a Gypsy fortune-teller in a painting as 'of good quality, and may be stolen' (1986: 23). As Gypsies have been explicitly criminalized in law, and punished by execution, banishment and 'rehabilitation', it is unsurprising that this label should persist where a prejudice is encouraged and reinforced by the state, newspapers and other wielders of power.

Going back further, the Gypsies were, of course, subject to genocidal Acts throughout Europe from 1554 to around 1783 (Hancock 1987: 16–29). They were enslaved, and later their very existence constituted a capital offence, such a policy being adopted largely in response to structural problems associated with vagrancy in the wake of social and economic changes in the larger society – the bourgeois fear of revolt and disorder (see Fraser 1992: 117). Gypsies, perhaps, were the necessary early scapegoats in the process of privatization of resources, enclosure of land, and proletarianization, which marked the terminal decline of feudalism (Acton 1994: 26–27). Indirectly Gypsies were squeezed by restrictions, operated by craft guilds, in the supply of certain handicraft skills traditionally associated with nomadism (Leeson 1980).

Theme 5: Overt Sexuality

The libidinous and promiscuous Gypsy is another persistent cliché in the archaeology of the stereotype. Within a patriarchal culture, it is mainly women who are the object of this particular projection: they are charismatically attractive, uninhibited and tantalizing, yet – crucially to make the stereotype work – unobtainable. The image of the Spanish flamenco dancer represents the distillation of the type, whose qualities are attributed to real Gypsy women:

> You dance, and I know the desire of all flesh, and the pain
> Of all longing of body for body; you beckon, repel,
> Entreat, and entice, and bewilder, and build up the spell.
> (Arthur Symons, quoted in Okely 1983: 202)

Although this (secret) explicit sexual fantasizing is largely a product of the Victorian period, Gypsy women were, from early records, perceived as implicitly threatening, perhaps over-assertive and conspicuous:

> The women of the band wandered about the town, six or eight together; they entered the houses of the citizens and told idle tales, during which some of them laid hold of whatever could be taken. In the same way they visited the shops under the pretext of buying something, but one of them would steal [...] [The] women went about in shifts and wore a coarse outer garment across the shoulder, rings in their ears, and a long veil on their head. One of them gave birth to a child in the market-place and, at the end of three days, she went on with the other women. (Cited in Fraser 1992: 72)

In *Antony and Cleopatra*, Shakespeare describes Philo as follows: 'His captain's heart [...] is become the bellows and the fan to cool a Gypsy's lust' (I.i.7–11). Kenrick and Puxon summarize the sexual stereotyping imposed by the majority: 'It is widely believed of course that Gypsies enjoy a better and fuller sex life than the average house dweller. The Gajo [non-Gypsy] mind alternates between the conviction that the Gypsies are just loose in their morals and therefore below contempt and the suspicion that Gypsies enjoy a natural and spontaneous love-life, enhanced by their handsome looks and romantic attraction' (1972: 39). They go on to point out the unreality of this mythology, as it contrasts with the tightly coded taboos of Gypsy culture and sexual morality. Okely (1983: 213–14) goes further, and concludes that both Gypsy and *gadjo* women harbour similarly idealized self-images and denigrating stereotypes of the 'other': 'we' are virginal, monogamous, abstinent and sexually in control; 'they' are prostitutes, promiscuous, available and sexually out of control (see Ní Shuinéar 1997: 28–30). One farmer in the eighteenth century referred to '[t]hese miscreants and their loose women, for no doubt all of them are so, as they lie and herd together in a promiscuous manner [...] a parcel of rogues and trollops' (quoted in Okely 1975: 55).

These are just some of the prominent themes in the early Western representations of Gypsies, although there are others, such as Gypsies as cannibals, child-stealers and 'polluters'. Their unique and complex languages have been dismissed as 'gibberish' or as 'thieves' cant', and the imagery used to represent them is often simplistic and crude. The larger society's responses to Gypsies were correspondingly unsophisticated: they were banished, further immigrations barred; people who were identified as 'Egyptians' could be imprisoned, transported, enslaved or executed. By the 1780s, it was being recognized that this barbarity was counter-productive: 'At last the evil grew too enormous, the complaints against them became so loud, that government was constrained to take official notice of them; they began punishing; hanging and beheading were not found sufficiently efficacious, yet it was necessary to go to the root of the grievance; it was judged expedient to banish them; a method more likely to render them worse than better' (Grellmann 1787: xiii–xiv).

The Evolution of Gypsy Stereotypes in North-Western Europe since the Eighteenth Century

The 'Enlightenment', it is argued, represented the transition from a culture of religious dogma and superstition, of an aristocratic hierarchy of power, conspicuously exercised by state and church, to one of scientific rationalism in technological and socio-economic affairs. The world was being reinterpreted and problems were to be identified and solved by the judicious application of reason. These paradigm shifts would affect the various approaches to minorities, including Gypsies: 'Perhaps it may be reserved for our age, in which so much is attempted for the benefit of states and mankind, to humanise a people who, for centuries, have wandered in error and neglect' (Grellmann 1787: xv–xvi).

Michel Foucault (1991) has argued that these shifts were revolutionary, but yet piecemeal, in that they occurred neither simultaneously nor universally: they took place by the application of reason and efficiency to particular areas of activity and knowledge, in specifications for design, training and rehabilitation. They were to enhance the efficient exploitation of human and natural resources – to know them, to assign them a place in the order of things. It is possible to view the changing societal responses to the Gypsies as one specific set of applications of these 'disciplines', as a means of reforming these 'primitives', an attempt to evangelize and modernize them – in short, to remove a threat and nuisance, and to assimilate them into the wage-labour workforce. Corresponding with the changes in the larger society, attitudes to Gypsies altered, at least among the new bourgeoisie. There was greater sophistication in the representation of Gypsies, and there were attempts at assimilation through cultural retraining, largely through the efforts of missionaries and humanists. Liégeois has argued that 'the gradual rise of humanistic ideas on the one hand and technocratic attitudes on the other combined to provoke a shift in the authorities' policy towards Gypsies. [...] The measures aimed at expelling Gypsies had been based on a repulsive image of the targeted group as inherently evil' (1986: 104–05).

There was a sizeable population that failed to conform to the imperatives of the Industrial Revolution: 'vagrancy' was synonymous with parasitism and delinquency (see Potter 1797), as evidenced by the numerous reactive statutes of the eighteenth and nineteenth centuries (Mayall 1988: Appendix 1). The Gypsies were a part of the nomadic, 'informal' economy, and perceived as outcasts who had escaped from, or been overlooked by, the industrial culture. This sustained evasion of the dominant spirit and priorities of industrialization – wage-labour, fixed abode, privatized land and natural resources, disciplined education and training – enabled particular projections and stereotypes to take root (McVeigh 1997). Although the portrayals ranged from genocidal denigration to hopelessly unrealistic idealization, they shared a perception of Gypsies and Travellers as distinctly 'other', which persists to present times. For a contemporary example, we need only refer to press accounts of the Czech and Slovak Romani asylum-seekers who sought refuge in Britain in 1997 and 1998. They were regarded as 'cuckoos in the nest' and as 'gold-diggers' – 'bogus' in everything they said or did. They were, quite literally, 'not one of us' (Clark and Campbell 2000: 32–33).

That Gypsies and Travellers were uniquely susceptible to mythologizing by outsiders is perhaps not that surprising. As a non-literate ethnic minority, with little if any power or representation in the dominant culture, they could be represented according to the requirements of particular writers, and their identities manipulated and distorted. The predominant perception was generally denigratory, and intolerant. However, during the nineteenth century, a peculiar idealization of the Gypsies developed, later rationalized by Victorian racialism. On the one hand, Gypsies could be seen, through the traditional fearful filter, as lusty criminals, con-artists, layabouts, and much worse:

> It is astonishing in what a state of fear and subserviency the rural population of this [Devon] and neighbouring counties are held by the Gipsy gangs, to whose application for relief, of whatever description required, the most ready acquiescence is yielded, lest damage should be committed by them in case of refusal. (*The Times*, 6 May 1826)[8]

On the other hand, they might be seen as useful (if peripheral), having a valued part to play. Take this example from the New Forest area:

> The farmers consider themselves, as to their homesteads and property, always as safe when Gypsies are encamped near them; but there is a fearful gang of poachers and deer and sheep-stealers all around the New Forest, which paralyses the confidence of the farmer in the belief of himself and his own [sic]. The Gypsies have ever been considered a dark and mysterious community. Those who know them and their ways, habits, and customs best, are the best to appreciate their claim to good feeling on the part of those who have experienced their singular ways. A farmer considers a Gypsy a good watchdog whilst the latter lingers around his premises; but a 'neighbour' he looks upon as being well worthy of watching. (*The Times*, 12 October 1842)

But then again, a month later, in the same area:

> it has invariably been noticed that when a horde of Gipsies has been encamped in the vicinity of [the] sheepfolds, one or more of the animals have been found dead in the morning which on the previous night appeared in perfect health [...] The fact is [...] that the Gipsies around the New Forest have been in the habit, for some months past, of resorting to the practice of suffocating the sheep on the farms in the vicinity in the manner above described [by forcing wool down the throat], evading thereby the suspicions of the farmer falling on them. (*The Times*, 14 November 1842)

These contradictory portrayals are not untypical of the early-nineteenth-century confusion about Gypsies. The duality was later resolved through the imposition of a hierarchy of racial purity, consistent with the

---

[8] Compare this with 1992 reports of special benefit payments to help New Travellers after a free festival at Castlemorton, in which the (false) impression was given that extra money had been found to encourage them to move on from the area (see e.g. the *Sun*, 1 August 1992: 'Hippy Scroungers Must Get Jobs or Starve').

racialist framework of the time, which created an idealized, romantic, and rather abstract 'race': a 'phantom people' of the imagination, 'degenerate hordes' on the wayside (Kenrick and Puxon 1972: 30). As long as one respected and admired the mirage of the 'true Romany', one was at liberty to dehumanize, denigrate and harass the people who were actually encamped on common or marginal land: they were no more than vagrants, or, worse, cross-bred Gypsies, who had deviated from the imposed stereotype, and diluted the precious *kalo-rat*, or 'black blood'.

Before going on to discuss the details of the representations, it is worthwhile to locate the schisms in the dominant culture that gave rise to the duality. Hobsbawm (who is not without his critics) acknowledges the importance of the Romantic reaction against the tide of industrialization:

> The poets of German romanticism thought they knew better than anyone that salvation lay only in the simple modest working life that went on in those idyllic pre-industrial towns that dotted the dream-landscapes, which they described more irresistibly than they have ever been described by anyone. And yet their young men must leave to pursue the by definition endless quest for the 'blue flower' or merely roam forever, homesick [...] The wanderer's song is their signature tune, nostalgia their companion. (1988: 319)

The Gypsies came to be seen as natural allies in the face of 'modernization': to the Romantic imagination they carried an aura, not just of medieval mystery and foreignness, but also of a golden age of naturally noble relations between individuals, families, tribes, animals, nature and God. To the Right they came to represent the feudal order as the lost ideal of social relationships, ripped apart by the ascendant bourgeois capitalism: 'conservative medievalism' (Hobsbawm 1988: 320). For the Left, the romanticization of the Gypsies represented them as primitives, a reminder of a supposed pre-authoritarian communism: 'the noble savage showing up the deficiencies of a corrupt society' (Hobsbawm 1988: 321). Hobsbawm describes a third strand of romanticism:

> Closely allied with medievalism, especially through its preoccupation with traditions of mystical religiosity, was the pursuit of even more ancient and profound mysteries and sources of irrational wisdom in the orient: the romantic, but also the conservative realms of Kublai Khan or the Brahmins [...] the bulk of the amateurs of the East and writers of pseudo-Persian poems, out of whose enthusiasm much of modern orientalism emerged, belonged to the anti-Jacobin tendency. Characteristically Brahmin India was their spiritual goal, rather than the irreligious and rational Chinese empire, which had preoccupied the exotic imaginations of the eighteenth-century enlightenment. (1988: 320–21)

Lorism and 'Race'

Arguably, it was this type of romantic Orientalism that was one of the most influential contributors to the myth of the 'true Romany', as expressed by Gypsiologists, journalists and artists. In reconstructing the stereotype, with fabulously concocted hierarchies of racial purity (Acton, for example, lists and discusses 18 different words used to identify or classify Travellers [1974: 60–80]), these labels supposedly denoted the proximity to the idealized strain of suitably 'exotic' Indian blood. The implications of romantic and classical racialism for political and social interventions by the state were profound and will become clearer when attempts to 'solve the Gypsy problem' are touched on later.

The stereotypes were, in essence, created and imprinted by the mid-nineteenth century: the romantics idealized the nobly savage 'true Romany', while rationalists saw depraved vagabonds, deprived outcasts or a 'useless race' (*The Times*, 19 July 1816). Perhaps the most influential projector of the romanticized Romany was George Borrow (1803–81), whose semi-autobiographical adventure tales were popular: 'He stood as the figurehead for the romantic elevation of the Gypsy to the status of chief protagonist with forces of progress and advance, resisting the crushing organisation of society and the routine and restraints of civil life. They stood for freedom against the tyranny of law, for nature before civilisation and for simplicity before complexity' (Mayall 1988: 72). Borrow portrayed the Gypsies as a 'dark wandering race' of close-knit companies and tribes, good at fighting, drinking and petty crime and cons, which reinforced the perception of the ordinary *gadjo* citizens as gullible, and overburdened with cares and property. Also, they exuded a mystical aura connecting them to a pre-civilized, communal relationship to a masculinist nature:

> two or three men on horseback are hurrying through the crowd, they are widely different in their appearance from the other people of the fair; not so much in dress, for they are clad something after the fashion of rustic jockeys, but in their look – no light brown hair have they, no ruddy cheeks, no blue quiet glances belong to them; their features are dark, their locks long, black and shining, and their eyes are wild [...] they do not sit on the saddle in the manner of common jockeys, they seem to float or hover upon it, like gulls upon the waves [...] the third is a very tall man with a countenance heroically beautiful, but wild, wild, wild. (Borrow 1991: 99)

During the nineteenth century, folklorists and Gypsiologists elaborated on the culture of the Romany (as they saw it). On the basis of their theories they were able to locate particular individuals and families within an imposed hierarchy of racial purity. It was believed that Gypsies had maintained their separateness by marrying only within their own 'race', and that their distinctive cultural characteristics were genetically inherited: physical appearance (darkness, dress), instincts (wanderlust, sexuality), 'purity' or 'depth' of Romani language use, inclusion in a 'secret fraternity' (which 'called to mind the secretive rituals and practices of freemasonry' [Mayall 1988: 76; cf. *The Times*, 5 October 1843]), and the practice of a complex series of rituals: 'The list of regulations is endless and, when accompanied by the range of other codes of conduct determining behaviour compiled by the lorists, it becomes easy to assume that ritual and ceremony dominated the lives of the Gypsies. They seemed unable to eat, sleep, travel, wash, drink or give birth without first consulting some omen or belief' (Mayall 1988: 77). They were represented as a dwindling racial minority – a threatened species – who would soon vanish from the scene, as evidenced by the visibly impoverished circumstances and alleged moral decline of the majority of Travellers. This notion was the catalyst for the members of the Gypsy Lore Society,[9] founded in 1888, which sought to preserve as much as possible of the 'lore' and language of the Gypsies, before they became extinct by miscegenation and political intolerance of their ways. Their members ignored political and social concerns, even when those they studied and observed were threatened, in the late nineteenth century, by proposed legislation to register them and their homes.

Thus, the romantic, lyrical, poetic portrayals of Gypsies were reinforced by pseudo-scientific means (including contemporary physical-anthropological techniques, such as head-measuring); and, in fact, this both confirmed the common prejudice against nomadism and reassured the majority that persecution of Travellers was not unjust: the 'true Romany', as described by the lorists, is never encountered, except by the lorists themselves.

Social and Religious 'Reform'

Besides the romantics and the lorists, there were others with a particular interest in the Gypsies. The social policy and religious reformers of the nineteenth century were concerned less with indulging in the Gypsy Lore Society hobby of 'Gypsying', or preserving an occult culture, than with 'rescuing' bodies and saving souls: the Gypsies were identified not so much in racial terms as in social and religious terms, as objects of charity and evangelistic fervour, ripe for conversion and assimilation.

---

[9] The *Journal of the Gypsy Lore Society* survives, now published in Massachusetts, despite various long interruptions. In 1999 the Gypsy Lore Society changed the name of its journal to *Romani Studies*, and it seems likely that the organization itself will be renamed in the near future. The relevance of 'lorism' is being increasingly questioned by Romani scholars in the twenty-first century.

For many of the early missionaries, the Gypsies – although often accepted as a racial group – were not romanticized. They were made subjects of surveys, whose aim was to gather information on their origins, numbers, nomadic habits and the like: 'Of late years some attempts have been made to reduce the numbers, or at any rate to civilize the habits of that vagabond and useless race, the Gipsies. In pursuance of such purpose, a society of gentlemen have been making all the preliminary inquiries requisite to a proper understanding of the subject' (*The Times*, 19 July 1816). In this report, 25 questions having been circulated around the country, the Gypsies are described as ignorant or reticent, sidestepping 'inquiries respecting their peculiar language, calling it gibberish', only nominally Christian. They are viewed not only in terms of the simplistic stereotypes discussed earlier, but also as a 'problem', which could and should be 'solved'. The techniques proposed to effect this solution were to involve compulsion: settlement, useful employment for adults (although the latter were often seen as beyond redemption), religious schooling and apprenticeship or domestic service for the children: 'Their being placed among a greater number of children, and those of settled, and to some degree of civilised habits, would greatly facilitate the training of Gypsies to salutary discipline and subordination, and the associations it provided for them out of school hours, being under the superintendence of a regular family, would, in an especial manner, be favourable to their domestication' (Hoyland 1816, quoted in Mayall 1988: 101).

Various missionary attempts at settlement were implemented around the country (see Acton 1974: 104–05; Fraser 1992: 199–200; Mayall 1988: ch. 5). James Crabb, a Methodist preacher, was intent on reforming the Gypsies of the New Forest and Hampshire through the work of the Southampton Committee. He was opposed to compulsion, favouring paternalistic, benevolent assimilationism, by 'teaching the "inconveniences, hazards and impropriety of a wandering life" [...] to be achieved by imbuing them with a sense of honesty and morality and instructing them in the Christian religion. When this was achieved, settlement would follow' (Mayall 1988: 107). A 'charitable' portrayal occurs in *The Times* (30 December 1842):

> The annual festival of the Gipsies of the New Forest was held today on the Rev. Mr. Crabb's grounds, about a mile from Southampton. On these grounds the families and tribes of the Gipsies were invited, according to yearly custom, to partake of a sumptuous dinner, and to receive various articles of clothing, to shelter them in some measure from the inclemency of the winter season. These presents are furnished by means of subscriptions of the wealthy in all parts of the country. At 2 o'clock nearly 200 Gipsies sat down to a handsome dinner of roast beef and plum pudding, and were waited on by the

gentry of the neighbourhood, crowds of whom were present to witness the singular scene. The swarthy beings proved by the quantity they consumed that a sumptuous dinner was a rarity to them; and they were so overjoyed at the sight of rich plum puddings, that they all rose, greeting them with tumultuous cheering. The Gipsy children, although many of them badly clad, some of them indeed half naked, appeared a fine healthy race. The clothing distributed amongst them consisted of blankets and fabrics fitted for under garments. The Right Hon. Sturges Bourne was present, and appeared to take the greatest interest in the festival.

The worthy efforts of Crabb met with limited success in the longer term (Acton 1974: 104), although some converts to the disciplinary system were reported: 'in the first year of the mission, six children had been settled at infant school, and by the following year were said to have "exchanged their restlessness of body and unfixedness of mind for habits of attention and self-control"' (Mayall 1988: 109–10). The notion of redeeming 'heathens' from their spiritual void, with the goal of conversion to useful citizenship, appealed to the bourgeoisie: good work induces a warm glow in the provider, and a grateful response in the recipient doubles the satisfaction. Unfortunately, most of the Hampshire Gypsies seem to have enjoyed their plum puddings while they lasted, and wandered off again when the charity stopped flowing. The evangelistic reforming passion faded in the face of poor results.[10]

George Smith (of Coalville, 1831–95) represented, in contrast to Crabb, a more secular (though divinely inspired) and forceful approach: he was successful in campaigning against conditions in the brickyards and on the canals (Hodder 1896). He had less success in lobbying Parliament for the regulation and control of the Gypsies; here, the notion of the 'true Romany' becomes politically and socially significant. Mayall suggests a convergence of interests between the secular philanthropists, such as Smith, and the lorists, and goes on to quote the *Weekly Times* (8 February 1880): 'For the genuine Gipsy tribe, and their mysterious promptings to live apart from their fellows in the lanes and fields of the country, we have a sentimental pity; but with such as these Lamb-lane people, off-scourings of the lowest form of society, we have no manner of sympathy; and we hope that a gracious Act of Parliament may soon rid English social life of such a plague' (quoted in Mayall 1988: 131–32). It is evident that the contradictory portrayals and confusion over who Gypsies 'really' were had implications for their treatment by the British State during this period. In many ways, this misunderstanding has not gone away and lives on today, leading to situations like that in July 1999 when the then Home Secretary, Jack

---

[10] In 23 years, only 59 Gypsies are reckoned to have been sedentarized by James Crabb's work (Acton 1974: 104).

Straw, made insulting and damaging claims about 'real Romani Gypsies' and those who 'masqueraded as "Travellers"' and 'act in unlawful ways'. He went on to suggest that 'many of these so-called Travellers seem to think that it's perfectly OK for them to cause mayhem in an area, to go burgling, thieving, breaking into vehicles, causing all kinds of other trouble including defecating in the doorways of firms and so on, and getting away with it, then their behaviour degenerates' (quoted in Clark and Dearling 1999: 14–15).

Whether being saved from their supposed heathen ways by the likes of Crabb, or being portrayed as a pre-Enlightenment 'useless race' and/or a 'threatened species', Gypsies had the useful function of showing the settled majority who they were *not*. That is, following historical assumptions of 'development', the civilized were sedentarist, independent and respectable, unlike the barbarians who were nomadic, parasitic and delinquent. Indeed, in the above quotation from the *Weekly Times*, we can see that 'real Gypsies', as championed by the lorists, were being contrasted with the moral degeneracy and perceived threat of the 'half-breed' Travellers who were regarded as a 'plague' to English social life (as Straw would argue). With regard to the former, their 'soon to be lost' culture and language were to be recorded and preserved for posterity, while for the latter, 'pretended' group, nothing less than complete isolation and/or total assimilation was required to keep the bloodlines of the 'real Romanies' pure. Clearly, Gypsies were deemed to be either saints or sinners with little or no middle ground for strategic manoeuvre or positioning.

Conclusion

This chapter began with a short reminder of an incident involving a group of 'Greek Gypsies' who found themselves in Liverpool in 1886. Although hoping to sail to the New World, they were refused this service and their mere presence in the city, although brief, provoked fierce reactions and overt public vilification. Just over 100 years later, similar incidents occurred – this time at the port of Dover with groups of Romanies from the Czech Republic and Slovakia, many of whom were claiming political asylum. My central argument here is that such episodes, and in particular the way they are presented, represented, reported and consumed in the British context, dig deep into a rich seam of already existing, historically developed – if unsophisticated – 'exotic' and/or demonizing stereotypes. The main themes and components within these stereotypes, although altering slightly with passing decades, have a great capacity to remain fairly rigid in their construction and to 'stick' – this in itself 'justifying' the repressive intervention that eventually comes in the form of state action.

It has thus been demonstrated how groups, families and individuals 'known' as Gypsies in Britain have had various identities constructed and imposed on them from 'outside' social actors, identities that often displayed one or more of the components and themes illustrated earlier. The collection of stereotypes tended to fit with particular roles into which Gypsies and other Travellers were being placed by the State and its agencies – whether as 'exotic noble savages' or as 'half-bred thieving wanderers'. The varieties on offer simply reflected the times and the prevailing social, economic and political fortunes at both local and national levels.

What is crucial here is the recognition of time, place and context.[11] Stereotypes are, once established, very persistent. But this is not to say that they do not take on new 'shades' and elements in different situations and contexts. They cross borders and time zones and their flexibility and adaptability ensure their continued usage, particularly as tools for social, political and legislative intervention by a nervous sedentarist state. By examining the historical evolution and construction of the Gypsy stereotype, in all its forms, and linking this with debates around (imposed) identity, we can see how a largely negative picture emerged.

In this context Gypsies are in many ways the perfect 'stranger' that the sociologist Georg Simmel (1950: 402–08) talks about in his short but brilliant essay: that is, a type of 'stranger' – like the Jew that Simmel speaks of in his own study – that can be made to fit as a scapegoat for any particular crisis. As Simmel notes, the 'stranger' has certain defining characteristics, including strangeness of origin and not being an owner of land. He writes:

> The Stranger is thus being discussed here, not in the sense often touched upon in the past, as the wanderer who comes today and goes tomorrow, but rather as the person who comes today and stays tomorrow. He is, so to speak, the potential wanderer. [...] He is fixed within a spatial group or within a group whose boundaries are similar to spatial boundaries. But his position in this group is determined, essentially, by the fact that he has not belonged to it from the beginning [...]. He is near and far at the same time.

Groups of Gypsies came to Britain, at least since the late fifteenth and the early sixteenth century, and they chose to stay. To this day many remain 'potential wanderers', as well as being 'near and far' from the settled, majority society. This is sometimes by choice and often by force. Likewise, Gypsies have certainly acted as convenient scapegoats in many circumstances where a 'stranger' was required to deflect a blow away from those attempting to hold on to some kind of power or status. Equally, however, it has continued to be the case that resistance has been

---

[11] See n. 3.

effective and sustained – Gypsies have not simply 'vanished', as many settled people have wanted them to over the years. As Woodcock rightly said back in 1865, severity has 'enraged' Gypsies and Travellers in Britain, but it has never 'subdued' them into a state of conformity and assimilation. Fighting for the right to 'difference' has been a long, uphill battle. For Gypsies and their children, some things never seem to change with the passing of time.

References

Acton, Thomas. 1974. *Gypsy Politics and Social Change: The Development of Ethnic Ideology and Pressure Politics among British Gypsies from Victorian Reformism to Romany Nationalism*. London: Routledge.

—1994. 'Modernisation, Moral Panics and the Gypsies', *Sociology Review* (September): 24–28.

Borrow, George. 1991 (1851). *Lavengro*. London: Constable.

Clark, Colin. 1997. 'New Age Travellers: Identity, Sedentarism and Social Security', in Thomas Acton (ed.), *Gypsy Politics and Traveller Identity*. Hatfield: University of Hertfordshire Press.

—2002. 'More than Lucky White Heather and Clothes Pegs: Putting European Gypsy and Traveller Economic Niches in Context', in Steve Fenton and Harriet Bradley (eds), *Ethnicity and Economy: 'Race' and Class Revisited*. London: Palgrave.

Clark, Colin, and Campbell, Elaine. 2000. ' "Gypsy Invasion": A Critical Analysis of Newspaper Reaction to Czech and Slovak Romani Asylum-Seekers in Britain, 1997', *Romani Studies*, 10.1: 23–47.

Clark, Colin, and Dearling, Alan. 1999. 'Romanies/Gypsies, Travellers or Nomads – What's in a Name?', *Criminal Justice Matters*, 38 (Winter/Spring): 14–15.

Crofton, Henry Thomas. 1888. 'Early Annals of the Gypsies in England', *JGLS*, 1.1: 1–16.

De Marly, Diana. 1986. *Working Dress: A History of Occupational Clothing*. London: Batsford.

Foucault, Michel. 1991. *Discipline and Punish*. London: Penguin.

Fraser, Angus M. 1992. *The Gypsies*. Oxford: Blackwell.

Grellmann, Heinrich M.G. 1787. *Dissertation on the Gypsies*, trans. M. Raper. London: n.p. (original *Die Zigeuner*, 1783).

Hancock, Ian. 1987. *The Pariah Syndrome: An Account of Gypsy Slavery and Persecution*. Ann Arbor, MI: Karoma Publishers.

—2000. 'The Emergence of Romani as a Koïné Outside of India', in Thomas Acton (ed.), *Scholarship and the Gypsy Struggle: Commitment in Romani Studies*. Hatfield: University of Hertfordshire Press.

Hawes, Derek, and Perez, Barbara. 1996. *The Gypsy and the State: The Ethnic Cleansing of British Society*. Bristol: Policy Press (2nd edn).

Hetherington, Kevin. 2000. *New Age Travellers: Vanloads of Uproarious Humanity*. London: Cassell.

Hobsbawm, Eric. 1988. *The Age of Revolution*. London: Penguin.

Hodder, Edwin. 1896. *George Smith of Coalville: The Story of an Enthusiast*. London.

Jarman, Alfred, and Jarman, Eldra. 1991. *The Welsh Gypsies, Children of Abram Wood*. Cardiff: University of Wales Press.

Kenrick, Donald, and Puxon, Grattan. 1972. *The Destiny of Europe's Gypsies*. London: Heinemann.

Leeson, Robert. 1980. *Travelling Brothers*. St Albans: Granada.

Liégeois, Jean-Pierre. 1986. *Gypsies: An Illustrated History*. London: Al Saqi.

Macfie, Robert Andrew Scott. 1943. 'Gypsy Persecutions: A Survey of a Black Chapter in European History', *JGLS*, 22.3–4 (July–October): 65–78.

MacRitchie, David. 1886. 'The Greek Gypsies at Liverpool', *Chambers's Journal of Popular Literature, Science and Art*, Fifth Series, 3.141 (11 September): 578.

McVeigh, Robbie. 1997. 'Theorising Sedentarism: The Roots of Anti-Nomadism', in Thomas Acton (ed.), *Gypsy Politics and Traveller Identity*. Hatfield: University of Hertfordshire Press.

Mayall, David. 1988. *Gypsy-Travellers in Nineteenth Century Society*. Cambridge: Cambridge University Press.

Ní Shuinéar, Sinéad. 1997. 'Why do Gaujos hate Gypsies so much, Anyway? A Case Study', in Thomas Acton (ed.), *Gypsy Politics and Traveller Identity*. Hatfield: University of Hertfordshire Press.

Okely, Judith. 1975. 'Gypsy Women: Models in Conflict', in S. Ardener (ed.), *Perceiving Women*. London: J.M. Dent and Sons.

—1983. *The Traveller-Gypsies*. Cambridge: Cambridge University Press.

Potter, B. 1795. *A New Dictionary of all the Cant and Flash Languages… Used by Gipsies, Beggars, Swindlers… and Every Class of Offenders…* London: n.p.

Simmel, Georg. 1950. 'The Stranger', in K. Wolff (ed.), *The Sociology of Georg Simmel*. New York: Free Press.

Thompson, T.W. 1923. 'Consorting with and Counterfeiting Egyptians', *JGLS*, 3.2: 81–93.

Vesey-Fitzgerald, B. 1973. *Gypsies of Britain*. Newton Abbot: David and Charles.

Index

The following terms recur throughout and have not therefore been indexed: England, English, Gypsy, Rom/Roma/Romani/Romany.